No Throwaway Boy

No Throwaway Boy

Abdul Lloyd-Bey

ISBN: 0692426329

ISBN 13: 9780692426326

Acknowledgement

This book is dedicated to my parents. Thank you for introducing me to the wisdom of maintaining a strong faith in God. Also, thank you for comfortingly loving and believing in me.

Thank you Sharoya, my daughter, for being the wonderful woman that you are and for being a strong inspiration in my life.

I would like to thank my son, "C", for reinforcing in me the knowledge of how important it is for fathers and sons to have a strong and healthy relationship.

I would like to thank Esmeralda Simmons for being a person who believed in me from the start and I will never forget your kindness and support. You are an amazing person.

Thank you Randolph "Randy" Jackson, for being one of the greatest inspirations to me. You are one of the most awesome human beings I have ever met.

Finally, thank you CG, my love and my friend. Thank you for being that amazingly supportive, loving and understanding woman that you are. Love you.

Table of Contents

A Note from Abdul Lloyd-Bey

THIS IS A WORK of nonfiction. It is my story as I remember it. All of the events and experiences detailed are true and have been put down as I recall them. Some names, identities, and circumstances have been changed in order to protect the integrity and/or privacy of the various individuals involved.

Conversations throughout this work have been recorded as I remember them, but they have not been written to represent word-for-word documentation: rather, I've retold them in a way that evokes the real feeling and meaning of what was said in keeping with the true essence of the mood and spirit of the event.

Introduction

I ALWAYS BELIEVED THAT I would die on death row. Where that thought developed, who knows, but it was there as far back as I could recall, six or seven years old, even. I recall telling a teacher that I could never be president, and when asked why, I told her, "Because they would kill me because I was Black." I was less than ten years old at the time.

I recall my dad asking, "What do you want to be when you grow up?"

I said, "A cop."

"Nah…you may get shot," Dad said.

Later, he asked the same question, and I said, "A pilot."

"Nah," Dad said, "your eyes are too bad."

By the time I got to high school, I had absolutely no idea what the fuck I wanted to be besides the motherfucker who ran that bitch (leader of the cool kids). I eventually ran that shit, too.

The block I lived on, in Bushwick, Brooklyn, was pretty close-knit, interesting families. We all looked out for one another. Many of the young people I grew up with on that block in Brooklyn, would all reunite as adults in various maximum-security prisons across the state of New York.

I attended elementary school at P.S. 299. My home life was pretty good, but I always felt crowded at home. There were too many people there, not enough space: eight kids, mother and father in a three-bedroom apartment, in Bushwick, Brooklyn, New York. I often preferred the streets. In the streets, however, you had to be alert so, I carried my knife, 007, razor sharp, as far back as I could recall, seven or eight years old.

My neighborhood had numerous gangs, and sometimes they marched the streets, in ranks, 100 deep. There were the Tomahawks, Savage Skulls, and Savage Nomads, to name a few. I saw them beat down many people, badly.

I formed my own crew at elementary school, and we practiced sequential marching in the schoolyard during recess and lunch break. It was only the guys from my fifth grade class, but still I understood early on that there was a need for togetherness; I was voted the leader. My second in command (DJ) some years later reportedly killed a man and was given a life prison sentence. Unbeknownst to me, he and I were on Rikers Island together as teenagers, but he was using his street name, not his real name that I knew him by. He was a notorious inmate on Rikers Island too, and his street name struck terror in the hearts of many motherfuckers.

Away from school and on my block, I rarely hung out with kids my age. I mostly hung with the older guys. We formed a gang there too, just the guys from the block, "Cornelia Street Demons." Being the youngest in the clique, I was not the leader but I was respected still.

There was always rivalry between the neighborhood blocks, i.e. Cornelia Street versus Jefferson or Madison. Madison was a tough block; many well respected young guys came from that block. Often, in the summer time, our entire block, so it seemed, girls and guys, would hit the park to engage in battles (usually friendly) with the other neighborhood blocks.

Our toughest elementary school guys would battle in one-on-one wrestling with their toughest elementary school guys. Then, middle school, then high school and the girls and other guys from your respective block would cheer for you as in the gladiator days; it was crazy fun. We would thereafter all return to the block and recount our wins and losses, congratulating the winners and laughing and clowning the losers hard. It was all in fun, though, and those were definitely fun times.

We all stuck together, on the block and when we ventured off the block. Summer times were the best. School was out for the year, daylight lasted a long time, ice cream trucks stayed on the block, and we played all kinds of games. We played basketball, handball, football, cocolevio, tag, tops, skelly, cards, just having fun. In the wintertime, we built snowmen and had wild, fun snowball fights; often times it was the guys against the girls or the older kids against the younger kids on the block.

Also, on my block, there was a categorization based upon family affiliations. On my block many were known by their families' names, Chapmen, Leftwich, Mimms, etc. Some family names were notorious, others pleasant, others tragic. There were many family tragedies among the families on my block. Looking back, almost every family known to me had suffered some form of tragedy, be it a killing, severe drug addiction, domestic violence, extreme alcoholism, or long-time incarceration. Everybody on the block was also very poor; that, too, was a fucking tragedy.

My dad was individually well-respected in the neighborhood. He was a strong, principled man. He was a long-time married man, no drinking, partying, or drugging, as many of the older folks of that time were doing.

My dad, too, was a product of the South, and he was raised with many of the Southern principles about family, community, and manhood. He lived by those principles and tried to impart them to his children. My dad was a man who would literally kill a motherfucker or die trying for his family. Most folks on my block knew it too, and they usually acted accordingly.

My dad kept guns in the home, many of them. Many folks in my neighborhood, they knew that shit too. Most folks in the neighborhood, of all ages, had a healthy respect for my dad, for a number of reasons, and thus, they too respected his children. I was given a lot of respect in the neighborhood while growing up; I was Mr. Lloyd-Bey's son. I was actually never comfortable being respected because of a relationship with anything or anyone, I always desired for people to respect me because of whom I was as an individual, period.

My friends of all ages also respected my father. They loved to talk to him, and he loved them back. Many of my friends and other young men in the neighborhood had no father in the home, or their fathers were unknown to them. They thus openly respected the fact that I did.

My father became, to many of them, a respected role model. My father, being conscious of the state of affairs in the Black community, embraced the role and became a mentor and inspiration to many young men in the neighborhood. Some of the toughest of the tough, the real bad boys of the neighborhood, looked up to my father.

My father held many jobs in my memory; he always worked hard. He was a city bus driver for most of my childhood. Those Southern principles about the man being the provider and protector of his family were serious with my dad.

My dad also was taking night classes at Brooklyn College, while working full-time, eventually earning his bachelor's degree. He went on to earn two master's degrees, while still working full-time, raising eight kids, and caring for his wife.

My dad left the bus driver job and went on to work as a para-professional for the Board of Education and thereafter became a high school teacher. He also would sell wares that came in from Africa, various woodwork and sculptures he received from his cousin Chuck, who was a merchant marine. He also made and sold various incenses, as well as custom jewelry that was made by one of his good friends.

Still, he never made enough to really accomplish all the things he wanted to do for his wife and children, and that definitely bothered him. I recognized this frustration early on and thus, I rarely asked for anything. As a kid, I recall always being fascinated with the stars and I wanted to study astronomy. I once asked my dad to buy me a telescope, and with the most pained expression on his face he told me that he could not afford it. I never asked my father to purchase me anything else after that. I figured that I had to find other ways to get what I wanted on my own.

So, at around eight years old, I would get up on Saturday and Sunday mornings at 6:00 a.m., wash, fix breakfast, leave the house by 7:00 a.m. to get to the neighborhood supermarket some blocks away to pack grocery bags for the cashiers. You had to arrive early or other kids would already have your place at the register, and you'd be out. I always arrived as the store was opening.

I would work from 8:00 a.m., when the store opened, to 6:00 p.m., or right before closing time. Often I came home with a pocket filled with quarters, dimes, half dollars, and a couple of bills mixed in. Sometimes, I came home practically broke, after a ten-hour shift, pockets practically empty, if people were not tipping that day.

My mom was always an amazing woman in my eyes, she was before her time. Mom was a homemaker, raising the children and keeping house. She was a very strong woman and a woman whom many of the girls in the neighborhood gravitated to. I loved my mom dearly and had a good relationship with her as a kid and a great relationship with her as an adult. I hated to see her without, because I sensed early on that she had the spirit of abundance, but economically, she did not have all she desired. I rarely asked her for money as far back as I can recall. I could never take the little she had and often offered her what I had, if I had anything to offer.

My parents both converted to Islam before I was born, thus, my name, Abdul. The conversion gave my parents and my family a novelty on the block; traditional Islam was pretty new to the African American community at that time. Both parents taught the religious principles to people in the neighborhood and converted a number of them to Islam. The principles of love of the Lord, self-sufficiency, love of self, family, and community were welcome ideas in a neighborhood that was filled with violence, alcohol, drugs, and self-destructive behavior.

I was introduced to the Mosque and the Muslim community as far back as I could remember. I was therefore raised around people from all over the world: Whites, Hispanics, Asians, and Africans. Under Islam, we were all brothers and sisters, so racism and prejudice was a foreign teaching to me. I knew it existed, but it was something we were taught never to embrace.

My father always wanted to have a house for his children, rather than an apartment, and when he found the chance to rent a home in Far Rockaway, Queens, he jumped on it. Moving to Queens was hard for me. So many friends and memories in Bushwick, Brooklyn, it was hard to move away. Yet, the last day in Bushwick was crazy fun. After the moving truck was totally packed, my friends and I were all in the hallway of my building reminiscing, laughing and cracking jokes, playing the dozens.

Kelroy, Bugsy (whom I would later meet in prison), Donna, and Lamont were in the hallway that day. Kelroy said his niece, Donna, who had buck teeth and was wearing furry high boots, looked like a "Russian rabbit with boots." On and on the jokes went throughout the night, hilarious and memorable.

My dad was ready to go, so I said my painful goodbyes. I climbed slowly into the moving truck, and we pulled off heading to Queens, leaving my hood and all of its pitfalls and distractions behind, or so we thought.

Upon arriving in Far Rockaway, Queens, I noticed that the whole feel was different. On my new block, there were many one-family houses, some unattached, others connected. No multi-family buildings or apartment complexes were on my new block. The new home consisted of a pretty beaten-down, one-family structure. It had two floors, a living room, dining room, and kitchen on the first floor. The second floor consisted of three bedrooms and a bathroom. There also was a basement that had a mid-sized room and small bathroom; this is where I would sleep, sharing the space with my two brothers, my younger brother and older brother, Kaheem.

The funny thing was, when Kaheem and I first went downstairs to the basement, there were voodoo dolls and small saucers filled with some form of white powder in the room. Dad saw it and warned my brother to not get any of that stuff on your person while disposing of it.

Reckless as my brother often was, of course, he had the white powder spill all over him. Some neighbors warned us that the previous tenants practiced some form of Black arts, devil worship, and that getting the powder on him would prove disastrous in the future. I do not know how true that was, but shortly after that incident, my brother's life began spinning tragically in the wrong direction.

About a year after moving to Queens, my brother was arrested for juvenile offenses. He claims to this day his innocence. He was sent to Spofford, a local juvenile justice facility in the Bronx and eventually to a state holding facility for juveniles. The facility was way upstate, nothing but farms, cattle, horses, and shit up there. We would make family visits up to see him, sometimes. My father was active in the fight to clear his son's name and get justice on his behalf. Yet, having limited financial resources, no private investigators, and no political connections, it was like David fighting Goliath with a slingshot, but no rocks. My father was battered, bruised, and disappointed at every encounter with the courts, juvenile justice facilities, and the entire legal process.

My brother, although upset by the allegations and the legal predicament that he was in, made it clear that he was not intimidated by the entire process and held his head high along the way.

Upon visiting my brother at the juvenile facility, it also was very clear that he was not intimidated by the juvenile correctional facilities, either. In fact, many of the detained juveniles and some staff were definitely intimidated by him. My brother was a very large, dark skinned, intimidating-looking young man. He stood a good six feet tall at fifteen years old, pushing two hundred pounds, solid muscle, when many of the other juveniles his age were often barely 150 pounds soaking wet.

Additionally, he was physically gifted – boxing, wrestling, basketball, football, you name it and he could do it, and fairly well. He was definitely not a straight bully and would challenge a straight bully in a New York minute. However, he also knew how to put the scare on a motherfucker if he thought it was necessary or possibly beneficial.

My brother, too, was pretty introverted, not extremely – he would socialize some, but most people usually could sense that he was perfectly content being by his motherfucking self. He didn't need to run with the crew, and if shit ever hit the fan, he definitely was a one-man wrecking crew, and motherfuckers knew it. Still, many people gravitated towards him; people liked strength.

I always believed that my brother preferred to be alone. It often appeared to me that he was just going through the motions in social situations, not upset when even the high-energy parties we often attended were over and he could be by himself. He was not that talkative. He definitely was a young man of few words, but people usually listened when he spoke, maybe because he was so damn big. More likely, though, it was because he was very insightful and very perceptive.

My brother also was the rare kind of big man, in that many big men actually do not enjoy fighting. Maybe because no one ever really bothers them because of their size, so they often actually do not even know how to fight. Not my brother; he welcomed a good fight, win, lose or draw. He was so confident and naturally skilled, there weren't many draws, and he usually won, pretty convincingly.

Upon visiting him in the juvenile facility, it was always good. I missed my big brother. The visits were usually all day, and I got a chance to play basketball, horseplay, and tour the facility that held my brother. I met his friends, other juvenile detainees, and the staff, all whom seemed to have love and respect for him. There were some tough kids there, from the roughest neighborhoods around New York City, including Brownville, Bedford Stuyvesant, Bronx, Queens, and uptown Harlem. However, my brother was definitely one of the most respected "juvys" in the building, respected by both inmates and staff.

I took in all the sights and sounds of the juvenile facility, always having a deep dark sense that I likely would be there one day. There was no fear or apprehension, just a sense of knowing, almost a certainty.

While my big brother was away, (he was three years older than me), I continued the process of adjusting to Far Rockaway, Queens: new school, new friends, everything. My friends from Brooklyn sometimes came to Rockaway for short visits and vice versa. My routine in Rockaway basically mirrored the routine I followed while living in Brooklyn. I hung with my peer group and classmates in school and was the designated leader. After school, I always hung out with the older guys, often much older.

In Rockaway, the dominant group and revered personalities in my neighborhood, unlike in Brooklyn, was not the street gangs, or hood tough guys, it was the football team. Football was a serious business in Rockaway, Queens, and the heroes, star players, and first-string guys were treated with lots of respect in the neighborhood.

There were project clusters in Far Rockaway, Hammel, Edgemere, and Redfern, to name a few. These places were separate from where my house was; there were no projects in my immediate neighborhood, yet they were definitely a short walking distance away. The culture of my new neighborhood was a bit different from the culture of the projects; I would soon learn them both.

A fairly large number of the star players of the area high school varsity football team lived in my area and some lived on my block. One was Jason, a short, powerfully built Italian teenager, about four years older than me. He was the starting nose guard for the varsity football team. There also was Artie, Flood, Big Brown, Snake, Kelroy, all were star players on the team or closely connected to it. They often referred to themselves as being from the "60s", referring to the general location where they lived, between Beach 60th Street and Beach 69th Street. I lived on 69th Street, I was from the sixties.

Saying you are from the 60s also informed the listener that you did not reside in many of the clusters of public housing projects that exist in Far Rockaway. The guys from the 60s, particularly those connected to the football culture of the high schools, were not extremely street; they were mostly decent, middle class clean-cut kids. They did their thing, though, in terms of smoking weed, drinking, and partying, but there was not a lot of straight criminality in terms of gun toting, robbing, and stealing. There was a lot of drug selling, mostly among a small circle of friends, and drug use within that same circle of friends, but nothing much really beyond that.

The 60s crew, as they were called, readily embraced me as one of their own. Upon my moving into the neighborhood and meeting them, I was readily accepted as their new little brother. I was still in junior high school, while they were in high school.

With my real big brother being away at juvenile detention, serving 18 months, I enjoyed being the little brother of the 60s crew. While countless high school teens, at the time, were willing to literally give their right arms to be embraced by the 60s crew – this again, was the varsity football team and the football team were the stars of the show – I was embraced wholeheartedly, protected and given a voice, among the crew. I was still only in junior high school.

I was always big for my age, usually the biggest kid in the class. I entered high school at six foot two, 185 pounds. I was strong, physically gifted, and talented at sports. Wrestling, boxing, and football were my preference. The 60s crew all recognized my physical talents and maturity for my age. However, even at my young age, I'm positive that they also picked up that I had a will, a drive, and a personality, that would soon make me as popular or likely more popular than any one of them.

Upon arriving in Far Rockaway, I was in the seventh grade. However, the school year was half-way completed and all of the seventh grade classes were filled except the academically gifted class. So, the new school informed my parents that I could sit in the gifted class and if I could keep up academically, I could follow that class straight from seventh grade into the ninth grade. I would essentially be skipped a grade. I was happy and I easily kept up academically with the class. I routinely scored in the top portion of the class and was eventually promoted from seventh grade straight to ninth grade.

I was anxious to finish junior high school so I could get to high school and really have some fun, my whole team was there. I finally arrived at high school, Beach Channel, 1980, and because I had been skipped, I was probably one of the youngest kids in the entire school. I was around 14 years old.

All the boys from the 60s, Artie, Jason, Flood, were happy to see me finally at the school. They were all juniors and seniors and stars of the football team, the popular dudes. They let everyone know right away that I was part of the 60s crew and introduced me around to all the people that mattered, the cool kids.

Upon entering high school, Jason, Artie, and Flood were my best friends from the 60s, and I spent much of my leisure time by one of their homes, and they often gathered with me in the basement of my home. Most of the time spent together with the 60s crew was spent laughing, joking, and smoking weed. They introduced me to smoking weed, and we smoked a lot.

It was so funny that, because I had spent almost two years with the academically gifted students during junior high school, I knew most of the so-called "geeky" kids; they were my friends. However, I also knew all of the major players at the high school, the so-called "cool kids". I embraced the geeky girls and geeky guys; they were the academically gifted, but back since junior high school, they were my friends. I defended them on quite a few occasions often to the so-called bully's surprise; how did I come to know and love these "geeks" so well and how the heck did they know me?, many likely wondered.

When the "geeks" saw me, they embraced me, and I genuinely embraced them. It seemed as if they always knew maybe because they really knew me, that I was always partly a certified geek at heart, a geek moving or being pulled sharply to the other side.

By the middle of my freshman year at the high school, although I was probably one of the youngest kids in school, I was without argument one of the most popular. I knew everyone who was anyone, and they all knew me.

During my freshman year, my big brother returned home from juvy and he was allowed to enroll at the same high school as me, and to finish the school year as a senior. He had been taking high school credits while at juvy so he only needed a few credits to graduate. He looked like a grown man among children. He had gotten even bigger, and still was nothing to fuck with.

I already had massive props, respect, in the school, and with him arriving there it would only increase; it did. The 60s crew embraced my brother immediately; he wouldn't have cared if they didn't. My brother liked them and they liked him, but they all sensed he was definitely more edgy then they were. Most could sense that he was one not to fuck with. Again, I already had massive influence at the school, but with big brother there too, a man amongst boys, it was over.

My brother, upon coming home after serving around 18 months in juvy, didn't hang with the 60s boys that often, that was basically my team. Although the 60s clique readily accepted him, my brother's preferences were mostly a couple of hard core dudes from the Far Rockaway projects, particularly Edgemere, who he had met and bonded with while in juvy. Those were his dudes. His dudes were running shit, very influential, in the area projects and they loved and respected my brother from the days in juvenile detention. My brother, upon being released from detention, swiftly established a reputation among the project dudes as one not to fuck with, same reputation he had established in juvy.

The high school I attended was racially mixed with most of the White kids coming from middle class, and upper middle class, and predominantly White neighborhoods in Breezy Point, Broad Channel, Howard Beach, and Ozone Park. Many of the Black students came from the large clusters of area projects that exist in Far Rockaway, while other Black kids came from more middle class areas of the Rockaway peninsula, including the 60s.

There was so much race and class dynamics at that school, more than a little bit. The White and Black kids often clashed over some racial issues, real or imagined. The middle class Blacks and project Blacks often had tension, but rarely was there violence, as it was sporadically between Black and White students. When race issues occurred, the middle class and poor Blacks were instantly united because the "nigger, go home" writing that was often found on Black kids' lockers and the bathroom walls probably referred to all Black people regardless of their economic status.

Strange thing, though, the football team, for the most part, didn't have as much apparent racial strife as the general student body did. Black players and White players often hung out together, ate together, got high and drunk together. Now, they all usually went home to their often fiercely segregated neighborhoods after school, but during school time, team members of all races mingled freely.

My best friend Jason was a short, powerfully built Italian kid from my block on 69th Street; Jason and his family lived about five houses down from my family's house. Again, Jason was the starting nose tackle for the varsity football team and Jason was definitely one of the strongest motherfuckers in the school – shit, one of the strongest motherfuckers I knew. He was benching 300 plus pounds like water and squatting anything you put on the rack. Jason was crazy respected by the White kids and the Black kids at the school, he was respected by everyone. If you ever heard the term "crazy ass-White boy" and were to look up the term in the dictionary, Jason's picture would be there. Jason was crazy as a motherfucker and he didn't give a fuck.

Jason also did everything to the extreme, whether it was working out, smoking weed, drinking beer, driving his car, whatever, he was going all out. Jason would often drive top speed, just to see how fast his car could go, while smoking crazy weed. You rode in the car with him at your own risk; his idea of slow driving was about 85 miles an hour.

Jason was definitely not the most gifted boxer; we all used to play box sometimes and I would give him hell. However, Jason was readily willing to take five punches just to give you one, and that one, if it landed, would likely end the fight. Additionally, do not ever let Jason grab you; he was so strong that the shit didn't make sense. If he grabbed you, it was big trouble.

Jason often hung out with a variety of different people, Black, White or whatever. However, Jason was from the 60s, so he was first and foremost one of us and we were absolutely down with him. It was so strange that during racial tensions that often flared up at the school, everybody would go to their neutral corners; Blacks on one side of the block at the school and Whites on the other. Then Jason and I would pull up in Jason's car, get out, look at everybody like they were on drugs (we were usually the ones high), and just bust out laughing. Jason and I both thought the racial bullshit was dumbass.

On more than one occasion, as the racial tension hit boiling points at the school, the school administrators would call me, Jason, and other influential Black and White students to the principal's office and ask our assistance to help keep shit from hitting the fan. We would help.

Jason and I would often sit around for hours talking about everything, from politics, to women, to race. I loved Jason because Jason was much older and had a mature, insightful perspective on most issues. Before coming to Queens, I rarely personally experienced racism. Jason, however, had lived with it and dealt with that issue among his friends and family, while living in Queens, all his life.

Jason told me that some people see race first and some people see people first. He said that he chose to see people and that if another person can only see race, then that person is limited and that I should limit my association with them.

Jason was a wise dude to be so young and, besides my big brother, he was one of the few dudes I ever looked up to. His family members were beautiful people. His mother and father, sister and brother always embraced me as if I were a member of the family. My family did the same with Jason. We spent a lot of time at each other's homes just raiding the refrigerator and kicking it.

At that time, Jason's older brother was away at prison for armed robbery offenses. Many people in the neighborhood did not know that, but Jason talked to me about it. Jason respected me and often confided in me, knowing that I would never betray the trust. However, Jason did keep a secret from me that revealed itself later in a really big way.

Before my first year of high school had begun, I was on the front porch of my home and I saw a family walk past. With the family was a very attractive, light-skinned teenage girl, apparently a little older than me. I just stared at her as we locked eyes. I smiled, and she smiled back. I noticed that they went into a house a few doors down from mine. The next day, I began questioning the homeboys, "Who was that girl, who lived in that house?"

The fellows went on to say that the people I saw were the Harris family, a very religious family, Jehovah's Witnesses, and that the father was one of the leaders of the sect in the Rockaways, and the head of a church. They informed me that they were extremely anti-social and protective of their children. The kids did not socialize with other kids on the block, unless the other kids, too, were Jehovah's Witnesses. Even then, the socializing was bare minimum, I was told.

The boys told me that daughter that I saw was one of their four children, and that she was fine, very attractive, but was kept under lock and key, untouchable. I thought about her that night – her eyes were amazing, sparkling green like a cat's. She had beautiful lips, full, red, sexy; I was smitten.

I never saw her much after that day until my arriving at high school; she, too, attended there. I loved the ladies, so I readily took classes that the ladies definitely would be in, cooking, language and dance; she was in the dance class too.

I was one of the few guys in the dance class, and I believe the teacher knew why I was there and so I got singled out often by the teacher to perform some dance move or pose. However, whenever the teacher was not looking, I would get in front of the class and do some stupid dance moves to make the class laugh and when the teacher turned back around, I would be standing there, all innocent looking.

Inga, the girl's name was, thought I was hilarious. I liked her style. She was well mannered, classy. Her posture, speech, and poise were always perfect. She didn't curse or use slang, my complete opposite. I cursed like a fucking sailor and made up my own slang words. My friend

Artie and I would get high and just start making up slang words to describe shit. I often teased her about her proper speech patterns and her book-on-the head-like poise. She teased me about my slang and mispronunciation of words. I often urged her to say a "curse word" just to see if she would do it, she would just laugh. I'd tell her, "I know you want to, just say it."

I spent a lot of time talking to her before class and after class and then by telephone. She often had to sneak to use the phone because her family didn't allow her to talk to boys. Some kids grew up in very strict homes; her home, as she made it sound, was beyond strict, that shit was like fucking prison. She could barely go outside, park, beach, movie, or talk on the telephone.

She told me that she was dying to just go chill on the beach sometimes, and I told her, well, we are going to do it. I do not remember how but she got out of the house one day and I took her to the beach. We walked the boardwalk, the sand, and ended up in the lifeguard chair. We talked and hugged and watched the sun set over the water, while sitting high up in the lifeguard's chair.

We began to spend more and more time together, before school, during school and after school. We would often cut class or totally ditch school, just to spend time together. The cat was soon out of the bag and the entire school knew that she and I were dating.

The 60s boys and others at the school were on the floor when they found out. Many others had tried and failed to get her attention. She barely gave guys the time of day. Now, she was spending many of her days with me, at my house, in my room, down in the basement.

A Life of Crime

MY LIFE OF ARMED ROBBERIES actually began pretty unexpectedly; I did not see it coming. One day, Jason and I and another one of our friends were hanging out smoking weed in Jason's car. Money was low, weed was low and Jason suggested that we pull an armed robbery. Jason had suggested this before, he wanted to rob an armored truck, but we would always just laugh it off. Looking back, Jason was never really laughing.

Jason was the type that always wanted more, bigger, and better. He had a brand new car while still in high school, but he always talked about being able to buy the highest end model, which of course was also the most expensive one. My personality drastically differed from Jason's. I didn't have a car going into high school, nor did any of my friends besides Jason. Thus, I would have been happy with any car, small, large, whatever. Yes, I loved fly things, but I was sensible. Not Jason, he needed and wanted the best of everything. That was my friend but he definitely had some issues.

While I was adjusting to Queens, my old Brooklyn friends were flowing in Brooklyn, equally engaging in criminal activity, mostly drug dealing. Again, while I moved into the stickup kid business, they moved into the drug game, heavily. Many friends and close family began experimenting with cocaine selling and using around the time I was in high school. Cocaine was flooding into many New York neighborhoods; before crack, there was freebasing, smoking cocaine. The cocaine business also had the tendency to bring with it serious violence. The streets were getting more violent. Gun violence, in particular, was increasing and guns simply became more available; I definitely had mine.

As Jason and I moved into the stick-up game, mostly fast food restaurants and supermarkets, the money was flowing nicely. I upgraded everything from my clothes, to my jewelry, to my guns.

As an 11th-grade student, now deep into the stick-up game, I came to school every day with tailor made clothes, designer jeans (I had countless pairs), and custom made jewelry, with diamonds in it. Every popular sneaker that was out, you name it, and I had it, in almost every single color. I kept my gun, cleaned and cocked. I was no bully, but I definitely believed in self-defense. I walked around with thousands of dollars in my pocket every day, and I went where I wanted, and bought what I wanted. If I ran out of money, not a problem, something would simply get robbed.

I met one of my other best friends, Darnell, when I first arrived in Far Rockaway. I was in the hallway of my junior high school and there was some commotion in the principal's office. Darnell came hurriedly out of that office and we basically bumped into each other. We later talked about the commotion and began kicking it ever since. Darnell was from the Edgemere housing projects, a notoriously bad place that was directly across the street from our junior high school. Although he was still in junior high, he was well known and respected in Far Rockaway. This, not only because he was a stand-up guy, he didn't take any shit, but also because he was a phenomenal DJ, he was no fucking joke; he was very good.

Darnell would get on the mix, turntables and mixers, and absolutely tear a party down. He was so talented that he was often invited to guest DJ at some of the most premier and exclusive night clubs throughout New York City, this while he was just a teenager. He would always invite me to hang with him at some of the nightclubs and parties that he guest appeared at throughout the city. I was a fourteen- or fifteen-year-old kid, hanging in the DJ booth, walking the dance floor and rubbing elbows with high-end celebrities at New York's premier nightclubs while lower-end celebrities and "regular folks" could not even get in; they were being turned away at the door.

Darnell also DJed at neighborhood house parties, park parties and at block parties throughout the city. I always rode with him to help him carry the crates of records, set-up equipment and then break it down. We met "mad" ladies, (large amounts), everywhere we went, and we had fun, we definitely partied hard.

Darnell had a large family too, a cool older brother, Jarrad, and four fine-ass older sisters, all of them were fine as hell, very attractive. One of his younger sisters would later date and have a baby by an extremely popular R&B artist; she was fine too. Darnell's family was mixed race, Black and Filipino. All of his sisters had that clear caramel skin, jet Black long silky hair and bodies of Southern-bred sisters; they had roots down South, Virginia; thick. They all were super cool though, and they treated me like family. I would come to their place in the Edgemere housing projects, and literally from a block away, you could hear the music blaring from Darnell's bedroom; the dude is mixing music and tearing shit up.

I arrive at his apartment and go to his room; he has the headphones on, head bobbing, in a fucking zone. He has more speakers, amps, records and other electronic equipment in that room than I have ever seen in my life; his set-up was ridiculous. The very first time that I visited his room, I was awestruck. Dude had thousands of dollars' worth of DJ equipment; some speakers were floor to fucking ceiling. I would often hang with Darnell, Jarrad, his sisters, and his sisters' friends in that apartment for hours, blasting music, smoking weed and having a blast.

Darnell, my clique and I soon started throwing parties in Far Rockaway at various venues, usually by invitation only. My house on 69th Street was a favorite spot of ours to throw parties. We had a large backyard and garage that we often turned into a club, invitation only, no charge. Darnell would bring all the equipment down, set up and then tear the party down. All the finest females from the area high schools and throughout the neighborhood always showed up. Darnell's girlfriend was the captain of our high school's cheerleading team, Monica. She was drop dead gorgeous. Most of the school's cheerleading team, as well as former team members always showed up to our parties. Some of the finest females who had graduated years earlier and moved on to college also showed up. Darnell's brother Jarrad, who became a dear friend along with each of his fine sisters, who I loved, often showed up. My Brooklyn cats would come through, as well as some of my Brooklyn girls. There was crazy weed in the place. My brother Kaheem and I would go to the Rastas on Franklin Avenue and buy that good weed by the pound. Dudes at the party had coke, pills, liquor, you name it and it probably was there; folks were partying hard.

My girlfriend stayed on lockdown, she couldn't get out the house to party. Although one time, she sneaked out of the house and came to hang out for a minute. The entire 60s crew always came through: Jason, Artie, Flood, as well as the area project dudes that I knew as well as those who ran with my brother. Some of the project girls got invitations too, but only the finest ones; we only gave out invitations to the finest young ladies; we discriminated like a motherfucker.

Our parties were always the talk of the school for sure and most parts of the neighborhood. One dude approached me and my friends days after the party, excitedly ranting on about how the party was off the hook, "Dulla had White girls and White dudes there and everything"; I just laughed. Most people at that time called me "Dulla," short for Abdullah, which was how my parents always referred to me.

Jason was using drugs heavily at the time, cocaine; that was his dirty little secret. He was blowing through money like water. While I had thousands of dollars stashed away and had purchased most of what I needed, Jason was broke. I got a call one day to meet up with him and he looked like hell and I told him so. He told me that he wasn't sleeping and that he was thinking about driving down to California and if I wanted to ride. I told him hell no, but I would catch up with him when he returned. Jason was impulsive like that. We would be sitting in the car in Queens, fucked-up, loaded gun, bags of weed, and his bottles of liquor, I didn't drink, and he would suggest that we immediately ride down to Maine to get some fresh lobsters, crazy dude. I was usually down for whatever, but California was definitely not a go. I was having too much fun in New York City.

Jason rode down to California solo. Months later, he had not returned and neither I nor anyone else had heard from him. His parents would say when asked that "he's OK, he's still in California." Anyway, I later learned he had pulled an armed robbery down there and had been arrested. He was sentenced to one year in jail.

Upon Jason's returning from California, we were all glad to see him, but he had changed some. He had put on some weight, not all muscle either. The innocence of a young, middle class guy was gone and there was a more hardened, less straightforward dude standing in front of me. Still, this was my dude, and we will ride together whatever.

Almost immediately upon coming home, Jason was suggesting we get to robbing places; I was in. My money was low; I wasn't doing crimes while Jason was away. We hit one spot and came off for thousands. I thought, "Yes, we're straight for a minute, no money worries at all." Less than two weeks later, Jason came around saying let's hit something up; he said that he was broke. His eyes were bloodshot red, he hadn't shaved in what looked like days and he looked bad and I told him so. He shrugged it off, claiming to be stressed. He may have been stressed but he was still also addicted to cocaine.

I had thousands of dollars stashed away, and although I enjoyed the rush and excitement of sticking up places almost as much as the money, that voice was ringing in my head, "Don't be dumb and don't be greedy." I began to duck Jason at every opportunity.

At that time, I was spending a lot of time with my man Artie. He was a clean-cut kid originally from Beaufort, Georgia; he was a genuine country guy. He was a stand-up dude though, well respected in the Rockaways. Artie was a few years older than I was, and he was the starting cornerback/safety for the varsity football team. Artie was still just a teenager like the rest of us; however, he looked like a grown ass man.

Although a high school student, Artie was basically raising himself and had been for years. He had a two-bedroom apartment in the Edgemere housing projects that he shared with his mom. However, she suffered from severe mental illness, and so, she was often confined to mental care units for months at a time, leaving Artie alone to basically fend for himself. The rare days that she was home he cared for her like a real adult. He cooked, cleaned, ran errands, did laundry, he did everything for the both of them. He loved his mom and did everything to make sure that she was OK. Sometimes, she would wander out the house and he would frantically walk around the neighborhood trying to find her and bring her back home before she was injured somehow.

He did all that while attending high school, making good grades, working part-time and being a star player on the football team; I had massive respect for Artie. I would spend many of my days by his place or he would come by me. We would sit and talk for hours about the lives we were going to have in the future and all the great things that we wanted to achieve.

Artie was a great influence in my life and thank goodness, although he loved me to death, his mindset was so strong that he never allowed anyone, even my crazy ass, to pull him too far off the straight and narrow. I recall, one day, while walking on the backstreets of Rockaway with Artie laughing and talking, when an older model car came cruising slowly down the backstreets towards us. The car slowed about 10 feet from us to allow Artie and me to pass, cross the street, we had the right of way. As we were crossing, the driver throttled the car, to try and frighten us, as if he were going to run us down.

I often carried a fake .357 Magnum to prank people, but often, to discreetly flash, so dudes would think I had my gun with me always. Anyway, I pulled the fake gun and aimed it at the car that was still in front of us and both the driver and the passenger simultaneously did some military type move, bending their heads down, placing their arms in positions to protect their heads. I immediately knew that they were police. They looked up and opened car doors, guns in hand, aiming. I had already sized up the situation and knew what time it was. So, I had already thrown the gun and my hands were raised and I was yelling, "It's fake, it's fake." Artie, throughout the whole incident was frozen stiff, like *what the fuck?* I felt horrible for Artie; I almost got us both fucking killed.

The police handcuffed me and took me to the precinct. I must have been fifteen at the time, but the police didn't believe me so, they called my house to verify my age. My big brother Kaheem picked up the phone and smoothly handled the whole thing. He told them I was a minor and that my dad was going to kick my ass when he found out. He told them that he was on his way there to pick me up so my dad could kick my ass. My brother came to the precinct, showed his college ID; he was a college freshman at the time and he looked twenty-five but he was barely eighteen. They released me to his custody, but gave me a Family Court appearance ticket.

My brother and I went home, smoked some weed and discussed whether we should inform Mom and Dad. My brother was my idol. Most of what I did was for him and others to respect my gangster, and my brother did. He was openly proud of his little brother and that made me feel good. When someone you look up to respects you back, it's a good feeling. My brother didn't have open respect for many dudes, so that made it all the better.

My brother and I, although we were three years apart in age, were very close. Originally, he was closest to my oldest brother, Shareef; they were thick as thieves. My oldest brother Shareef, the story goes, smoked a bag of bad weed one day and went on a mental trip, never to return. He was in and out of mental care units from about nineteen years old until adulthood. Before mental illness set in, my brother Shareef was the man. Shareef was tall with male model good looks, top student brains, brawn, style, charisma, humor. He was the complete package. He wore the best clothes, dated the finest women and had the respect of all the dudes in the neighborhood, the street dudes and the geeks. My brother Kaheem looked up to him and was Shareef's shadow, they were mad close. I was too young to run with them, but I always watched how they moved and I took notes.

Shareef was always in academically gifted programs. He was an A student at Brooklyn Technical High School, one of the most elite high schools in New York City. That school only accepted academically gifted students and Shareef was at the top of the top. However, he was still street to the bone gristle. He smoked weed, sold weed, partied, ran with the crew, and boned mad, fine chicks, street to the bone.

Before Shareef had the mental breakdown, my other brother began also hanging with a new to the neighborhood dude named Xavier. Xavier came from a huge ass family and all of them were wild; cool as heck, though. I don't know how many children were in that family, but it was definitely a bunch of them.

Xavier became like a second big brother to me and I guess to my brother too, although they were pretty close in age. My brother looked up to Xavier, and that says a lot because again, not many dudes did my brother ever look up to.

Xavier was crazy. He was high yellow complexion, medium height with a slim build but he was freakishly strong. Fairly mild-mannered, at least compared to his other brothers who were buck-wild from the time they came out the house to play to the time they went back home.

Xavier was the type of dude who didn't fear anyone, and if you ever fought him you had to practically kill him or you were in trouble. Xavier well knew his own physical abilities, but simply by looking at him, his slight build and fair skin, most people would have no clue; light-skin dudes were often seen as soft.

One day, Todd, a much older, big muscle bound prankster, was on our block pranking the younger teens and pre-teens as he often did. Todd pranked Xavier by pulling his floppy hat down over his eyes and calling him names as Todd laughingly ran away. Xavier told the big group of us standing around that he didn't like pranks and that if Todd pranked him again, he was going to fuck Todd up. I and others knew Xavier was dead-ass serious, but I would have not bet money on Xavier in a fight against muscle-man Todd.

Days later, my brother and Xavier were hanging in my building lobby just kicking it, when Todd walked into the lobby. I didn't see the prank, but later heard that Todd blew cigarette smoke in Xavier's face and simultaneously pulled Xavier's floppy hat down over his nose to lock the smoke in.

The part I saw, as I was coming down the stairs, was when Xavier, in one swift motion, picked this big, muscle-bound dude up, and slammed him face first into the hard ass granite floor of the hallway lobby, WWE wrestling style. He then proceeded to whip Todd's ass. My brother finally got Xavier off of him but that ass whipping was ugly.

Days later Todd came on the block and both his eyes were still practically closed shut from the beating and his bottom lip was swelled up like a balloon. Xavier had sent a message as one of the newer kids on the block, and the block had heard it, loud and clear.

When my brother was a teenager, you would have to search far and wide, to find another in his age group, who could straight beat him, hand to hand. One out of a massively huge group of teens could potentially do it. Xavier potentially was that one and I believe my brother knew it. He didn't fear Xavier, as some may have, but he had a big-time respect for him.

Xavier was not intimidated by my brother even a little bit; in fact, Xavier openly talked about how they were best friends and how best friends always eventually fought. It was almost like Xavier was looking forward to the day – that boy was crazy.

After we moved to Queens, the relationship between Xavier and my brother grew distant. They still remained best friends for a while, but my brother was about fifteen years old at the time, no car, and the large distance between Rockaway and Bushwick on the subway made it impossible for the two to hang tough like they had in the past. My brother, besides with me, never really clicked again with a dude as he did with Xavier.

My brother and I were always fairly close but I was too young to really hang. However, after he came home from juvy, I was a little older and we hung tough. He and I shared the basement space in our Queens home and we had big fun down there. We had the place decked out nicely, always kept weed, music and women flowing through there. It was a big one-room setup. He had his bed on one side of the room and I had my bed on the other. Oftentimes he'd be laying up doing his thing with one of his girls and I'd be in my bed with her best friend. Other times, I'd come home with a girl, ready to do the thing and the door would be locked. My big brother is in there with some female who doesn't want to share the room.

Other times, my brother and I would spend hours in the basement smoking weed and just talking about life, the future, women, everything, sometimes until the sun came up. We also always found time to work out, whether we were high or not. We did pushups, dips and slap boxed until we were drenched in sweat, exhausted. My brother was good with his hands, a good fighter, and I was good too. I had grown by that time taller than my brother. I was six foot two, 195 pounds whereas my brother was six foot one about 205. Although my brother was three years older than me and definitely stronger, hand to hand, if I couldn't take him, he definitely would get a very close fight, and he knew it. We would hit up all the clubs and parties throughout New York City. If it was a party, Manhattan, Brooklyn, Queens, we were in there, fake ID and all.

Jason was back from California and the robberies began soon thereafter. I later began to duck Jason as often as I could because although I had no experience with drug addiction to realize he was on drugs, I knew that something was off. Jason had recently pulled a solo robbery as well. I had kind of suspected that and it came to light when I heard of a neighborhood spot being hit. Upon casually inquiring one of the employees described the robber, the person described was definitely Jason.

The day we got busted, Jason had come to me about a score that was too big for him to pull off alone; he couldn't cover everyone and grab the dough. He confessed that he had done some work solo and I told him that I had already known. I informed Jason that I would roll with him, but every instinct in my body said no. When we arrived at the place, everything was wrong. It was located on a busy street, many people were in the place, traffic lights were up and down the strip, and it was a good distance from the nearest highway.

When we walked in the establishment, everything was wrong. The two managers noticed Jason; he looked like a drug addict. Then they noticed me, I looked out of place walking with him. One picked up the phone and began to dial. Jason said, "Let's do it," and we pulled out on the dude and told him to put the phone down. Jason did what he did, collecting all the receipts, pulling out the phones, and we headed out. It was too sloppy and people noticed the robbery and started fleeing in different directions.

Usually, we would calmly walk out of the establishment, but we knew the police had to be on the way, so we ran, another no-no. When we arrived at the car, a person was staring, others were pointing in our direction. We got in the car, and standard procedure was that I sit in the front seat and lay the seat flat, creating the appearance that a lone White male was in the car. However, this time, detectives saw us flee the store and they followed us to the car. Almost immediately upon laying the seat flat, I heard Jason say, "They on us, Du, they got guns out." Out of the corner of my eye, I saw Jason place both hands behind his head, like he was giving up. Detectives were around the car with guns drawn. I knew the days ahead were going to be different, but I had absolutely no idea how different they would be.

Months before my arrest, my brother Kaheem had been arrested on a gun possession charge. They sentenced him to one year in jail and I was missing him like crazy. He was one of the few dudes besides Jason who enjoyed venturing out to wherever. We rarely stayed in Queens. Around that time, I was often ducking Jason, so I was rolling throughout the city solo quite often.

I still knew a number of the club owners and bouncers from hanging with my dude, Darnell, and at the spots where I didn't know anyone,

I usually talked my way in or flashed one of my numerous fake IDs. I enjoyed partying with grown women because they were more mature and understood and related to my personality more than teenage girls did. I always came through fly as a motherfucker, tailor made clothes, fly shoes, and thousands of dollars' worth of jewelry. Some old dudes would hate but most showed me love and respect.

I always knew that most dudes weren't on my level, even amongst these old heads. My attitude was always "never let a motherfucker front on you," old or young. I kept my gun with me more often in those days; I just sensed the streets were becoming more dangerous. When I arrived at the club, I would put my gun in a brown paper bag and then locate an abandoned building, alley, or dark area, where I would tuck my gun. The place had to be as close as possible to the club.

After passing through the metal detector, partying, smoking, and having fun, I'd collect my firearm, go grab a bite to eat, and often chill with a lady I had met in the club. My favorite spots in Manhattan were Studio 54, Bonds, and the Paradise Garage. The Garage was crazy because I would get there sometimes at 11:00 p.m. and leave the spot at 8:00 a.m., and people would still be partying, and some just getting there. That place was off the hook.

One day, while at school, I ran into my old girlfriend and she said that she had to talk to me. She and I had taken a break from dating. There were so many obstacles to us spending quality time together and the penalties for her breaking curfew to see me were too severe to handle; her parents didn't play. Anyway, she said that she was pregnant and that she and her parents had decided that they were going to keep the baby and raise the baby alone, meaning without me. She told me that she was ordered to have no more contact with me and that she would notify her parents if I tried to approach her again.

My mouth was on the floor. I asked her whether this was all decided without my input or opinion. She said the baby was like a gift I gave to her and once she had it, she could do whatever she wanted with it, she was gone.

Being young, I did not understand all the dynamics of the situation, but I knew enough about her crazy ass, religious fanatic family to know that she, without doubt, was under extreme stress from home and at church because of the pregnancy. I still had feelings for her and even after all of that, in my mind, she was still my heart and she was having my baby. So, I decided to give her some space, but I notified my parents so they could intervene, parents to parents.

Days later, my parents and her parents met for the first time to discuss the pregnancy. Her parents went on to lecture my parents about how I had corrupted their daughter and that this entire affair was my fault. What Inga's parents honestly did not understand was that they had corrupted their own daughter with their extremely oppressive child-rearing. The human heart longs to be free, not caged up. In my opinion, the restrictions they placed on her since she was a child until her teenage years encouraged her rebellion. Inga's mind was made up to rebel long before I came along, that I know, and she had rebelled in her own ways a number of times before I came along. Our relationship was not her first rebellion, although it was likely her most sustained and her most intense. Inga's parents would later learn that her rebellion would continue in a big way, too, even well after I was out of the picture. What a shock.

Her parents then went on to detail the financial arrangements they wanted from my parents, but access to the baby they detailed would be practically nonexistent. They then told my father that the child would be raised as a Jehovah's Witness. Dad definitely didn't agree with that. Talks broke down and no negotiated settlement was reached. Inga's family adamantly refused to allow me to have any contact with Inga or with my son.

Not long after discovering Inga was pregnant, another young lady I had briefly dated after breaking up with Inga informed me that she was also pregnant. P was an older girl who lived in Hammel housing project, in Far Rockaway. I actually met her while visiting her apartment with a friend of mine, Kelroy. Kelroy urged me to walk with him to meet her and raved about how cute she was and that he was going to put her in the bag, make her his new girlfriend. When we arrived at her place, she definitely was cute, but she didn't seem that into him, it was more like he was a friend, not a boyfriend. Kelroy was definitely deluding himself. P was obviously not romantically interested in him at all. Kelroy eventually picked up on that very apparent fact and moved on.

Some weeks later, however, a friend of mine from school, Janee, informed me that her friend, P, wanted to meet me. She described her friend for me, and Janee said that I would definitely like her. Janee arranged the meet-up and it was P, the same P who had my boy's nose wide open some weeks earlier. P and I talked a while and I definitely wanted to know about her relationship with my dude, Kelroy. She said there was none, he was a friend, who likely wanted more. P and I started talking, she was very cool. She was a very motivated young lady and she was determined to make something out of her life. I liked her. P and I began a short whirlwind romance.

I was surprised to hear that P was pregnant; however, I was often so reckless during those days that it wasn't a shock. Here I am, a high school sophomore, with two babies on the way, and potentially serious baby momma drama. Both Inga and P were still students at the school and word on the street was that they used to be friends. So, people were talking about how I knocked up two best friends. People started taking sides, some supported Inga while others supported P, and I had to work hard to keep things from exploding. With herculean effort and numerous interventions, often with people who didn't have jack to do with the situation, the drama was basically contained. Much of the tension came from people who were not feeling Inga and her family because they felt that they flipped on me after she became pregnant. Yes, that was true, but I understood the dynamics. Inga could not stand next to me even if she wanted to, the pressure from her church and family was too severe. Thus, I kept silly people out of her face and out of our business.

In the summer of 1981, Inga gave birth to my son while, two months later, P gave birth to my daughter. I named my daughter. Inga's family named my son. Both of my children were good looking, just like their dad. In the early days, after my son's birth, Inga would allow me to sneak by to see him, when her parents weren't home. One day, they caught me leaving and they gave her hell, and threatened to have me arrested for trespassing if I ever came by again. Inga and her family never allowed me to see my son again.

I didn't know anything about family court and father's visitation rights back then; all I knew was that, in time, I would see my son. For now, I couldn't put any undue pressure on Inga's life. She often looked extremely stressed, so I fell back. However, P always allowed me to see my daughter, she welcomed it. Even when I went to jail, she made sure that I had ways to contact them and that my daughter stayed in contact with me, too. Often times, P and I went out with our daughter as a family. Some thought we were still a couple, we weren't. We were just two young people committed to doing right by their daughter, the best we knew how. My daughter stayed at my home many days and nights, too. I enjoyed being a father. My daughter was my pride and joy.

When the police handcuffed Jason and me, they placed us in the back of the police car. They drove us to the police station and placed us in a holding cell. Detectives and other officers would periodically come by the cell to peer in at us. One of them peered in at us and said, "Salt and Pepper, we've been looking for you for a long time." Another detective came in the holding cell area, walked over to where I was standing, eyed me up and down, and said to me, "What the fuck are you doing here? You had the fucking world by the balls." I never forgot that cop and his words. For some reason, they stuck in my mind for years to come. At the time, I just thought, *"What the fuck does this cop possibly know about me?"*

I had just turned seventeen and Jason was about to turn twenty-one, so they processed us as young adults and drove us over to Rikers Island, jail, the part for defendants under age twenty-one.

Ironically, I had just been on Rikers Island less than two weeks earlier, visiting my brother who was serving a year on Rikers for a gun charge. I usually visited him every other week or so, bringing him money, clothes, and putting money in his inmate account. The craziest part of the visit was, I always visited fly to the bone, mad jewelry, and money on me, and the visitors' bus was usually filled with dudes and females from all over the city, rough and tough individuals, including other stick-up kids for certain; I rode up with my gun. When the bus pulled up to the Rikers Island visitor's area, I went inside, where we were offered lockers before going through screening, and onto the actual visit. I placed my gun and other valuables in the locker, then moved on to the screening. When the visit was over, I would collect my gun and other valuables from the locker and head out.

When Jason and I were transported to Rikers Island that night, I knew my brother was there, but in a different unit. I believe he was in the sentenced part, C76, while I was in the waiting trial or pre-sentencing part, C74. I knew he would know I was there soon enough. Word spread quickly behind bars.

Nothing about prison frightened me, nothing. I had been groomed for this practically my entire life. I was more anxious to get the process going more than anything else. Finally, I am here.

In the summer of 1982, I was finishing up summer classes at Jamaica High School and was scheduled to graduate on time. Actually, because I had skipped a grade, I was really scheduled to graduate a year earlier than most, just turning seventeen. After the arrest, that never happened. Actually, before the arrest, I was doing pretty well, working, attending class more regularly, and spending a lot of time with my daughter.

I had accepted an after school job at Burger King, over on the turnpike in Queens. My dude, Darnell, soon followed and we worked there together. Darnell, being fair-skinned, was often asked to work the register; I had to work in the back. It was an unwritten policy at that store that fair-skinned Blacks were allowed to work the front register, but darker skinned Blacks were not. They're lucky they didn't put my black ass on that register anyway; I would have been robbing those motherfuckers' blind.

Darnell and I found other ways to hit them up though. We would move chicken patties and whopper patties out of that place by the crate, "Fuck 'em." On our days off, we were making whoppers and chicken sandwiches at home, extra cheese.

One day, I'm sitting with the manager while on break and Darnell comes out of the back kitchen area and his gym bag is so fucking heavy, he can barely carry it. The manager is like, "What the heck you got in that bag?" I tried to cover right away because I knew what was in there, all kinds of Burger King shit. So, Darnell explains just clothes and things and I chime in some bullshit to try to throw her off, but she was adamant that he had to open the bag. I push back harder. "How you going to tell that man to let you search his personal stuff?" She was like, "Open it or you cannot come back." Darnell bounced and resigned.

After Darnell left, I got cool with another dude from Far Rockaway, Redfern housing projects, who also worked at Burger King, my dude, Black. Black was a green eyed, quiet, smooth dude. Ladies loved him and he was a standup dude. He basically ran solo; he and his girl were usually locked at the hip. He didn't run with a crew. However, he would step to his business, address threats, solo or with his big brother, who, through reputation, was apparently the real deal. I met his brother a few times at the store when he came to see Black. I had the 411 on both of them from my dude, Keith. Keith lived in Redfern, too, and he introduced me to the major players living in Redfern housing project. He schooled me early on to never sleep on Black. He said, "Don't let that quiet shit fool you."

Black would later kill a man; I believe it to be over an incident with Black's girl. This happened a few months before I was arrested and Black was given a life sentence. I later ran into Black in Attica Correctional Facility, where he and I were the best of friends. While in Attica, Black's brother was murdered, the story goes, in a brutal fashion. He was tortured and mutilated in his own apartment. They found his body in the bathroom tub; he apparently was there for a few days. I gave Black space so he could grieve, his brother was his dude for real. It was similar to me and my brother, the one person you would choose to ride or die with. I knew what he was going through.

When my brother heard that I was on the Island, he sent a kite, written note, saying simply, "Hold your head and don't let crab motherfuckers front on you." That was our motto as long ago as I could remember. "Do not let a motherfucker front on you." I lived by it and, if necessary, would die by it, fuck it.

I finally got to the housing unit where I was to be housed, I believe, 4 lower. It was night so everyone was locked in. In the morning, in the day room, I got to see the other dudes on the unit. Queens's dudes had that unit on lock, mostly dudes from Jamaica, Queens. The Island was cliquish, meaning that everyone basically represented their borough, Queens ran with Queens, Brooklyn with Brooklyn, etc. The entire prison system is like that to a certain degree, very tribal.

I had roots in two boroughs, Brooklyn and Queens, and although I had love for my Queens cats, I didn't naturally click with them, never really did. In prison, Brooklyn claimed me as one of their own for many reasons, and I always represented Brooklyn to the fullest.

Right away, the Queens's dudes in the housing unit thought I was from Brooklyn, but later realized after a short back and forth that I lived in Queens. I guess that made me somewhat safe, at least for the moment; it was still early morning. Shit almost hit the fan right after lunch though, when I came into the day room, a place where inmates from the unit can mingle. The day room had about four separate tables, each large enough to seat four. There were about twenty dudes on the unit, all gathered in the day room. After lunch, I arrived in the day room close to first, soon followed by others. I sat at the table the closest to the TV and was watching TV. Some scrub approaches, saying I had to move and that I could not sit at that table. I thought he was joking but he said it again. By that time, the entire unit had arrived to the day room and the kid stopped talking to me and began talking to four or five dudes who looked like they ran the unit.

One was a big dude about six feet, 220, my brother's size, obviously the leader. The other was second in command, about five-ten solid muscle, then two or three others. They went on to explain that "new jacks," new inmates, could not sit at their table, touch the TV, and a list of other "house rules." I'm looking at these dudes as I am still sitting at the table, like, *you are fucking bugging.* I had already sized them all up, and none of them were on my fucking level. I understood what they were saying, basically that there is a pecking order and that new inmates in jail and on that unit are at the bottom. However, mankind, too, has a pecking order and among mankind, I am at the fucking top. So, now, we definitely have a problem.

The big one, hand to hand, could not beat me with ten tries, none of them could. Like he was reading my mind, the big one said, "The rules are the rules, and in jail, you are not going to get a fair one," meaning that they would jump me. It was still a problem though. My mind would not allow me to bow to the will of a lesser man, even if it was four or five of them so, "what will be, will be," and the big one knew it.

Right then, the second in command looked at me real hard and said, "Yo, you look mad familiar. You have family on the Island?"

I said, "My brother is on the Island."

He asks his name and I said, "Kaheem."

He asked, almost in an awed tone, "Big Kaheem's your brother?" Funny thing is, my brother once told me that he meets dudes sometimes and they speak with "awe-like tones" when they talked about me or upon finding out we were brothers, maximum respect. I just laughed because I knew the awe-like tone he was speaking of. I saw it before, and this dude was an example of it.

The second in command told me that my brother and I looked just alike; many people did confuse us as twins. He told me that he and my brother were in juvy together and that my brother was his man for real. He then asked the big leader, "Yo, you know my man, Big Kaheem, from the 6 building (C76), right?"

The leader was like, "Yeah, yeah, I know Big Kaheem." The second in command went on to tell me that my brother had respect throughout the Island and that he would never allow anyone to front on him. He said, "Your brother wouldn't allow it and don't you allow it either." In an instant, I was received to the top of the pecking order; I sat at the table whenever I wanted to, no problems.

My brother had been on Rikers for a few months already so he was established. He knew many people there and many people knew him. Upon my arrival, my brother and his people began sending the word that I was there and that I was people. For the most part, besides minor incidents, I had no real issues on the Island. However, since my brother and I were little boys growing up in Brooklyn, his friends were my friends and his enemies were my enemies, too. If he went to war, I went with him, no questions asked. We'd often talk about the reasons for the fight only after the fight was actually over.

I recall often, while being in the second and third grade, coming out of school at 3:00 p.m. and seeing a large, raucous, cheering, and jeering crowd. I would part the crowd, and see my brother and some big dude, battling. I immediately dropped my book bag and I jumped in. On other occasions, I would part the crowd and there's my brother, fighting two or three big dudes, sixth graders. I'd drop my book bag and immediately jump in. My brother is three grades ahead of me, so, these are sixth graders while my little ass is in second or third grade. I didn't give a fuck, you jump on my brother and we are getting it on. Actually, I was already used to fighting bigger dudes, by regularly play fighting with my older brothers, and often real fighting with older dudes on my block, so handling sixth graders as a third grader was not a big deal for me.

While on Rikers Island, my brother and I were called to court once or twice on the same date. He was facing some criminal charges in Queens separate and apart from the charges Jason and I were facing. Court day on Rikers Island was a straight nightmare. They would wake us up for court about 4:00 a.m. or 5:00 a.m. then begin moving us from one cramped holding cell to another to another one. There may be twenty-five inmates to one small holding cell. There would be one filthy, shit and piss covered toilet in the cell for twenty or more dudes to share. If you had to shit, you do it on that dirty ass toilet with twenty other dudes watching; there were no doors and no privacy.

There would be one or two small benches in the cell, enough space for four of the twenty-five men to sit down. You would often be held in these holding cells for hours at a time, either waiting for bus transport from Rikers Island to courthouses in the Bronx, Brooklyn, Queens, Manhattan or Staten Island or you were held in the outrageously nasty cells upon arriving at court, waiting to see your lawyer and then the judge.

After seeing the judge for two minutes, it's back to the filthy holding pens for more hours to wait for the return trip back to Rikers. Again, you have been up since 4:00 a.m., and the return trip to Rikers doesn't occur often times until after 9:00 p.m. So, dudes are kept locked in these cramped, crowded, disgusting holding pens, usually with backed-up, smelly toilets for at times 16 hours or more. There was so much tension, anger, and frustration in those pens. There were few benches to sit on so there's basically no place to sit except on the filthy-ass floors. Men often stood crowded in these pens, shoulder to shoulder with bodies, fighting the summer heat, and the smell of piss and shit were constantly in the air; it was inhumane. To only a fool's surprise, there were fights in those holding pens, lots of them.

In August of 1982, my brother and I ended up in one of these filthy-ass, crowded, hot, and smelly holding pens. We both had a court date in Queens. This was one of the first times I actually got to see my brother because he was confined to a different building and on a different part of Rikers Island than I was. Rikers Island was large, having numerous separate inmate housing unit/buildings and different classifications of inmates. So, my brother and I literally could be on the Island for years together and never actually see each other. That is, unless we both had the same court date, as we did that day, and thus, we'd meet in the courthouse holding pens.

It was so good to see him that I didn't notice the noise, the smells, the heat, or the hours locked in the cell. We were in our own little space, just talking about everything. He looked good, and he was in good spirits for a prisoner. For both of us, we believed, our present state of affairs was just something we had to deal with, and we would. Neither one of us looked at it as a big motherfucking deal.

After talking for hours, my brother said, "Yo, Du, I'm tired, I wanna grab a seat." Looking through the crowded pens, I could see that one bench was occupied by some dudes sitting and talking, while the next bench was occupied by one dude laid out sleeping.

My brother approached the bench with the sleeping dude and asked him, "Can I sit here?" Dude was like, "No," claiming that was his bench. That was prison; dudes claimed everything as their own, the telephone, TV, tables, benches, and sometimes even other people. Dude gave the wrong answer to my brother's question though, and I knew it. See, when my brother asked, "Can I sit here?" he was actually trying to be nice. Dude, as dudes in prison often do, took niceness for weakness and gave my brother a disrespectful response. A response that had to be addressed immediately and it was. Before I could get over there to say a word, my brother physically slid dude, by his feet, off of the bench onto the floor. It was on. Dude got up and swung once but it was futile, it wasn't even close. Police heard the commotion and stormed in, grabbing me, my brother, and dude, placing us all in isolation cells. Dude ranted on and on while in the cell, that he wanted blood, and that he was going to hit my brother up first chance.

This fight happened in the court holding cells. However, when we got back to Rikers Island from court that evening, they put us all back in the same area again, but different cells. They often did that on Rikers, put known warring factions together. Some say it was negligence, others say the C.O.'s enjoyed and encouraged the drama. I believe it was mostly the latter. Working in a place like Rikers or living there for too long, you can easily lose a piece of your soul; I would come to see that reality again and again.

Anyway, when they opened the cells to march us for strip search, I scan for my brother, I see him and we connect. Dude then appears from nowhere coming toward me and my brother. I jaws him, hit him straight in the jaw, and we start fighting. C.O. s rush in, break it up, and they put us all in isolation cells again. We sit there for hours and, eventually, they move us all back to our respective units.

This dude is still sending word to anyone who would listen that he got jumped and we didn't give him a fair fight and that he wanted revenge. He was a soldier though, not a general, and people who knew my brother and me began working hard to squash the beef. This dude apparently ran with respected dudes on the Island.

He tried to keep it going by sending word that he got jumped but everyone spoke up that he had a fair fight with my brother and lost. Then, he had a fair fight with me and lost again. Folks were sending the word, from all over the Island: all fair, no foul, so let it go. My brother and I got word that after numerous interventions from respected inmates that it was "beef squashed."

Days passed, and things were quiet again on the Island, besides the usual flare-ups here and there but the beef with this dude, as numerous other beefs with other dudes have been, it was over; or so I thought. My brother was old school and raised me with the same old school values. If you go to war, people get hurt but once the truce is signed, the war is over, and that's it. Those were the rules, however, my brother still didn't trust the dude and told me so, even though most of the jail assumed that the truce signaled that the beef was over.

I believed in the truce but I also believed my brother's gut feeling about dude, so I watched him but not closely enough. One day, while in the prison yard shooting hoops and talking with a few dudes in my new clique (I had begun building one from scratch and it was coming along), I heard the guards order the yard closed. That meant that inmates had to line up with their respective housing units and march as a unit into the building as your housing unit is called.

I knew that the dude's housing unit and my housing unit often attended the yard together, but I didn't see dude enter the yard that day. He made himself invisible. As the crowd in the yard was walking toward the line of their respective housing unit, I stopped to talk to an inmate who I vaguely knew from around the Island, not one of my people. The dudes from my unit I had been walking with kept walking, not even noticing that I had stopped to kick it with this other kid. Even if they had noticed, they probably would have kept walking anyway because as far as they knew, our unit had no beef, no reason to be on red alert.

All I felt was a violent bang to the back of the neck and I instantly fell face down to the hard concrete. I heard yelling and shouting and saw people running this way and that way. I was wide awake but I could not move a muscle. I saw numerous guards all around, and heard them shouting, trying to clear the yard, but I still couldn't move.

I had my hands in my pocket and my mind was telling them to move, but they wouldn't. Although I was lying face down on the ground, my legs felt as if they were being pulled upward toward the sky but I knew no one was actually touching me. I didn't know at the time the extent of the injury but I knew it definitely was bad. I could sense from the decrease in noise that the yard had been virtually cleared out. By this time, a few officers were around me, asking me if I could move, and I heard another on a radio asking for medical assistance in the yard.

I recall eventually being lifted from the yard on a gurney and being carried through the lobby area, where I heard the receiving room officers saying, "Fuck him, let him die." The receiving room officers were notoriously brutal and sadistic motherfuckers, and the two Black officers who were in charge were the worst. Everyone on Rikers Island knew these two bastards and feared them, hated them, or both. Their feelings, thoughts, and words didn't move me. I didn't know them, although I knew of them, didn't want to know them, so fuck 'em. I was more concerned about the injury.

I lay on that gurney for hours, in a dimly lit corner of the jail, untreated; I was practically ignored. A nurse came by once and asked some basic questions and then was gone, no treatment, no nothing. Any time I saw an officer pass by, I would ask if they could get me to the hospital. Most kept walking. One told me that they were waiting for transport to the hospital. I just waited. Hours later, some officers appeared and said that they were transporting me to Bellevue Hospital. They handcuffed me, shackled me, and strapped me to the gurney at the waist and the feet. I couldn't run away if I wanted to. I still couldn't move a muscle from my neck down. The transporting officers were three White officers, ignorant rednecks, and they called me every kind of fucking dumb nigger motherfucker in the book. They wanted me to tell them about the attack, but not so they could do anything about it but simply so that they could have a war story about how niggers attacked each other when they got home. They didn't care one bit about me and I didn't waste my little energy engaging their bullshit.

Upon arriving at Bellevue Hospital, approximately six hours after the stabbing, the officers wheeled me on the gurney into a waiting area, and I waited there for another five hours or more, waiting to be seen by a doctor. When the examining doctor finally appeared, it had to be close to midnight. I had been stabbed earlier that afternoon, twelve hours earlier.

They took X-rays, gave me a spinal tap, and ran a number of other tests. All of them, I cannot recall. The doctor finally informed me that it appeared that the injury was caused by an ice pick and that the ice pick had punctured my spinal cord. The doctor informed me that there was serious injury to the cord and that there was a lot of swelling around it. He said that was why I could not move. So, I asked the doctor exactly how long this paralysis, as he called it, would last. He informed me that as the swelling around the cord went down, I would likely regain some movement but he couldn't say exactly how much. The doctor said, "You are lucky to be alive but there is a very good chance that you may never walk again." I looked at this dude like he was on drugs. I'm walking, fuck that. I didn't even let that register into my psyche. I totally rejected that bullshit.

I remained in Bellevue Hospital for weeks and for the first two weeks, I was totally confined to the bed. I could not move a muscle from the neck down.

Around the second week in the hospital, I began regaining movement in my upper body, arms, shoulders, and then hands and fingers. However, nothing in the legs, I could not move them at all. I often lay in the hospital bed for long periods, just staring at my legs and ordering them with my mind to move. Nothing. The frustration that this caused was intense. Why the limbs were not following the instructions of the brain was bothering me. I later learned from the doctor that although the mind was sending the legs the message, the damage to the cord was not allowing the legs to receive it. I was just hopeful that if the swelling went down a little more, maybe then, the message would get through.

Around the third or fourth week in the hospital, I woke up one morning, and I could move my legs – only a little, but they moved. The next day, I could also move the feet but I couldn't wiggle my toes, I had no movement there. I knew intuitively that if I ever wiggled those motherfucking toes, I was walking next. Days later, they wiggled.

Feeling happy, I slowly slid my legs out of the hospital bed, placing my feet on the floor for the first time in weeks and braced myself with my upper body. Here it goes. I stood; I fell, banging my head on something. I laid on the floor thinking, this ain't going to be easy but this is going to happen, I'm walking.

Another inmate in the room with me helped me up and got me back in the bed. This dude was crazy as hell, and funnier than all outdoors. He kept me laughing with prison war stories; he was a prison veteran, in and out of jail since juvenile detention. He was in the hospital because his ear had been bitten off during a fight with another inmate on Rikers Island. He told me that he looked down and saw his ear on the floor dancing around like it was at a fucking party. I told him that probably was the nerves in the ear being still alive and not knowing what was going on.

We laughed and laughed during those hard days and we bonded at a different level. I later learned that people who you meet in your bleakest hours in life (for example, hospital recovery wards), you often bond with at a level that an average person could never understand. Maybe because you see them at their most vulnerable moments, mentally and physically, and they see you, too, yet rather than taking advantage of each other, you lift each other up. The love and the absolute trust that develops thereafter exists at a level that the average person could never comprehend. It's literally like a brotherhood, the love and the trust runs that deep.

In fact, I ran into this same dude years later, in Clinton, an upstate correctional facility. At the time, Clinton was one of the most notorious prisons in New York State and this same dude was the primary muscle for one of my more recent enemies. The enemy was handled and my clique wanted to know whether this dude should be touched, too. My clique, when I asked, told me dude's name, but it didn't register and his appearance, as did mine, had changed significantly since we were teenagers in Bellevue Hospital, many years earlier. However, one day, he walked past my cell, and I glimpsed his face more closely. I didn't recognize the face, but I then glimpsed the ear and it all came rushing back. I couldn't allow the dude to be hit up, so I let it ride. I never told him how close he was to being hit. He most likely never had a clue. That hospital bonding ran deep.

Weeks after the stabbing, I was standing with the help of a walker but still I couldn't walk. However, I felt in my bones that it would happen, I knew it. My family was pissed off, my brother wanted blood. My attitude was "shit happens," you simply try to make it right.

My dad saw me for the first time when he came to visit me in the hospital; I was wheeled out to him on a gurney. Lying flat on my back and handcuffed to the gurney's railing, we were separated by a security glass, him on one side and I on the other, and we talked for a while. However, I was very weak and because of the spinal injury, I had no real control over my bladder function for a good while and when the urge to pee came, I was helpless to control it. I peed all over the floor, and my dad was through. His anger was palpable and I understood it. He couldn't continue the visit; he told me that he had to go.

My father always believed that many of the ills that came my way were because of his poverty. He felt that I had potential and he always told me, "You are going to do something very special." He told me that, "be it through marriage or some means," he didn't yet know. He told me this as a child and even while incarcerated, he repeated it as if he had a vision. My dad was a very spiritual man and often simply sensed things, and was often pretty accurate. However, the only vision he was experiencing now, as I peed on that floor, was anger. As the nurses and doctor came out to tend to me, he had to leave. My dad took anger with him deep into his later years about the way the criminal justice system treated his sons. At that moment, he was a very unhappy man.

My dad always said that if you do the crime, you have to pay. However, he felt that the system was extremely brutal towards me at every turn. The fight he had to wage to get me bare basic medical care after my injury was more than enough proof that something was off within the system. He believed that if he had just a little bit of money, everyone within the criminal justice system, from the courts to the hospitals and medical providers, would have treated him and his children, although they went wrong, at a minimum, like humans should treat one another. He believed that in his heart and it pained him that he didn't have money and power to fight the system, and it pained him that the system appeared to respond best to those who had money and power in the beginning.

He also believed that his temperament and my refusal to hang my head low before any man made the overt and blatant hostility toward me worse. My dad believed that you should speak truth to power whenever power is being misused or abused. The thing is, when the powerless speak truth to power, power often doubles down, because abuse of power is often the manifestation of a diseased heart. Someone once said that "power corrupts and absolute power corrupts absolutely." I believe the corruption spoken of is the corruption of the heart.

So, when one speaks truth to power, it's not like in the movies, where people break down in tears, repent, and accept the truth. No. In real life, when you speak truth to power, be prepared for them to become indignant, and possibly determined to crush you. They are going to try to bury you under their feet; that is how it goes in the real world. In the streets, in prison, and every fucking where, if you challenge power, be prepared for the retaliation.

However, my dad apparently believed that you could touch a man's heart with pure truth, from his mouth to their hearts. I love my dad but I didn't buy that stuff he was selling. I believed that these peoples' hearts were too messed up, so the truth did nothing but enrage them. These people were worse than dudes on the street because at least you knew what dudes on the street were about. The people we were dealing with hid their true selves behind expensive suits, uniforms signifying authority, and respectable titles. In my mind, these were the worst type of motherfuckers.

After about a month or more in Bellevue Hospital, I was released, wheelchair bound, and sent back to Rikers Island. The doctors told me that there was nothing more they could do; however, I would need intensive physical therapy. My dad fought to have me kept at Bellevue because he knew that once I returned to Rikers Island, getting the intense physical therapy that I required likely would not happen, and he was correct. The prison refused to agree to transport me back and forth from Rikers Island jail to a rehab center at Bellevue on a daily basis, which was needed; they were not doing that.

Upon leaving Bellevue, they first transported me, wheelchair bound, back to the building where I was stabbed, C74. They pulled up to the reception area and the reception room officers came out; they were notorious for being bags of shit. They said, "Is that the kid who got stabbed in the yard?" They went on to curse me out, asking why I didn't "just die." They went on to explain to the transporting officers that "wheelchair bound motherfuckers are housed in the prison hospital down the road, not in regular housing units." They went on to say, "That motherfucker don't want to come in here anyway." I just looked at them with the look that I heard that I will often give to people, the "Fuck you, because you aren't on my level" look. I learned early on not to waste time arguing with assholes, a rule I live by to this day; it's a total waste of time and energy. However, I was thinking to myself as they were talking, *I am not afraid of prison, not even a little bit.*

Looking totally confused and lost, the transport officers rode around, and pulled up to the hospital unit on Rikers Island. The hospital unit was a large, dingy building with different floors and various wards. On the floor, I was eventually transported to, there was a ward to the left of the elevators when you came off and another ward to the right. When you entered either ward, it was a dormitory style set-up, with approximately twelve beds, headboards to the wall on one side of the ward and the same on the other side. In the middle of the floor, you had tables where guys sat, ate, or whatever, and in the front of the ward was a TV. In the back of the ward was a ping pong table and at the far end, where my bed would eventually be, was an open patio, caged in, of course, where guys could go outside to smoke or just sit around. The ward's entry door was heavy solid metal and when it shut, it made that real prison door closing noise.

There were no correction officers inside the wards. There was a desk outside of the ward, where a correction officer sat, for eight-hour shifts. Inside the ward, hardcore prisoners ran that place, period. Again, when I first arrived at the ward, before I was sent upstairs to a ward, reception officers greeted me with questions about my injury and medical needs. They asked my age, and upon realizing that I was barely seventeen years old, they informed me that they didn't have a ward for minors, only adults. They told me that the minors were kept separate from the adults for their protection and were placed in individual cells, in isolation. I informed them that I did not want to be in isolation and that I would take my chances being housed with the adults.

Rikers Island at that time had a strict isolation policy, meaning that if you were under twenty-one years old, you housed with other inmates they considered minors, other inmates under twenty-one. This was a strict rule, one I was now asking them to break. The hospital had very few minors, so they had no individual minor wards, I basically would be locked in a cell with no one to socialize with and kept separated from other inmates. That sounded too much like "PC" (protective custody). In prison, we said PC stood for "punk city," and I definitely was not going to any environment that even looked like "punk city," not happening. I convinced the officers, who were pretty decent, that I could handle myself with the adults and was willing to sign a document relieving the prison of liability, which seemed to be their main issue. Eventually, they didn't compel me into an isolation cell and they allowed me to go upstairs to the ward with the adults.

When I arrived at the ward, I instantly thought, maybe this wasn't the best idea. The hospital ward was fucking filthy. It was filled with trash, cigarette smoke, and noise. The officer showed me where my bed was, last bed in the back of the ward by the patio, where numerous inmates were already gathered, talking, smoking, and blaring the portable radio that was a staple on each ward. The guard gave me some dirty sheets that looked like someone had used them for days, a dingy white towel, and a bar of stinking soap. He gave me a small box of cereal and a hot little container of milk. He then walked away, down to the front of the ward and out the door, closing it, as it made that loud ass prison door closing sound.

I just sat there for a minute, stunned, thinking, *what the fuck?* In the ward, there were countless flies, swarms of mosquitoes, and little annoying gnats were everywhere; they constantly flew into my ears. Rikers Island is surrounded by water, which exacerbated the situation. It was summer time on the Island, hot, blazing summer, no AC, and that ward had to be 100 degrees, with no breeze anywhere. I could barely breathe in that bitch.

I placed the cereal and milk on top of the small cabinet that was located next to my bed, cubicle area. I turned for a second to place the dirty sheet on top of the bed and when I turned back toward the cereal, a roach had already crawled onto the box. I swatted it away and opened the cabinet, thinking it may be safer in there, roaches swarmed out every which way upon being exposed to the light. *This is going to be crazy*, I thought.

As I looked up to scan the ward, I saw two dudes heading toward me. One was a short, heavily muscled guy, about 26 years old, no shirt, short pants, and a cast on his leg. The other dude was tall and slim, approximately 27 years old, with a full fucking body cast; he looked like a walking mummy. The short, muscle bound one approached and said, "What it is, young blood?" He had that Brooklyn swagger and accent, I recognized right away. I said, "Everything is good." He told me his name was CB and that his dude was "Skip." CB was out of Brownsville, Brooklyn, and Skip was out of Bed-stuy. CB asked how old I was and I told him that I just turned seventeen. CB asked, "What the fuck are you doing up here?" I told him the situation, about my injury and about the isolation cell and that it looked like PC, and that I wasn't going near nothing that looked like PC. CB and Skip looked at each other, looked at me, and just shook their heads like, "This dude is the real deal or just fucking crazy."

I later learned that CB was there because he had been shot during an armed robbery gone bad. There was a major shootout, after CB robbed a worker at an illegitimate establishment and the owners all appeared as he was exiting. They were all armed. The owner's son shot CB with a .357 Magnum; it's not pretty what a .357 does to the human body, CB's leg below the knee was blown almost completely off. CB returned fire, allegedly fatally wounding the owner's son. The owner's son had made a name for himself in the streets, and CB had, too. CB had respect in the hood and in the penal. CB also had respect on that hospital ward, big respect.

Skip, too, had been shot. His shooting was at the hands of the police. Skip was a stickup kid, CB called him the ladies' man, though. CB was straight-up, no chaser while Skip was smooth and slick as can be. I clicked with both of them but more so with CB. Skip was like CB's right hand man, but CB took such a quick liking to me that I believe Skip felt a little threatened, although I was just a kid.

I was tired upon arriving at Rikers hospital. I was not even close to full strength, and I tired easily. CB began barking orders to this dude and that dude, and clean sheets appeared along with clean pillowcases and pillows. I couldn't make the bed because I still couldn't stand for long or move too much, so CB and Skip did the bed for me. I crashed as soon as my head hit the pillow. I awoke in the middle of the night to a stifling heat, mosquitoes swarming, and gnats buzzing annoyingly around my ears. Then I heard a paper rustling sound on the floor by my bed. I looked down to see that somehow the mice had grabbed my box of cereal and had completely opened the cereal up on the floor. The little motherfuckers were running around everywhere.

I simply pulled the sheet over my head and tried to sleep this nightmare off. At sunrise, I heard CB's voice. "Yo, get up, you want breakfast?" The breakfast cart was rolled in early every morning, too early for most people to get up and eat. CB was a military dude, Navy, so he was accustomed to rising early and working out, and he maintained his routine even in jail.

The inmate in charge of the breakfast cart was a huge trustee, sloppy wannabe gangster from Harlem, about 340 pounds. He was rude to most everyone he was supposed to be servicing, but I read him as a bitch ass motherfucker, fronting on dudes in the hospital because most were too physically weak to get in that punk ass. He had no physical injuries. He was simply an inmate worker. CB read him the same way and later told me that day, "As soon as they take this cast off, I'm fucking him up."

Less than a week later, dude came to serve lunch and he was yelling and barking orders in the front of the ward. I looked up and saw CB's face, and he had that same look that Xavier had after he beat up the neighborhood prankster that day in my building's hallway. CB had that "I cannot take this fronting fat motherfucker anymore, and this shit can't wait until the cast comes off" look. CB got off his bed and started walking unsteadily, but determinedly, cast on one leg, toward the front of the ward. Dude is nearly twice CB's size, so I hop in my wheelchair and start rolling toward the front of the ward. Skip catches my eyes and he comprehends what's going on.

This big dude is oblivious and walks into the ward's bathroom, CB follows him in there. I get to the bathroom door first and open it. All I see is this 340 pound bear going up in the air, almost ceiling high, as CB picked him up, and in what looked like slow motion, this dude came falling down from ceiling-high, crashing to the ceramic bathroom floor. The entire hospital ward shook from the impact. CB was on him, banging him out. The other ward inmates arrived at the bathroom with canes, crutches, anything to hit this bastard with; people were tired of his bullshit. That scene looked like something straight out of a comedy; correction officers had to rush in and save this big ass dude from a bunch of fed-up guys, with casts, canes, and crutches.

CB was my dude, he was the real deal and everyone knew it. He had a great heart and he hated bullies; he, too, always rooted for the under-dog. We were so similar in spirit; I was the exact same way. If there was a basketball game, boxing match, whatever, I knew who he was rooting for and he knew who I was rooting for before anyone even asked. We both usually rooted for whoever was not supposed to win.

The hospital ward was crazy because we were basically approximate-ly twenty-four inmates confined to this small pen dorm area with the open patio in the back and practically no police supervision, twenty-four hours a day. The only time our day was interrupted by the door up front opening was the serving of three meals, and for the "head count" that the officers did three times per day at the same exact time, to ensure no one had escaped, so we knew when they were coming.

This was a hospital ward, but doctors almost never came up there, that I can recall. A nurse would come to the ward with medications three times a day; that was basically it. We basically took care of each other and if we didn't, inmates would likely simply die up there. That place should have been shut the fuck down and every administrator there should have been locked up. This is a hospital, but they didn't change the sheets but maybe once a week.

If an inmate was so injured he couldn't get out of bed to get new sheets when the sheet man arrived, too bad. We had to clean the floors, bathrooms; everything or that shit would not get done, it was a dump. They dumped injured inmates there and if they got better, fine, or maybe released, even better, one less inmate they didn't have to totally fucking ignore. So, we had to look out for each other. If a bandage needed changing or bedpan needed dumping, or whatever, we looked out for each other, other inmates often did it.

Those summer days were hot and long, but we found ways to pass the time and often had crazy fun. There were inmates there who were experts at making moonshine. They would make liquor that was good and it would have you sloppy drunk. All kinds of drugs were up there and barely a day went by, the year or so I was there, that there was not liquor, weed, dope, coke, acid, pills or something on that ward. Sometimes all that stuff was there at the same time and in large amounts. I stayed weeded up. I didn't care much for anything beyond that. I was also like the little brother on the ward and so, I was allowed to smoke weed, cigarettes and drink moonshine if I wanted to without condemnation. If CB, Skip or the any of the other numerous older inmates who respected me and watched out for me ever saw me trying to go anywhere beyond that there would have been condemnation. I wasn't interested in anything else anyway, but still, they wouldn't have condoned it if I had wanted to.

Prison is funny in that, similar to the early days in the rap music industry, many of the guys who get the maximum amount of respect are guys who were known to have been shot some time in their life. How a person being shot gives them street credibility, I'm not exactly sure, but I am positive that to a certain degree, it does. Rikers Island hospital was the temporary home of numerous shooting victims either by the police or other street dudes and so, I knew many of them and many of them knew me. We formed solid friendships and trust, often based on necessity. Friendships outsiders could not easily comprehend because they had never experienced the horror that was Rikers Island hospital. That place is unforgettable.

Also, on the ward, we had so much free time on our hands. We were locked in that dorm literally, twenty four hours a day, every day, for almost a year in my case. We all passed most of the day playing cards, watching sports, smoking weed, or just talking. For instance, after a year of sitting with CB, sometimes from sunset to sun up, smoking, drinking, laughing, and maybe some crying, there probably was not a person on the planet who knew more about him than me, no one. I knew his family, friends, travels, hopes, dreams, but what likely made him and many, many others trust me like they trusted no others was, I knew of their crimes, charged and uncharged. Many of them thereafter went on trial and I never walked in the courtroom as the surprise witness, hoping my testimony against them would get me a reduced sentence, never. Since I was a young man, people had the tendency to confide in me, in whispered tones, things I often did not need to know, nor did I want to hear.

Dudes trusted me to hold water and to be a standup guy all throughout my time behind bars, again, sometimes to the point that I was shocked and on occasion uncomfortable they trusted enough to tell me some real stuff. Stuff that, if it got out, their reputation or even their freedom would be in severe jeopardy.

CB was about to start his trial for murder. If he was found guilty, it was over, he was looking at a life sentence. Every day of the trial was intense and nerve wracking. The day the verdict came in, CB returned to the hospital ward with a solemn look on his face. Everyone basically sensed it was a "guilty" verdict, so no one uttered a word. CB sat down, head towards the floor, then looked up and said, "Not guilty." Everyone exhaled, and hugged CB, knowing he likely would have a second chance at life. CB always maintained he acted in self-defense and didn't intend for anyone to get hurt and I believed him. The jury, too, believed that the people didn't prove CB fired the fatal shot that took the life of another so, they simply found him guilty of robbery and lesser offenses. He was later sentenced to 8 1/3 to 25 years. Some years later, he and I would reunite, in a maximum-security prison in upstate New York. CB's legal situation was concluding as my own legal woes were just about to get significantly worse.

One day while in the hospital ward, Corrections Officers approached and instructed me to get dressed because there were some detectives from Nassau County there and I was being re-arrested. The detectives informed me I was being taken out to Nassau County, Long Island to be arrested and charged with numerous counts of armed robbery offenses out there. This caught me off-guard. I had been in the system for months and no one ever came concerning anything. I was being offered 2-6 years in prison by the Queens County prosecutor's office, and I already had close to a year on Rikers Island already so I'm thinking, "Take that 2-6 and possibly be home in another year."

When I arrived in Nassau County the situation was crazy. They took me to court and appointed me an extremely old legal aid lawyer who obviously was not interested in me or my case. He just kept mentioning he was retiring. The way he handled or mishandled my case, he might as well have been already retired. He just wanted me to plead guilty and be done. He gave no impression he was even going to try to fight this case, not even a little bit. My case was assigned to Judge Gooden and he was a big piece of work. He and my dad, who was actively involved in my legal affairs at that time, continuously clashed. My dad was pushing hard, to anyone who would listen, to get me the medical attention I needed, I was confined to a wheelchair after suffering a spinal cord injury for nearly a year with practically no physical therapy being rendered. That fact was eating my dad up, as well as the fact that nobody was actively trying to help or take my injuries into consideration during penalty discussion. Neither my injury nor the fact that I was not receiving close to adequate medical care, to the powers that be, was not even a minor factor in their deliberations; they simply did not give a damn. The Nassau County Assistant District Attorneys, the judge, the court officers and the jail's corrections officers looked at me with not a hint of mercy, pity, or concern, none.

As a 17-year-old kid, I wasn't looking for mercy from them, and they all looked incapable of rendering that anyway. However, in my naiveté,

I believed they at least would be basically close to just; not merciful, but just. My dad however believed that they would be just and if pushed, with truth, they too would be merciful. We later discovered they would not be either.

I was hearing on the streets that my co-defendant Jason had retained a well-known Nassau County criminal lawyer, who also was a neighbor of Jason's and a long-time friend of Jason's family. Jason and I had been re-arrested and charged with additional armed robbery cases in Nassau County. However, Jason's attorney made a severance motion which at the time I didn't fully comprehend. I later came to understand that severance motions are often used when a co-defendant is about to do their own thing. They are going for self-preservation.

After the court granted the severance motion, instead of appearing in court, Jason and me together, same day, same time, Jason and his attorney began appearing in court on days I was nowhere in sight.

The days I did appear in court, Jason was nowhere in sight; however, the hostility level from everyone from the judge, to the district attorney, to court officers had drastically intensified. I had gotten word from my attorney that they were now offering Jason five years flat to run concurrent with his Queens prison sentence. Jason would only serve 5 years in prison.

Since Jason was a predicate violent offender, he had previously served time for armed robbery, and he was four years older than I was, I was seventeen years old and he was twenty-one, I assumed my plea offer would come in between 3-5 years, max. When my attorney received notice of my plea offer, he notified me that the offer was 10 years flat, "take it or leave it"; my plea offer was twice that of Jason's.

My head was spinning. At 17 years old, ten months seemed like a lifetime, ten years, I honestly couldn't even comprehend that number. That was more than half the time I had been on the fucking planet. My dad was flipping and he gave it to the judge, not disrespectfully, but intensely and thoroughly.

I later discovered, behind the scenes, a deal had also been made, for Jason to quietly plead guilty to a solo robbery he had committed and that his brother was falsely arrested and convicted of. Still, the judge and the district attorney slapped Jason on the wrist with a five-year flat sentence. Then, they turned around and, to satisfy the intense "get hard on crime" emotions that were sweeping Nassau County at that time, focused their every effort on completely and thoroughly making me the fall guy.

The biggest impediment to doing their dirty deeds with impunity was my dad, who would not stop telling them, in open court, for every spectator to hear that "what you are doing to my son is wrong." The judge threatened my father with having him forcibly removed from the court and with arrest, but my dad wouldn't stop. He simply started sending messages to the judge and the district attorney through my lawyer. I had been appointed a new lawyer by this time, a young Legal Aid. The guy was right out of law school. The messages that my dad instructed him to communicate to the court made him uncomfortable, but he usually said it. My dad wrote letters to the judge and called the judge's chambers, again so much so, the judge told him he better stop or he would have my dad arrested. My dad wrote the governor asking for intervention on more than one occasion. The Governor never responded. My dad was bitter about that for many, many years. My dad felt that because he was a loyal voting member of the Democratic Party, the Democratic governor should have at least responded to his pleas for help, nothing. I wasn't surprised. I never had faith in politicians, ever.

While going back and forth to court in Nassau County, it became apparent that my appearing in court, still wheelchair bound, was a great inconvenience for the Nassau authorities, so they got a court order to have me moved from Rikers Island to the Nassau County prison ward. So, they transported me to court one day in Nassau. Right after Court, they immediately transported me over to Nassau county jail, without telling me, I would not be returning to Rikers. CB and Skip, however, and thankfully, secured all of my personal property, letters, family pictures, etc. and safely forwarded them to my family.

When I arrived at the Nassau prison ward, it was another dump. That place was ridiculous. No way should that place have been allowed to stay open or be called a hospital ward. Doctors were invisible, inmates ran the ward, it was filled with cigarette smoke and dirty conditions. They put me on twenty-four hour lockdown for the first few weeks I was there, I cannot recall the reason they gave but it was really punitive. My dad was pressing them to get me medical assistance and they hated that. They were not really equipped to render real medical assistance. The place was a joke. The judge eventually was shamed in open court into agreeing to allow an outside doctor to evaluate me and send a medical report to the jail and the court. They never followed up on the doctor's medical recommendations anyway, so that really accomplished nothing besides making them angrier because the doctor verified all of my injuries thus making them look more inhumane for what they were doing and refusing to do. It didn't make them feel guilty, though; they had no guilt, it was simply an embarrassment.

The weeks they kept me in solitary confinement locked in a small cell, sitting in a wheelchair, 24 hours a day was the first time I really stopped and began to think. I thought about the hurt and pain I caused many through my actions. I thought about my children, and their mothers. I thought about my life and the many mistakes I had made. I thought about the whys and the hows. I thought about God, and I asked for forgiveness for all I did. I sensed I was about to go on a journey that was going to be crazy, so I asked for his strength and I asked for his guidance.

I began to read enthusiastically first, while on Rikers Island. CB got me into reading novels. He read a lot and had stacks of novels in his area. The first book I ever read from cover to cover was "Eldorado Red" by Donald Goines, CB gave it to me. It was a short reading about a ghetto gangster, but it was good and I was hooked. I began to read all of CB's novels; the books about gangsters in the hood kept me fascinated the most. Then I branched out into espionage, and dramas, all fiction stuff.

While in solitary confinement, I was going through books like water. Other inmates on the prison ward who were not in solitary confinement would pass by my cell and drop off books, food, and stationery, anything to help me maintain myself while locked in.

After weeks of solitary confinement, the authorities in Nassau County finally allowed me out of my cell to join the regular prison ward. However, again, like on Rikers, they had no prison ward for minors so I was placed in the prison hospital ward with the adults. Again, I am the youngest dude on the ward, I am still a teenager. I was there with old school gangsters, pimps, pushers, extortion kids, you name it, and they were there. However, CB and the adults I had lived with on Rikers Island for about a year had schooled me so well that these dudes were amazed I was so young but carried myself like an old-school cat. I knew a lot about bidding (serving time). I knew when to talk, and when not to talk. I knew how to spot a short con and long con. I knew how to stay out of the C.O.s' faces, even though I still often clashed with them. It was just too hard for me to "Yes sir" and "No sir" to a punk-ass C.O., this, especially when I mostly didn't respect them because they mostly did not show respect for me or any of the other inmates under their care. I knew that "Yes sir" and "No sir" was probably the best way to keep them out of your face; I simply refused to do it.

Nassau County C.O.s were different from Rikers Island C.O.s only in that on Rikers Island the racism was there, but because so many Black C.O.s worked there they were particular about when they gave it to you. In Nassau County, the C.O.s gave you "Nigger," "Nigger," "Nigger," from the time you came through the door to the time you were released. It was almost a hatred of Black people exhibited by most of the jail's staff in Nassau; it was ridiculous. They jumped me once or twice and threatened to get me often. Actually, the Black C.O.s at Rikers Island were often worse than the White ones. A Black C.O. on Rikers Island attacked me once because I wouldn't answer a question he asked. I was in a wheelchair at that time; he didn't care. Power often corrupts even though many of the C.O.s I encountered, Black and White, were already corrupt to the fucking bone. Some, however, I watched change, from very decent people to corrupt individuals, as they became acclimated to the C.O. lifestyle. The slow transformation is an amazing thing to see.

While going back and forth to Court in Nassau County, I would often see a young Mexican, White looking inmate in the holding pens. He and I talked often; his name was Devine or "Devine-God-Allah." He was facing serious charges as a very young guy and he was being housed at Nassau county jail not with the adults but with the minors, ages 16 to 21. Devine took an immediate liking to me during our hours-long discussions while in those holding pens. Devine, too, was one of the most influential prisoners in the jail, being one of the undisputed leaders of the five-percent nation, a religious group (many called them) which was very prominent and influential within the penal system at the time.

While on the Nassau hospital ward, frequently, inmates were admitted after being victims of extremely brutal beatings at the hands of other inmates. Often times, too, the distributor of the beating was a single inmate called "Wild-Out." It was rumored he was a talented professional prizefighter who simply preferred street life to a career in boxing, but he was rumored to be a good fighter, very good. He was also Devine's older brother and one of the most feared inmates at that jail.

During my time at the Nassau prison ward, after tons of prayer, exercise (I did strengthening exercises intuitively), and through strong faith and the grace of God, I was getting stronger by the day. I began walking with a walker, then crutches, then without assistance. I was still fairly weak and I tired easily but I was walking. Eventually, I abandoned the crutches totally and was walking unassisted for longer periods. Desperate for space in the hospital ward, I was ordered transferred out and eventually sent to probably the worst and most notorious housing unit in the jail. I had heard rumors of the unit, apparently the jail had absolutely no control over it and it was rumored to be violent in the extreme.

I arrived at the entrance to the unit, after being discharged from the hospital ward. The unit I was being transferred, had a long corridor with approximately 22 cells lined on the left hand side. Looking towards the end of the unit, I saw a TV, which was on MTV. There were a few tables with decks of cards on them as if a number of card games were recently in progress but had been interrupted abruptly. On the right hand side of the unit were bars, which lined the length of the unit. As the officer opened the front door of the unit to allow me in, carrying my basics, towels, soap, slippers, I heard a loud voice from the far end of the tier, someone said if that inmate is not "God-body" (a part of the five-percent nation) he can't live here; "only God-body can house on this unit," he said, others chimed in their loud agreement. The C.O. is looking at me like, "This is some crazy shit."

I begin sizing up the situation. They were putting me in cell number 12 or so. So, when all the doors opened, there would be at least 10 dudes to my right and 10 to my left. The officer looks hard at me again like, "speak now, say you do not want to go in, or forever hold your peace." I don't say a word, I enter the cell. The officer walks away looking back at me like, "You are dumb as shit or crazy as fuck." I immediately remove my boot and began assembling my knife; I have a wicked blade under the tongue of the boot. I make strips of string by tearing my bed sheet and place the short metal blade between two toothbrushes, tying the tooth brushes tight with bed sheet string, turning the tooth brushes into the handle of my knife, with the blade sticking out far enough to definitely lay a motherfucker down. No way am I going to get them all, but I am definitely going to lay one of them down, there is no doubt.

While still locked in, one or two of the unseen inmates are calling out to me asking me questions, I stay silent. I already know what it is when the doors open, no use yapping. When the doors open, I step right out so I won't get caught in the cramped quarters of the cell. I got my hand on my blade, but kept my hand in my pants pocket. I scan left then right; there's a small crowd of hostile inmates on either side. Through the crowd of inmates to my left walks a Mexican-White looking inmate, wearing a red do-rag and a stern look on his face, it's Devine-God-Allah. He sees me and instantly breaks into a big smile, and says "Yo, Dulla what's good?" All the tension in the air is released as Devine introduced me as his "big brother"; everybody fell back.

Devine looked up to me, real dudes usually recognized real dudes and often there's mutual respect. Devine was interesting in that he was one of the undisputed leaders of the five-percent nation partly because he genuinely was the best versed in the teachings, but he also genuinely sought and respected knowledge. Devine thought I was one of the wisest young dudes ever, and upon meeting me, he immediately looked up to me and often sought my advice about things. Most of the dudes on the unit were all twenty-one years old or under. I was too. However, they all felt I was dealing on a different level and soon they all came to seek out and respect my advice on all kinds of issues.

I was housed on that unit for a long time, often being the only non-five-percenter allowed to stay there in peace. Any other inmate sent there usually got "beat down," run out, or carried out. Devine ran that unit with an iron fist, and the respect and fear the other five-percenters and inmates throughout the jail had for him was ridiculous. Everyone knew that when Devine flew into one of his rages, I was one of the few people in that jail who could talk to him, or maybe his big brother, Wild-Out, whom I soon came to meet.

Wild-Out was running with his clique on a different unit, mostly non five-percent nation dudes. Wild-Out's unit and Devine's unit were both extremely violent. Every day, dudes were getting laid out on those units, often over senseless things. I told Devine about that. I told him, "If you are going to lead, then lead dudes to do the right thing," because the inmates would follow Devine's lead. Devine did lighten up a little bit with the running of all non-five percenters off the unit. I stayed in his ear on that because that shit was senseless and ignorant. Devine was young though and he enjoyed exercising his power, but again, power often corrupts and there definitely was some corruption there. Generally, though he was a decent dude and was genuinely trying to grow.

When Wild-Out was surprisingly transferred to our unit, I had only heard lots about him, but I had never actually met him. When I first saw him, I was like, "That's Wild-Out." He didn't look intimidating or dangerous as people said, not even a little bit. I soon found out how deceiving looks could be. Wild-Out wasn't on the unit but for a few minutes before he robbed this dude's cell, while the dude was down the tier on the phone; Wild-Out cleaned him out, took all of his personal belongings from his open cell. When the dude returned to his cell he asked who went in his cell, Wild-Out said, "I took it. Come to the back (away from the officer's sight) and take it back, bout for it", (fist-fight for it).

I was like, "finally, I am going to see the infamous Wild-Out get busy, fight". I still had a bit of ignorance in me, too, although, I actually thought the dude could handle Wild-Out; the dude was bigger and completely unafraid. Dude, being diesel, heavily muscled, swung first, a blow swung with such force, it would have floored a horse. Wild-Out smoothly slipped it, ducked under the blow, as if the punch were in slow motion. He simply dipped into a crouching position allowing the vicious blow to pass harmlessly over his head. Wild-Out then swiftly came out of the crouch with an equally vicious left hook, landing it squarely on the dude's jaw. Dude swung again, same result, he hit nothing but air. He couldn't hit Wild-Out, and I soon discovered that was part of the magic. Wild-Out had perfected the art of hitting without being hit. That shit was fucking beautiful to watch, but deadly as a motherfucker. Dude had no chance, and he got knocked out.

Wild-Out, upon moving to the unit, soon approached me and introduced himself. He told me, "My brother loves the hell out of you, man." I told him the feeling was mutual and that Devine was my little dude for sure. I respected Devine because, although he was not even vaguely physically gifted as Wild-Out was, he had such a powerful mind and personality he actually had more influence in the jail and over other people then Wild-Out had. Devine's personality was magnetic, charming and at times, many times, he was very manipulative. Wild-Out had massive respect though mainly because of his fearless heart and physical gifts. Devine had massive respect because of his mind, his heart and his personality. He was honestly an intellectually gifted young dude, always seeking more knowledge of self. Devine was on a journey, honestly seeking to better himself and so was I. It was an honest journey and although I was a bit further down the road than Devine was in many areas still, we both had many miles to go. I saw a lot of myself in Devine and although I was barely twenty years old, I believe he saw me, if not as a person he aspired to be like, but definitely a person he honestly admired.

Wild-Out and I became close friends. I had been studying Islam more intensely upon leaving Rikers Island and I was becoming more versed in the religion day by day. I didn't socialize much with the Muslim community though, because I was still somewhat doing my thing. I didn't want to be a hypocrite. One day, Wild-Out confided in me he always wanted to be a Muslim, but he said he could only study with a person he respected. He asked me if I would teach him the religion; I agreed. I taught Wild-Out the basic principles of Islam and he and I soon after began attending Muslim services together. He later converted to Islam to his brother's Devine's absolute delight. Wild-Out wasn't a five-percenter as Devine had tried to get him to be for so many years, but to Devine, Muslims were righteous people and he was happy for his brother, and even happier I was his mentor.

Upon converting to Islam, Wild-Out was, however, still Wild-Out. I advised Wild-Out, as I always tried to influence his brother Devine to do, that was, to stay away from straight ignorant things. My philosophy was, if you considered yourself a wise man, why get involved with or initiate ignorant and senseless things. In the penal system there would be ample opportunity to deal with enough real issues, people plotting to harm you or yours.

So, when real things hit the fan, then by all means, do what you do. Again, while serving time, more than enough real things will definitely hit the fan so, you don't have to look for it or create it, it will surely come. Serving time is weird, though, because sometimes incarceration is so boring that there's always the urge to simply start drama just to break up the boredom. That urge sometimes is very strong, particularly when you have power and massive influence, and that we had.

At court, I rejected the plea offer of 10 years. Although both the prosecutor and judge supported that plea offer, it was one that I would never willingly accept. I was guilty as sin, no doubt, but I refused to be bullied into holding the bag. I saw what they were trying to do. They were preparing the way to cover up their shame in that they were letting Jason off with a slap on the wrist, I would thus be the sacrificial lamb; I would be the one made to pay. Also, at that young age, I was 19 years old, a teenager, 10 months sounded like a long time, 10 years sounded like forever. However, the judge warned that if I failed to take the plea of 10 years and if I were thereafter convicted, after trial, I would definitely receive more than that. I refused to be bullied, fuck it.

Again, I was assigned a court appointed attorney on the Nassau County charges; a very old one and then a very young one. My family didn't have the money to hire an attorney and my ill-gotten gains were virtually depleted, the thousands that I had stashed away were basically gone. I hadn't saved much of that money; I used it to survive the first year in jail, buying basics. Had I foreseen these Nassau County charges coming, I would have been much smarter with that money.

Anyway, the old Legal Aid attorney was a joke. I often wondered if they intentionally assigned me the worst attorney that they could find. He had to be eighty years old and all he talked about the few times I had the opportunity to talk to him was that he "couldn't wait to retire." He had no fire, no passion, no enthusiasm, nothing. He appeared to be simply going through the motions so he could pick up his last checks before he retired.

Not knowing much about the law at that time, I really had no idea how badly he was actually managing my case. My mere instincts were telling me that he didn't care much about me or my case. The thing is, as I later learned, even if your client is absolutely guilty, you still have the obligation to defend them zealously. That zealous defense takes many different forms, but it should be there. Your goal is to protect the rights of your clients whether they are guilty or innocent. If this zealous defense is not there, the issue of fairness, equity and justice gets lost and the integrity of the system is severely undermined. The American criminal justice system is a powerful force and it can crush a person, even unintentionally at times, if that person is not properly represented by strong counsel. Without zealous representation of all criminally accused, unjust and unbalanced outcomes will often be the end result.

My attorney gave no resistance to the runaway train that was coming my way in the form of a mercilessly over-ambitious prosecutor, one who never once looked me in my face and hostile judges who often didn't even try to hide their absolute contempt for me and for my family. Additionally, the attorney apparently had no legal strategy in preparing for plea bargaining sessions and definitely no strategy for a trial. Guys back at the jail often referred to the judge, the prosecutor and the legal aid attorney as the "devil's triangle," and I was getting a first-hand look at why so many people felt that way. I was toast.

Back at the jail, things were the same old, same old. Dudes were getting beat down every day; the jail was violent as hell. The thing with our housing unit was that the jailers actually knew full well that if you put a non-five percenter inmate on that unit, chances are they were going to end up in the infirmary, but they kept sending them there. It was messed up because I never liked senseless violence and the violence on that unit was intense and often completely senseless. I saved a number of dudes from beat downs, but it wasn't totally my house, so I couldn't save everyone.

That unit again was so arranged that if an inmate got sent there, chances are they were going to get what the five-percenters referred to as a "universal beat down." That essentially meant the person would be viciously attacked and severely beaten when their cell was opened, by sometimes 10 or more people. For many years after leaving that place, whenever I met any man, I wondered how that man would respond to a situation where they knew that when the cell doors opened that they would be viciously beat down; would they yell, would they scream, would they fight or would they call the officers and asked to be placed in "protective custody" before those doors ever opened? I witnessed too many men do all of the above.

When I turned 19 years old, under a fairly new jail policy, the jail had started classifying 19 year old inmates as adults. Previously, inmates had to be 21 years old to be classified as adults and moved to the adult units. At 19 years old, they thus moved me from that extremely violent unit, which was for minors, to an adult unit of the jail. Everyone on this new adult unit was however mostly around, twenty-five years old and older. Other inmates there were very old men. After serving so much time at Rikers Island hospital around much older inmates, I fit comfortably right in. This, too, was a very violent unit, but not as senseless as the unit I had left behind. Many of my "juvy" dudes were up there already, on that unit; they had turned 19 years old some months before me. Many of the older dudes didn't always like us around though; they viewed most "juvys" as too wild, irrational and very unpredictable, which mostly was true. However, I was pretty level-headed for a teenager and I got along well pretty much with most of them.

I did start to notice though that, on this new unit, dudes were getting jumped on and beat down periodically and it always was by the same dudes, older Latino dudes, my man Flaco and his clique. Now, I basically paid it no mind because they didn't want it with me and never brought any noise my way. We kicked it, played cards, no beef my way, nothing but respect. I had met Flaco some time ago when he and his man, another young Latino dude, were moved into the old juvy unit that I was on and they got simultaneously beat down pretty viciously. Flaco's man got his head split open to the white meat by a mop ringer, blood was every fucking where. Flaco had suffered serious injuries too. Although I didn't take part in that beat-down, Flaco knew I was a well-respected affiliate of that clique; he didn't want any beef with me.

Anyway, while on the adult unit, one day Flaco and his Latino clique were surrounding a big Black dude and were about to jump him. A much older Black inmate, career criminal, ran to the Black dude's defense, even though he didn't even really know the big Black dude. The defender was a well-respected inmate at the jail and they didn't really want it with him. So, it became a standoff and Flaco and his clique backed down.

Confused, I later quietly asked him why he came to this dude's assistance when he really didn't know the dude like that and the dude was basically "a nobody" which is a cruel term used for inmates who had no rank or status within the jail or prison. This, particularly, when Flaco was cool with both of us, and Flaco claimed the dude had violated, it wasn't some senseless attack. The inmate informed me that "if you notice, all the dudes Flaco and his Latino clique ever have beef with, claimed violated, and then robbed and ran them off the unit, they were Black."

He went on to explain that Flaco and his clique, some older Latino dudes, were racist motherfuckers and that they were trying to run Blacks off the unit one at a time. He went on to tell me that as soon as they had clear numbers over the Black inmates on the unit their true colors would come out. I started to reflect and saw that what he said was definitely true, no Latino inmate had been run off the unit by Flaco for any reason. The Latino inmates were playing slick-ass racial politics, and conscious as I thought I was, I didn't even see it. From that day on though, throughout my entire time in the system, I stood with the brothers against the racial politics. No more brothers would get run off that unit, or any cellblock I was on anywhere, due to racial politics, not without me standing with them.

Again, I had previously stood up and protected many people at that jail, "nobodies" included, but it was never based upon race. I did it simply because it was the right thing to do, based upon the facts as I knew them. It didn't matter if the person I stood with was White, Black, Latino or whatever. These racial politics were absolutely new to me, but it was definitely very real; and I thus had to pay attention to it.

The Trial

In my naiveté, I actually believed that the offer of ten years in prison, as a plea offer, in Nassau County, was so unfair that someone, somehow, somewhere beyond the judge and prosecutor, would intervene in the process and the offer would be considerably reduced; I was very wrong. The frustration for me, however, was that, although I was one hundred percent guilty, and fairly remorseful for the foolish decisions I had made, the disparity in plea offers between myself and Jason, based upon the facts, was so huge, that I simply could not go along with it; I just couldn't. I knew, even at that young age what the judge and prosecutor were doing. I was the sacrificial lamb, and I wasn't playing along.

I informed my new attorney, a young legal Aid, that I'd rather take my chances at trial; reluctantly, he said "OK." The first trial and the second trial were both a joke. Since there were numerous charges against me, occurring on separate dates, times and locations, there were separate indictments and therefore separate trials. My defense attorney had practically no defense against the charges. In all fairness to him, however, there was no really strong defense to put on; I was admittedly guilty as sin. I was simply going to trial on the principle of what I believed to be right and wrong. Although I was absolutely wrong in what I had done, I believed the prosecution and judge were equally wrong in what they were trying to do.

A sense of fairness and justice has always been deeply embedded in me, so much so that the often asked question to criminal defense attorneys, "How can you defend a guilty person?" is easily answered with, "Justice is a gift for the innocent and for the guilty." Simply because a person is guilty of a bad act does not thereby simply mean they are a bad person or more specifically unworthy of just treatment.

The first trial, in Nassau County, before Judge Terry ended quickly with a guilty verdict. The judge thereafter sentenced me to 4-12 years in state prison. The second trial before Judge Harrison ended equally as quickly with a guilty verdict, and I could have sworn the judge, for the first time, smiled. Judge Harrison despised me and he despised my father even more, and sentencing day was his opportunity to finally show us exactly how much.

I knew that the sentence was going to be heavy handed because of the open hostility and enmity the judge had towards me and more particularly towards my father; he sentenced me to twelve and a half to twenty five years. The prosecutor with a straight face and no shame asked the judge to run the sentence consecutively with the previous 4-12 year sentence. A consecutive sentence meant that I would first serve the 4-12 years and thereafter serve the 12 and one half years. Therefore, I would be incarcerated for a minimum of sixteen years. Again, this is the same District Attorney's office that bent over backwards to ensure that Jason was given a five-year prison sentence; these were some treacherous people, and they knew that I knew.

The judge stated very sarcastically that he thought that twelve and half to twenty five years was sufficient. I sensed that he believed that I wouldn't last that long. He believed that he, essentially, had just given me a death sentence. He looked hard and long at me with his sarcastic smile on his face as I showed him absolutely no emotion, none. I left the courtroom that day feeling that I was royally messed over, but I had put myself in that predicament and so I had to deal with it. The judge believed that I couldn't do 12 and a half years. He believed he had taken my life. I was going to shock that motherfucker, no doubt about it. My mind was absolutely made up in that regard. Some of my family was in the courtroom that day. My dad was there too, and he wasn't happy.

I was soon thereafter transferred from Nassau County jail, on Long Island New York, to the state prison reception facility for inmates under twenty-one years old, Elmira Correctional Facility. When I first arrived at Elmira Correctional Facility, my big brother was already there serving a short prison sentence. I was in the reception area of the facility, which was separated from his area. He was in the area where guys were serving time. The reception area at Elmira was for guys simply being received into state prison; they stay only for a few weeks and are thereafter usually shipped out to other state prisons. My brother, however, was actually serving his sentence there.

I knew they weren't going to keep us together, so I knew I would be gone soon, although we saw each other in passing every now and then and communicated through kites (hand written notes). I was then shipped out of Elmira as expected, chained at the hands, waist and feet, to Coxsackie Correctional Facility, a state prison for inmates under the age of twenty-one years old.

Coxsackie

COXSACKIE HOUSED HUNDREDS OF INMATES, many lifers and young men, many who were serving extremely long prison sentences. Most of the inmates were from the five boroughs of New York City, but Brooklyn dudes were in the building in large numbers; I mostly ran with my Brooklyn dudes. The day I had actually moved from Brooklyn to Queens, and I was with my clique in the hallway of my building laughing and cracking jokes, saying so-long, my dude Bugsy, funny dude, was in the hallway with us. He was now at Coxsackie serving a long prison sentence; he and I were on the same unit together. Other inmates from my neighborhood were also there as well as a number of my big brother's people. Many of the dudes from Nassau County were there as well, five-percenters mostly; I had no beef at Coxsackie, basically. After being there for about a year, I was accused of being involved in a major brawl among a number of inmates. I was sent to solitary confinement and thereafter transferred out of Coxsackie and sent to Attica State Prison; I had just turned 21 years old.

Attica

WHEN I ARRIVED AT ATTICA, that place was unbelievable. I was still in solitary confinement, so they marched me straight to the solitary confinement unit. They opened the dark, stinking cell and I was escorted in. Looking around, I was shocked at what I saw. There was human feces all over the walls, along with blood and mucus as if someone with a bad cold was coughing up globs of mucus and hog spitting it all over the walls. The mucus had blood in it drying or completely dried all over the walls of the cell. The guards refused to have the cell cleaned. I tried to clean it the best I could, having no soap, rags or sanitizer.

Attica at that time housed the worst of the worst and it was definitely not the ideal place to send a 21-year-old inmate. There were numerous other facilities, less dangerous, and potentially less corrupting than Attica. However, by that time, I was on the prison administration's radar because I would continuously challenge the mistreatment of myself and other inmates within the prisons. They didn't like that and, thus, they didn't like me.

Upon arriving at Attica, I was definitely one of the youngest inmates there. However, I had been well schooled by CB and other older inmates and thus, I wasn't as green, (naive), as many of the other younger inmates were. Many people from my old Brooklyn neighborhood were in Attica when I arrived; they welcomed me and then schooled me to the particulars of that facility. Also, my dude, Black, from Far Rockaway was there. He and I had worked together at Burger King before he killed a man and was given a life sentence.

Black, upon learning that I was there, used his influence with the C.O.s in the prison kitchen, "mess hall", to have me pulled to the kitchen unit to work there with him. That was real cool because the mess hall work assignment was considered the plum assignment in the entire prison. Prison food is usually extremely bad, but Attica's food was often inedible. They would serve food and nobody actually knew what it was; it was eat at your own risk.

However, while working in the mess hall, we had access to the food coolers, and there was food in the coolers that the Attica inmates never saw. We had access to hamburgers, blocks of cheese, chicken, rice, and food seasoning, which was a luxury item in prison. We cooked our food often separately from everyone else and some of the inmates were exceptional cooks. The kitchen crew ate very well; not so for the rest of the prison's inmates.

Also, the kitchen workers were housed separately from the rest of the prison population. They had their own unit with all kitchen workers on it, and it was considered an "honor unit". There were many privileges offered on that unit, frequent yard access, phone access, clean cells, little tension and rarely a single fight. Inmates came there and they stayed for years, serving comfortable prison time. I didn't like the unit upon arriving there. I have never been impressed by prison perks and cushiness, and I definitely wasn't about to kiss any C.O.'s ass in order to have continued access to these perks; like some of these dudes were doing with a smile.

The C.O.s knew that I was a little different as soon as I arrived; the inmates did too. Black tried to shelter me as best he could but that shit was futile. First, many C.O.s at Attica were racist to the extreme and there was no subtlety with their racism. They would openly make horrible racial jokes, referred to inmates as "dumb-ass niggers" and would quickly and routinely jump Black inmates, beating them half to death. There were rumors, too, that many of the inmate deaths at Attica, including some of the so-called suicides, were actual murders at the hands of a bunch of renegade racist C.O.s. So, I knew whom I was dealing with when we crossed paths.

Also, most of the inmates in the unit were so desperate to stay there that they would tolerate almost any disrespect from staff or other inmates. They didn't want to do anything to get kicked off this so-called "honor unit." I told Black that I likely wouldn't last long on that unit with all the "buck dancing", "tap dancing" and "yes sir, boss" that was going on, I wasn't doing it. What also bothered me was that these same "yes sir, boss" butt-kissing inmates would turn around and talk to one another or other inmates like dirt; massively disrespectfully. One inmate in particular, who kept his lips puckered for frequent C.O. butt-kissing, was in charge of the new kitchen workers; I was one of the new workers. He spoke with total disrespect to everyone. Again, he knew that most inmates didn't want a confrontation with him, because he was so totally in with the guards, from butt-kissing, snitching and cooking them food. It was known to everyone that he could, with one whisper to the guards, have any inmate transferred off that unit.

One day he tried to scream on me; I immediately checked him. I told him, "Watch your mouth." Black quickly intervened and it didn't escalate; not that time anyway. For a few days, the dude kept his distance and I tried to keep mine, however we had to interact. He was in charge of the kitchen area. He instructed me to do something one day and thereafter made a comment about "Are you stupid or something?" He continued on about how he was a real "bad man" and thereafter he got in my face barking, I stepped in his face barking back. Black heard the commotion and came running from the back of the kitchen to separate us, but it was too late. The dude pushed me and I floored him. He lay on the floor bleeding heavily from his nose and mouth.

The riot squad came rushing in, grabbed me, handcuffed me and walked me to my cell. They put me in the cell and locked the door. Black later arrived by my cell, just shaking his head. Black told me what I already knew. I was going to solitary, "keep lock", and I would be transferred off that unit; he was right. I was given one month cell confinement and transferred to what was then the worst unit in Attica, A Block; the other inmates called it, "Vietnam." I was on A-block for practically no time when a young inmate got murdered. He allegedly had passed a flirtatious note, written by his friend, another inmate, during a family visit, to the girlfriend of a third inmate. That third inmate, however, had allegedly already murdered two people on two separate occasions while he was behind bars. The man was a killer, and the young inmate should have known better. A friend of the killer thereafter murdered the young dude who passed along the note for that transgression. Attica was extremely unforgiving like that.

When I arrived on A-block, many of my people, mostly guys from my old neighborhood, Coxsackie and some good Muslim inmates I would often socialize with were already there and they told me, "We knew you were not going to last long on that kitchen unit." I just shook my head. A-block was "buck-wild", murder, extortion, rape and robbery. The place was crazy. However, I had a buck wild clique and we could hold our own against anybody.

I didn't have much trouble while in Attica besides a few little beefs every now and then. There was one incident in the yard where I was caught in some bullshit. I was made aware, upon entering the yard, that some Muslim inmates I socialized with had some beef with a hard-core, well-armed crew of Latino and White inmates. They had us outnumbered at least two to one in that yard. That was very tense. It was resolved without any bloodshed, but it definitely almost went there that evening. After a little more than a year in Attica, I was told to "pack up." I was being transferred to Eastern Correctional Facility.

Eastern Correctional Facility

I ARRIVED AT THE EASTERN Correctional facility, which was a maximum-security facility for only "well-behaved" inmates, sometime around 1988. I arrived there from Attica Correctional Facility, which was one of the most notorious prisons in the State of New York, and maybe even the country. Eastern had a boxing gym and boxing team and they supposedly were very good. I went to the gym to see them. The heavyweight champion was in the ring at the time, Kaybar, a big, six-foot-five-inch, 260 pound, jet black, very intimidating looking dude, no laughs, and no smiles, nothing. He was beating the blood out of some under skilled sparring partner, while me, my wild-ass homeboy from Attica, Quawi, and a dangerous former-professional fighter, Saif, sat on the benches close to the ring watching the action.

I made a comment, louder than I had realized that "I'd fuck that dude up", referring to the heavyweight champion. The fighter's trainer overheard my comment, and assertively stepped up to me asking, "You think you could fuck with my man?" I told the dude, nah, "Your man can't fuck with me." I was young, cocky, and just coming down from serving hard time in Attica while working out four to five hours a day, every day. Although, I had never been in the boxing ring before and was not really a heavyweight, I was only about 193 pounds, I knew for sure I would beat the brakes off of that dude.

The trainer said, "The ring is right here, we can do this right now." I told him, "Let's go." I walked over to the equipment cabinet, strapped on a protective cup, headgear and gloves. My man Quawi, who was a seasoned amateur fighter, would serve as my corner man. As I "geared up", the heavyweight champ and the trainer looked at me like, "You've got crazy heart but you are about to get it." I stepped into the ring, and it felt funny. The ring floor wasn't solid so I couldn't firmly plant my feet, it was like walking on top of a big mattress. I put my mouthpiece in and looked across the ring at this big-ass dude and he and his trainer looked back at me like they knew something I didn't know.

Before the bell rang, Quawi said, "Bey, work his body, he's soft in the gut." I nodded my head, thinking, "I'm knocking this dude the fuck out." The bell rang and we met in the middle of the ring where I rocked him with hard lefts and harder rights to the jaw. I wobbled him twice in the first round and he was bleeding from the mouth. The gym was packed with inmates, playing basketball, cards, and just kicking the breeze. After the first round had ended, the basketball games, card games and all inmate activity in the gym had stopped and the inmates crowded around the ring to watch the facility heavyweight champ fight a walk on.

Kaybar, the champ, and his trainer's secret they knew and thought I didn't, I later learned, was, they believed after a few rounds in the ring, even if I was extremely skilled and very confident, I would likely tire and become vulnerable. This was because I hadn't yet learned the art of "pace." That is, fighting too hard early, and not fighting relaxed and thus running out of gas late, becoming tired in the latter part of the fight. However, I was in tremendous condition and my corner man Quawi, an experienced fighter, knew the boxing game. He told me after the second round, "Bey, stop going for the knockout, you're gonna burn out. Just beat that ass."

Kaybar was too ring-savvy to knock out. When I hurt him, got him on the ropes, or began banging his body while up close, he clinched, grabbed me to prevent me from punching. When I rocked him from a distance, he immediately started dancing on his toes, staying away from me, to clear his head. So, I settled down, as Quawi suggested, and just began to pick my shots as they presented themselves. I stopped pressing.

The average amateur boxing match is three rounds, but Kaybar and I fought six rounds, the first three, mostly in the middle of the ring, toe-to-toe.

After the bell, ending the last round of the fight, we met in the middle of the ring and hugged, there was mutual respect. He was a little better than I thought, and I was a lot better than he thought. However, after that bout, the prison was talking. Some said, I had won, others said he had. However, most agreed that based upon what they saw, I could definitely take his title, if I wanted it, with just a little formal coaching.

After several months at that facility, Kaybar and I had become good friends. We also became sparring partners. I never challenged him for his heavyweight title. However, I did fight for and won the "Cruiserweight" title, 190 plus pound class, defeating an uptown street dude named "Knockout." Sparring with Kaybar and others every day definitely got me ready for my championship fight.

Fight day at the prison was crazy. The entire prison population was invited to the event, which was held in the huge gym, adjacent to the prison yard. It was a major event. Corrections Officers, staff and prison administrators came out to watch the fights and a lot of betting was going on. My supervisor in the stock room where T, a super respected, older, street hustler, and I worked, made a big bet against the supervisor in the area of the prison where "Knockout," my opponent, worked. He told me with a smile, "Don't lose, Bey." I told him, smiling back, "Easy money."

I walked to the ring with my clique, Quawi, Saif, and some other dudes I rolled with from Attica. I came into the ring to the LL Cool J song, "Momma Said Knock You Out." In the front row was my dude T the hustler and his Harlem clique often yelling excitedly, "Beat that ass, Bey." I know T had money on the fight and all his dollars were on me, no doubt. My opponent was short and stocky, built like a baby Mike Tyson, and was an intimidating inmate presence around the prison. His strategy, obviously, was to use his extremely powerful punches to end the fight early, but he definitely never perfected the art of "pace." I boxed him the first round while the crowd cheered for him or for me. He bulled in, I clinched. He threw haymakers with all of his might while I boxed, slipped and moved. As I looked at him in his corner after the first round, I saw he was gassed, extremely tired. Quawi said, "He's tired Bey, knock him out." I stopped him in the second round. After the fight, my big brother T, was, "Beautiful pace, Bey, that's how you fuck a nigger up." Again, while at Eastern, Kaybar and I became good friends, so I never challenged him for his title, although I certainly believed I could take it.

At Eastern, I also became a certified, Literacy Coach, trained to teach people how to read. My new prison job assignment as a literacy coach took me to a remote part of the facility where they held classes for inmate students who couldn't read or write or who were studying and progressing towards taking their GED. Upon entering the classroom for the first time, I saw Kaybar was one of the students and he was in the group with the difficult students, students who basically could not read at all.

Kaybar was big, jet-black and very intimidating looking. He looked like one of those huge New York City club bouncers, just more scary-looking. The teacher prepped me that he was not progressing rapidly and that he needed tons of work. However, my sense was everyone in the room was a little intimidated by him, the teacher included and thus no one really pushed him too hard. I agreed to work with him. He looked surprised to see me there. This may be because he knew of my boxing skills and I ran with a well-respected prison clique, mostly the Brooklyn dudes. He likely thought, *how could he also be an academic instructor?* Initially, he was a bit thrown off.

So, I told him a little about myself beyond what he already knew, including that I had earned my GED behind bars and had begun taking college classes thereafter. I told him I had read my first book while in jail and that my reading had gotten better through reading. I told him I was serving 12 ½ - 25 years and I wanted to get a second chance at life upon release and my goal was to earn a college degree. We talked about boxing and sports and he began to open up to me about his life as so many inmates over the years often had done. He told me he was embarrassed that he never learned to read or write and that many of his actions stemmed from that insecurity. I had noticed upon first meeting him that he had this menacing disposition that said "keep away"; which was definitely part of his insecurity. Additionally, he was big, and jet-black, that classic "Boogie man" that many in America are programmed to run from, and never embrace. He was that big black African–American Boogie man, the image that is so ingrained into the American psyche, and so, he lived up to the part. He became that "Boogie man" in demeanor, scary, and intimidating.

Getting to know him, however, when he removed the mask, he was funny, witty, self-deprecating, and kind-hearted. He laughed like a little kid. Kaybar was simply a frightened, insecure young man who needed a hug from a world that would never give it to him. They were too afraid. He was that dude America feared on sight, while giving him no explanation as to why.

I began to teach Kaybar how to read and write, and he was appreciative. He was even more appreciative that I kept his secret that, he was illiterate. I continued to teach him and spar with him, although in the gym, he wouldn't take full shots at me even when he got the chance. He had huge respect for me and often didn't spar with me as hard as he could have. I definitely wouldn't ever challenge Kaybar for his heavyweight title, the title which was one of the few things that made him feel good about himself, I would never try to take that away.

Eastern Correctional Facility was cool in that it was super laid back, not much drama of the physical kind. That allowed me to focus on getting my mind right in that I could read, write, take college classes and maintain a peaceful state of mind. However, sometimes the facility got too laid back and dudes seemed to forget at times they were in prison. They talked recklessly, they didn't work on their post-release plans and they talked to the guards as if they were friends. The thing is, I believed there always should be a line between the guards and the inmates and the Eastern inmates often forgot about the line. The level of "snitching," straight telling on other inmates was epidemic at that facility, so I trusted few people there. I kept my circle small. I wasn't into anything illicit, however, I was always aware that shit could hit the fan at any time in the penitentiary. If I had to defend myself, I didn't need my so called right hand man claiming I was the aggressor, then cutting a deal, for a "get out of jail free card." I rolled with a few thorough dudes and if shit popped off, we would ride together, no talking, no deals.

The administration, guards and officials knew well that I wasn't an inmate who bought into the "Happy Nappy", Eastern's nickname among inmates, ideology that many of the inmates at that facility bought into. I always knew I was a caged man no matter how many so-called privileges they threw my way. Until they gave me the privilege of opening the prison door so I could walk out, I was in prison, and there was no forgetting that.

I fell out with the administration and the guards because of this mentality pretty often. They would do dumb stuff to annoy me and sometimes I ignored it, but other times I resisted it. One time, when we fell out big time, I refused to take a prison ordered blood test as they wanted me to work in the kitchen. I refused to work in the kitchen, been there, done that, and I therefore refused the blood test and the kitchen assignment. I was given 90 days "keep lock," cell confinement. I was thereafter punitively ordered transferred from one of the so-called best prisons in New York State, Eastern Correctional Facility, to one of the worst prisons, in New York State, Clinton Correctional Facility, in Dannemora New York. However, prison was prison to me and I was simply trying to do my time and go home. I really didn't give two shits where I served the time. They didn't seem to comprehend that shit, though, so they wanted my time to be as hard as possible. Fuck it, let's go. With punitive transfers, they do not tell you beforehand what prison they are shipping you too, only that you are being "shipped out."

Before leaving the Eastern Correctional Facility, however, an older, African-American guard, who was very cool as far as C.O.s go, passed by my cell and said "Be careful up there." I knew right then, (he was not supposed to tip me off, it's a security risk), they were sending me way up into the mountains. Since I had already served a stretch in Attica State Prison and knowing the administration wanted me to suffer or maybe even be killed, that's real talk, I knew they were sending me to Clinton.

My relationships with the jail and prison administrators, from my first days after my arrest were often and usually extremely contentious. They hated my guts and there absolutely was no love lost on my part towards them. Many of the jails and prisons I was confined to were infested with employees and administrators, who were openly hostile, antagonistic, racist, sadistic, or all of the above. Many of the staff in these facilities were worse in their exhibited morals and conduct than all but a small handful of the inmates they had custody of. Additionally, the general culture in prison, in order to stay under the radar of the guards and administration was simple, "Go along to get along." The problem for me was, I was not raised that way. I was always taught when someone is treating you like shit, you are supposed to, at a minimum, bring it to their attention: "You are treating me like shit." Since jails and prisons at the time generally treated you like shit, I therefore often had an issue. I actually did try to fly under the radar at moments, but the conditions within those facilities were so messed up that my spirit would not allow me to do it. So, their radar stayed locked on me almost all of the time.

The guards smiled broadly as they chained me at the hands, waist and feet and put me on the bus for a long fucking ride to Clinton.

Clinton Correctional Facility-Dannemora

I ARRIVED AT CLINTON AFTER a nearly six-hour ride. It was way up north by the Canadian border, far from New York City. The place was an absolute shit hole. The place was dirty, gloomy, loud, hostile and violent like a motherfucker.

However, upon arriving at Clinton, I was still in the box, solitary confinement, serving a ninety-day stint, of 23 hours a day lockdown for the beef I had with guards and the administration at the prior facility where I was housed, Eastern. So upon my arrival at Clinton, they marched me directly to solitary confinement.

Upon arriving at Clinton, I had only about four years left to serve before a possible release date. I had already served over eight years of a 12 and a half-year sentence. Of the thousands of inmates at Clinton, I knew that many of them were lifers and they were never coming home. I also knew that at the time I arrived at Clinton, the facility was being used to house the worst of the worst and that place was definitely dangerous. I would have to be on point. Clinton was about an eight-hour ride from New York City limits, way up in the mountains of New York State. The weather was brutal in the winter and many of the thousands of inmates housed there were just as brutal all year around. The feeling of tension was always in the air, in every part of the facility, and it was so thick you could cut it with a knife. You could almost smell it in the air.

The solitary confinement area was crazy. The cellblock was dark and dingy, with no windows and no ventilation. It was freezing cold one minute then hot as hell the next. Upon talking to an inmate in the cell next to me, who had been in solitary confinement for a few months already, I learned of some of the inmates who were confined to that unit. He mentioned the name of the man who had stabbed me. I was done talking. I had no steel; I had just arrived. I knew the yard would be opened soon for the day. They allowed those in solitary confinement out to the yard for one hour a day. I knew he would have access to steel. He had been at the prison for a while. He was likely cliqued up too and he would have soldiers with him. My possible advantage was that he didn't know I had arrived, and I could possibly creep him and split his head with a rock in the sock.

However, if I knew he was there, then he likely knew that I was there and he would be ready. I heard the guards say, "Get ready for the yard." I knew that if his clique was tight and they had good steel, I would likely die in the yard that day. The cell doors opened, and I stepped out, armed with a hidden sock. I would quickly snatch a rock once I hit the yard. Upon entering the huge yard, I scanned it quickly, looking for signs of this dude or any threats at all. I could be attacked by an unknown soldier, someone trying to make a name for himself.

I scanned the small bands of inmates to my left then to my right, then those in the distance and those close by. I saw nothing apparently threatening. I recognized some faces of dudes I had met in other facilities, but I didn't acknowledge anyone. I just kept scanning, again nothing. I finally acknowledged a guy I knew from another facility by face only and we kicked the breeze a bit. I subtly dropped a few names of dudes we may have both known and then I subtly dropped the name of the inmate who had stabbed me. He mentioned that the dude was recently there, but had been transferred out some time ago; he believed he had been released.

He went on to say that the dude was never really a general, but simply a soldier and he had turned himself around. He allegedly was on some real chill shit, no more wannabe gangster shit. I don't know the truth of any of that shit; I don't know. What I did know, beyond a shadow of a doubt, was that even though the dude wasn't there, I knew, in this crazy place, there would be other situations to come.

In my eight years of incarceration, I served many months of that time in solitary confinement, for one issue or another. Some inmates hated solitary confinement, being away from the general population and the small privileges that were available there such as television, telephone calls, extended prison yard visits, and visits to commissary, where inmates could purchase cigarettes, candy and other little things. However, others mentally couldn't stand to be confined to a cell about the size of a small apartment bathroom for 23 hours a day for weeks, months or even years at a time. Some would actually hang themselves before going or upon arrival. Others would noticeably mentally deteriorate, begin talking to themselves, cutting themselves, or shitting on themselves and refusing to wash. While others would have to be put on what we called "the juice", Thorazine, and other mental medication that turned vibrant, talkative men into silent walking zombies, all of which is some fucked-up shit to see.

As a young man in my early years of incarceration, I actually enjoyed solitary confinement. I welcomed it. I enjoyed being alone, just me and my thoughts. It gave me a stillness that I had never experienced in all my life. It forced me to stop and think; there wasn't much else to do in solitary confinement. As I aged, however, and began to better understand myself and the world around me, I didn't enjoy it as much. I was just extremely tired of prison by the end of my sentence and I simply didn't enjoy much of anything, and definitely not solitary confinement.

As a younger inmate, however, I often used solitary confinement as a strategy to break up the monotony of prison life. Prison often was literally as boring as watching paint dry. At times, I did or said things knowing I would likely get sentenced to a week, or two-weeks, a month or whatever, on "keep lock" (23 hours confined to my cell). That time on "keep lock" usually gave me time to clear my head and depressurize.

I would use that time to think, write, read and meditate. I generally would read between seven or eight hours a day, every day during my period behind bars. While on "keep lock," however, I generally read between ten to twelve hours a day. I would also go on frequent fasts, eating only one meal a day, or not eating any food except only every other day. Sometimes my fast would include absolutely no talking at all. The longest no talking fast I ever did was for thirty days, and it was quite easy. My goal was to have as much control over all aspects of myself as humanly possible. I may not ever be able to control the world around me, but I was determined to get complete control of myself.

I was nearing the end of the 90 days solitary confinement at Clinton, most of which I did reading, fasting, exercising, and meditating. At that time in my incarceration, I had easily read well over a thousand books. I began my prison reading with fiction like Donald Goines, Robert Ludlum, and Sidney Sheldon. I then moved into non-fiction, particularly World, Western, American and African History. I fell in love with autobiographies. I found the lives of other people fascinating like Nelson Mandela, Steven Biko, Dr. Martin Luther King, and Malcolm X. I devoured books on psychology, sociology, theology and law. Through reading, I was often transported from the prison cage in which I was confined, to distant times and fascinating places far away. I loved it, I needed it and so I read.

Upon completing the 90 days of solitary confinement at Clinton, I was transferred from the solitary confinement unit to a general population housing unit. Clinton was a huge prison with many housing units. They had the north side of the prison completely separated from the south side, and prison administration ran the sides like separate facilities. Inmates from each side rarely saw each other and yard, mess hall and programs, inmate work assignments, were done with only inmates from the side you were housed. The north side of the prison was strictly run and notoriously dangerous. They sent me to the north side.

I walked the long trip from the dingy, dark, solitary confinement unit to the general population area, finally reaching the new housing unit where I was assigned. The cellblock was designed as a long corridor, about 50 yards, with, on the left, approximately 30 cells, side by side, numbered approximately 1-30. The entrance to the tier and the guard's station was at the front of the tier, by cell 1. The width of the corridor was, however, very narrow, about three and a half feet. To the right was a caged in tier. I guess the caging was to prevent a person from falling off the tier, as some tiers were very high up. More likely the caging was to prevent a person from getting thrown off the tier. My assigned unit was two tiers above the ground floor tier and there were also two or three tiers above my housing tier, same design.

I was assigned a cell toward the far end of the tier, cell 20 something, which had some benefits, but also some inherent dangers. One benefit was that I had to pass nearly each cell before I reached mine. So, I used my peripheral vision to subtly scan those cells for potential enemies. I didn't have many but I still had a few. You have to be discreet upon scanning a cell because looking into a man's cell is seen as disrespectful and likely will get a "what the fuck you looking at?" from the occupant.

I didn't see any threats, but there were some cells behind me I hadn't passed, so when the cells opened, I would have to be on alert. I listened intently to the conversations being had by inmates talking "on the gate" (inmates stand at the cell doors, the "gate," talking to other inmates on their respective tiers or on other tiers, as that inmate also stood on their "gate"). You could learn a lot about a dude by simply listening to their gate conversations. They often told their whole life stories "on the gate," some real stuff and some embellished bull. At times, I heard things that had men in tears laughing, funny stuff, and other times it simply sent my antenna up. Everyone knew, I rarely talked "on the gate." I didn't like my business in the street, so I didn't do it, but I would often listen. The street wasn't talking, not that day anyway.

When the cells opened, inmates poured into the narrow corridor waiting to be told to line up for the mess hall, the inmate dining facility. My plan going forward was simple, lay low, keep my nose clean, avoid the prison politics and bull, serve the four years I had left on my sentence and go home. I didn't see anyone that I really knew on that tier, friend or foe, and that was cool with me. In all my years of serving time, if I had to put a fist or knife to a dude, it was almost always me standing up for someone close to me because others were coming at them for some unjustifiable reason. Very rarely did I personally have a beef.

When I hit the yard for the first time, it was crazy. Hundreds of inmates were in the huge yard. Everybody that I knew and was pretty cool with from years of bidding (serving time), was in the big yard and all of them had brewing beef with somebody. The tension in the yard was so thick you could cut it with a knife. In the yard were dudes I knew from Rikers Island hospital, Nassau County lockup, Coxsackie, Elmira, Attica, and from my last stop, Eastern Correctional Facility. There were dudes I had grown up with from my old Brooklyn neighborhood and dudes I went to public school with. There were dudes who were cool with my brother and dudes who knew my whole family and I knew theirs. I immediately thought, "How am I going to keep my nose clean in this environment? How am I going to be able to lay low?"

The yard was huge, a couple of football fields in size and rectangular in shape. In the middle of the yard was a football/soccer field. There was a huge hill at the far end of the big yard/field and another big hill on the right of the ball field. The hill sloped way up and overlooked the big yard/field. On those hills, overlooking the big yard/field was assigned food courts, dozens of squared off and numbered areas assigned to certain inmates for the purpose of hanging out, viewing yard sporting events, and for cooking. Each court had an outdoor woodstove, pots, pans, and cooking utensils. Wood could be ordered and supplied to each court to burn when cooking food. Only four or five inmates were allowed on each court at any given time. So there were some big cliques who tried to get ownership/assignment of as many courts side-by-side as they could. This would allow all members of their clique to be close to each other and they would all be neighbors. Many beefs and stabbings occurred over who would or would not be assigned to a particular court; age-old territory fights.

When you first enter the yard, you march out with your unit. When my unit arrived at the yard, hundreds of inmates were out there already. Almost immediately people recognized me and started approaching. They filled me in on "what was what" and "who was who". Many men in the big yard were "lifers", they would never be released from prison. The drug crews were "very strong" in that prison I was told. They had drugs, money and power in that facility like a motherfucker. They had many soldiers who would hit a man up on command just to stay ingratiated with the drug kings, and thereby get cheap drugs or a cash payout. Many of these soldiers, once upon a time, were thorough dudes not to be fucked with. Some were ex-professional fighters, hit men for drug crews on the outside and even some military veterans, with real combat experience. Now, they were simply drug addicts, serving massive time and selling their services to the prison drug kings.

As I stood on the sideline of the main yard surveying the landscape, and sizing up people and crews, a short, stocky, Muslim inmate passed by me while walking the yard with two other sternly serious looking Muslim inmates by his side. They all wore Kufi headgear (Muslim headgear) and held prayer beads in their hands. He instantly did a double take upon seeing me and called out excitedly, "Abdullah Bey" which was the name that most inmates knew me by. I said, "Kadeer?" and gave him greetings of peace, "As-salaamualaikum."

Kadeer and I had served time together in the Attica Correctional Facility some years prior. He was a dangerous individual, martial artist who could easily take a man's life with his bare hands. He was older than I was, as was many of the seriously respected inmates in those days, and he was one of the most respected inmates in Clinton. I had earned his love and respect during an incident in Attica yard when the White and Hispanic inmates were cliquing up to wage war against the Muslims over some minor earlier incident. They had overwhelming numbers on us that day in the yard. My position was "let's go," no truce, as some of the other Muslim inmates were talking about. My position was based upon a belief that if five blood brothers ever went to war against ten friends, although the brothers were outnumbered two to one, they would fight harder and more fiercely because they were brothers and they would defeat the opposition even while being outnumbered. The Muslims at Attica were a close-knit community and were genuinely like-brothers. Kadeer was of the same mindset as me, although we were out-voted and a truce was agreed upon rather than war. We gained massive respect for each other after that day, and he and I remained close friends serving time together at that facility.

Kadeer went on to walk the yard with me that day, catching me up on all the things that were going on in his life the past few years, as I did the same. He went on to tell me that the state of affairs with the Muslim inmates at Clinton were in complete disarray. He said that the Muslims had good numbers in the facility; they were well over 100 strong, but they were severely fractured. He said the brothers in charge of security, Wazirs, were strong, fierce, dangerous old heads, older inmates, mostly lifers, but extremely insulated. They were focused, Kadeer said, mainly on protecting their small circle, consisting of approximately ten inmates, and the Imam, the Muslim religious leader in the facility.

As we walked the big yard, Kadeer told me they did not have patience with the hordes of younger Muslim inmates, many of whom were new converts to Islam, and thus still very wild. The new converts were former street dudes, stickup kids, drug dealers and musclemen from drug crews. Kadeer said these young guys, who were raised on hip hop, were not embraced by the present Muslim leadership of the old heads, who found hip hop mostly distasteful and the majority of the hip hop generation often offensive. Kadeer said the community was severely separated, old versus young, and although the Muslims had good numbers in the prison, they were not respected because they didn't move as an organized unit. Kadeer went on to say that the prison was dangerous for a Muslim's health and that a number of Muslims had been severely and unjustifiably attacked with no retaliation or fear of retaliation coming from the Muslim prison leadership.

Finally, Kadeer said, "Abdullah Bey, the old heads, the young heads, Muslim and non-Muslims respect you. You have to take over the security team. You have to take the position of Wazir." I told Kadeer that I couldn't do it. I told him that I was "too short," possibly going home in four years and to be Wazir of security was a huge responsibility because the lives of over one hundred men would be in my hands. Kadeer said, "Abdullah Bey, I trust you, and I'll support you, and I know you will do well by everyone."

"Fuck," I thought as we walked and talked, "I just want to chill and go home." I knew I could organize this team in no time into the crew nobody in the prison wanted a problem with. We had the bodies, numerous young, strong, strapping dudes who enjoyed whipping ass. However, everybody was in their own corner, doing their own thing. I knew I could change that.

I knew that if I took over security, in no time, the Bloods, the Crips, the violent Hispanic gangs, racist rednecks and even the extremely strong drug crews would not be able to touch us and would want no problems with us. However, I also knew the hard and dangerous work that it would entail to get us to that point. I was possibly going home in four years and to do this, take over security, would definitely put that in jeopardy. My life and freedom would be in serious danger; there likely would be bloodshed whether, it be with the prison gangs or prison drug crews. People likely would be laid down. However, to do nothing would definitely put my life and the life of my friends in even larger jeopardy, because at that time, at that prison, it was hunting season on Muslim inmates. They were that weak, and unorganized and thus, they were easy targets.

I told Kadeer that I would give it some thought. I asked Kadeer, "What about the brothers who were presently running security for the Muslims? Would they willing step down?" He said, "We can ask them to." I laughed. Kadeer said, "Let me introduce you to the Imam. He just came to the yard."

The Imam was a young, slightly built inmate from upstate New York. He was funny, likeable and very well versed in Islamic teachings. He was wise. He was also well-respected among the prison administration and he had the ear and respect of the prison warden. What many people do not know about Islam, primarily because of the fierce anti-Islam propaganda on the news and in movies these days, is that most prison/jail administrators in New York City and State usually enjoy having large Muslim populations in their facilities and on their cellblocks and units. The prison Muslim population is actually one of the most peaceful of inmates. Many inmates, too, will tell you that they prefer to live amongst Muslim inmates above any other inmate population. The Muslim inmates generally keep peace in the cellblocks. No raping, stealing, extortion, and senseless violence will be going on, that is, if the Muslim inmate population in the area is strong. Therefore, when Muslim inmates are around and they have influence in the area, that area is likely the safest and least violent and crime-ridden area of the facility.

The Muslim population at Clinton was not that influential when I arrived there and the Imam went on to explain that he, too, was concerned with the state of affairs, particularly in the area of security. Muslim inmates were constantly at risk of harm in that facility. The Imam joined Kadeer and me in our walk around the yard and they introduced me to the head of security as well as his security team, who had also entered the yard.

I knew the head of security from my time in Attica. His name was Rafeek, and he knew and respected me. He was a former Black Panther and was serving a life sentence for a murder that many claimed was a frame-up by the FBI. His team, too, was mostly former Black Panther Party members and former Black Liberation Army members. A few who were also recognized by many as political prisoners. They were men who many claimed were falsely imprisoned because of their political views and their commitment to the liberation of people of African descent in America and around the world. These were hardened, old-school inmates who didn't take any mess and were respected to the fullest throughout the state prison system.

The main issue with them, however, was that, it was a new day. These hardened warriors had been incarcerated at that time for over 25 years. There was a new generation of inmates entering the prison system and they were far less politically conscious than the inmates from Rafeek and his team's era. This new crop of inmates were mostly young, wild, and totally politically unconscious. Many of these new inmates didn't read, debate, talk politics or have a clue as to what the Black Panther Party was. They didn't know anything about civil rights, the march on Washington, or anything related to Black people's struggles in America or anywhere around the world. This ignorance was, if not a turn-off to Rafeek and his clique, definitely a put-off. There was a poor connection.

Rafeek knew that I had a sense of his world because he and I would often talked while serving time together years ago in Attica. He and many of his comrades would sit-around and talk and I would be there listening, asking questions and trying to learn and understand where they were coming from. They recommended books and I read them. They held group discussions and I listened intently because I understood that these dudes were living American history. History books, when talking about the Black Panther Party and the Black Liberation Army, whether one agreed with their ideology or not, would mention these men who I was literally standing next to. I understood the significance of simply listening as they spoke. These men respected my search for knowledge and my maturity level and spoke openly and freely around me. I often challenged them on some of their old ideas and many of them had definitely evolved in their thinking and they openly discussed their evolutions.

I left the yard that day after saying so long to Rafeek, the Imam, and the other members of the security team. Kadeer parted with a salutation of peace to me, saying, "Abdullah Bey, think about it." I returned to my cell and thought about it. I knew I wouldn't challenge Rafeek for the position; I had too much respect for the process of bringing us together and an open challenge to Rafeek would only tear us apart. I also understood Rafeek and his frustration with the young dudes. I'm sure Rafeek knew that many of the younger inmates were going to rally around me. He knew that they respected me and that I knew how to vibe with them, no matter how wild they were.

I came up running with wild, young dudes, Devine, Wild-Out and countless others in my years of incarceration. They related to me and I related to them. My close affinity in age with them made it easy to sit with them, and my somewhat mature edge allowed me to encourage them to be their best self. In me, because of our closeness in age, they saw their own possibilities. The young dudes saw in me that, yes, I love books, and reading and education, and civility, but still, I was "not the one" to mess with and they respected that. I also had no beef with the hip hop generation, I was a part of it.

The older inmates also knew and understood that I was on a search for knowledge and self-improvement. I was committed to it. They knew that I was well-read and well-taught. I had actually learned much from Rafeek. They knew that I had values, morals, integrity and was a principled young man. They also knew that I was well-respected throughout the prison system and they also mostly had a healthy respect for me. They also knew that the hordes of young, wild dudes at the prison were going to ride with me. They would follow my lead.

The Imam sometime later came by my cell. He held an institutional pass, giving him privilege to roam the entire prison unattended to handle Muslim Community business during certain hours of the day. He had the complete respect and trust of the prison administration. The Imam told me that a number of inmates had spoken to him about me, including Kadeer, who was a loyal and trusted friend to the Imam. The Imam said that he wanted me to consider taking over the reins from Rafeek. He said that he had spoken to Rafeek and that he was open to it, no resistance. Rafeek was an older inmate and he maintained the position because he was best suited at the time to do it. I told the Imam, as I had told Kadeer, that I didn't want it and the reasons why. The Imam told me to "think about it."

I later ran into Rafeek, and he and I talked. He was a strong dude, mentally, physically and spiritually, but he was tired, and wanted a break. His thing, however, was that he was not going to step down for someone he didn't believe had the ability to get things done. He said that he trusted me. I knew, and Rafeek knew, because we had talked about it years ago, that the old and wise should sit and guide while the young and physically strong should stand and fight, not vice-versa. He knew that the set-up as it presently existed was not ideal. However, he didn't trust many of the young inmates there to lead. He trusted me. Rafeek said that he would step down if I agreed to take over. After long thought and internal struggle, I agreed.

The Imam soon after introduced me to the Muslim community as the Wazir of security and that if the Imam or his assistant was not around, I was in charge. Also, in all matters related to security, I was the final word, period. Rafeek and his team offered assistance in any area where I needed them. I thanked them. I told them, for now, just relax, and know that, I got it.

Surrounded by Killers

I IMMEDIATELY BEGAN PUTTING TOGETHER my security team. Young dudes, who were previously not involved in security matters, immediately began offering their services. They wanted to be involved and I wanted them involved. Many of them were lifers. I knew that if things really hit the fan, I would need them on the front line, ready, willing and able. I hand-picked dudes to be on my first team, including Kadeer, my inner-circle, my security team.

We had our first security meeting in the big yard. We huddled up as I began laying out the plan to keep us safe and alive in an extremely dangerous and hostile environment. Doing this correctly was literally a matter of life and death. I looked around the huddle and I was pleased with what I saw. I was surrounded by killers, but these were the only men I trusted to protect my life and the lives of my people. If things hit the fan, I couldn't choose Boy Scouts.

The word spread quickly throughout the prison that Abdullah Bey was the new Wazir of security. That is how the prison was; certain news traveled quickly. Many pledged support to my leadership, Muslims and non-Muslims. The thing is, many non-Muslims strongly supported the Muslim community because they were not swayed by the widespread anti-Muslim propaganda. They believed that we truly were men of peace and righteousness.

Some also pledged support because they actually saw themselves as Muslims. However, the prison lifestyle that they openly lived would not allow the Muslim community to embrace them. These men were usually using or selling drugs, or involved in gambling, extortion and other frowned-upon activities. Still, they truly believed in the teachings of Islam and privately considered themselves Muslim, just not great ones. Others pledged allegiance, mostly non-Muslims, vowing their support in times of prison conflict. They volunteered to act as spies embedded in the enemy camps because their childhood homeboy had converted to Islam and so, if their Muslim homeboy, and the Muslim community had beef, they would ride with us. A number of inmates, both Muslim and non-Muslim, volunteered to be "Raad" (hit men). These were the inmates, mostly lifers, who would lay a dude out if necessary and take any and all consequences, no matter how serious the injury was to the victim. Raad were totally secret; only the Wazir usually knew who these men were. Oftentimes, Raad didn't even openly socialize with the Muslim population, and thus they could get close and touch practically anyone in prison without them seeing it coming. After a short time in the position, we had a formidable force configured and everybody in the prison knew it.

To make sure everyone in the prison was aware of the new leadership and, consequently the new rules, I or my assistants met with the leadership of other major players at the prison, including gang leaders, drug lords, and other cliques that had strength and influence at the prison. The message my assistants and I delivered was clear: the Muslims are men of peace; however, no one within that prison was going to run over us and there will be serious repercussions if anyone tries.

I also established peace treaties with most of the major players at the prison and got their word that if they had beef with any Muslim inmate or any inmate under our sworn protection, including numerous non-Muslims, they would notify me of the issue; they would never shed their blood.

At any given time there were at least fifty Muslim inmates in the big yard and if I gave the order for everyone to come out to the yard, including our non-Muslim supporters, our numbers would swell to close to one hundred men. No one else in that facility could bring that many men to the battlefield to match us, not the Bloods, Crips, Latino gangs, five-percenters, or drug kingpins; it wasn't even close.

Most of the people at the prison saw the new swagger, and they believed, but if anyone doubted our numbers or our unity, I squashed that nonsense by periodic shows of strength. I demanded that all Muslims, upon entering the yard, every day, congregate at the far left-hand corner of the yard to do a short opening prayer and to inform our security team of any potential beef amongst us or others that we needed to be aware of. The first time I gave that instruction at least seventy brothers came to the yard that day and the looks on the faces of the other inmates when they saw that show of unity and togetherness was priceless.

I had my new security command team with me, about ten strong, mostly young inmates, some wild and anxious for whatever. Rafeek was there with his older, mellower, but dangerous ex-security team, giving us their full support, encouragement and cooperation. The Imam came to the yard to lead us in prayer, happy to finally see young and old, wild and learned, all standing together as one community. It was a good day.

The other prisoners took notice of our new standing in that facility and I was told they had begun amassing steel, numerous knives to war against us. More specifically, it was the Latino gangs. This information came from numerous sources, including my man Yaya, who was the chief assistant in the prison metal shop. Metal shop was a place where you could make better knives and blades than the old Samurai warriors carried. That's why many of the prison gang-bangers fought to get assigned there.

Yaya told me that he saw the gangs feverishly making and stashing knives. You had to make them on the low because guards are constantly watching, but they were more determinedly making them and slowly sneaking them out to the yard. The thing is, making them unobserved is definitely hard, but sneaking them out of the shop, through security checks, is even harder. So, they could only move them to the yard maybe one or two per week.

Yaya, however, was the chief instructor at the metal shop and had been there for years. He was a favorite of the guards, a true "trustee" who was beyond suspicion and for good reason: he was a geek to the bone. Geeks and I have always connected, back to my junior high school days so I had love for Yaya and he absolutely respected me in return. Again, I don't know what Yaya did to get to prison, forgot to pay child support or something, but beyond that I couldn't see him ever committing a crime. Yaya likely never made a knife in all his time at that metal shop like the Latino gangbangers often did and he definitely never smuggled one out. However, I desperately needed knives and lots of them.

This reality, a need for good knives, came apparently clear early on as the new Wazir. I got into a beef with another inmate who called himself Muslim and hung around us, but was rumored to be involved in all kinds of nonsense activity, including heavy drug dealing in the prison. One of my assistants and I approached him on it and he started barking aggressively, eventually pushing my assistant when they went nose to nose. I tried to break them up, grabbing the dude so the guards wouldn't notice and thereafter send my assistant to solitary confinement; he already had a bad prison record. Dude believed I was attacking him and he proceeded to bite me viciously on the shoulder. I laid him out.

Immediately after that incident, the dude was locked in his cell and questioned about the incident while my assistant and I slipped away. Dude was also on my cellblock. So when I arrived back on the cellblock, I saw him talking on the gate with another inmate, D, who claimed to be a friend of mine. I didn't say anything to either of them, and I kept it moving. Later, the next day, as I approached his cell, I saw that he was still locked in. He was on the gate again, talking to D. D tried to back away from the gate when he noticed me coming. Something was cooking, and I had to stay on point.

While I was returning from the yard that evening, as I approached the dude's cell, it was pitch black inside his cell, but D was on his gate and looking down the tier. I could see D's hands hanging outside of his cell. He was spying. I hesitated, just the right amount, as I passed dude's cell, because he had tied a wicked knife on the end of a broom stick and was standing on his bed within his cell and he harpooned me with it as I passed by. My slight hesitation saved my life because the knife hit right below my left breast. I hustled quickly past the dude's cell as the guards started coming down the cellblock, having sensed that something was popping off. I quickly went to my cell because if you are stabbed in prison they automatically put you in protective custody and thereafter ship you to a different facility. I wasn't leaving, not until after I got hands on this dude.

As the guards walked up and down the cellblock looking for signs of an injured inmate, I sat on my bed reading a book as if everything was fine, but my chest was throbbing. As the guards passed, I removed my outer shirt and then T-shirt, which was spotted with blood. There was a small puncture hole right next to my heart. That was a close call. I cleaned it and began sharpening my knife. I didn't sleep at all that evening. I wanted this dude badly. When the cells finally opened for breakfast, the dude didn't come out of his cell. That's cool. "I'll catch you at lunch time; you cannot stay in that cell forever," I thought. Before lunch time arrived, however, I looked down the cellblock and saw numerous guards around the dude's cell, and they were escorting him off of the cellblock. He had whispered to the guards that his life was in danger and that he wanted to be moved to protective custody.

At lunch time and later in the big yard, I connected with my clique, some of who were on the cellblock and others who were not and filled them in that I was ok, although I had a serious fever. I also told them that D had to be touched because he definitely was involved in my stabbing. He was the one who told the dude I was coming before the hit. A number of people volunteered to get him, but I told them, "I got this." The thing is, in prison, if you allowed a stabbing to go unchecked, against you or one of your people, it opened the door for other attackers to step through, so my life and the people rolling with me would then be in danger.

Also, my thing with D was that we were supposed to be friends. He and I kicked it, (talked about serious issues) on many different days.

Therefore, in my mind, he had sold me out, and although he knew the other dude, because I believe they were from the same neighborhood, he should have, at least, stayed neutral. He had to get it.

When the cell doors opened for dinner, my clique was on point. They already knew what was going on. D hung with a decent clique and he was pretty respected in the prison. Still, D had to be addressed. He and his clique stood waiting for the gate to open for mess hall. I came down the cellblock, knife in hand but hidden. D's clique was not really on red alert because I'm sure D never told them about the snake shit he had done. However, D was definitely on alert even if it was simply guilt. He saw me approaching and quickly reached in his pocket. I hit him hard and he fell. However, I didn't trust my blade because he had on a thick jacket of coarse material. So, I moved in to hit him again, but he had quickly scurried to his feet and began running toward the front of the cellblock to the guards. I fell back. I didn't chase. I wasn't trying to go to the box, solitary confinement, for this snake-ass dude. I dropped the knife off the tier to my little man who was a trustee, and was waiting for the knife drop on the tier below. He quickly made it disappear. I knew I had put a good hole in him, but I definitely didn't get him like I wanted to.

D was still walking. He walked slowly to the mess hall with a mass of other inmates and guards nearby, obviously injured, but he hid it well. Returning to the cellblock from the mess hall, he quickly locked into his cell. Yard was in a few hours, so I would simply finish it when the cells opened; one of us was going to the emergency room that day. Word spread quickly around the prison of the incident and inmates from all over the prison were sending words of support and encouragement to me as well as to D; he was a fairly popular dude at the facility.

Inmates were coming by my cell, kicking it with me, sending me kites, letters, and they were doing the same for D. I saw from my cell when an inmate, a punk dude named L, slipped D a knife. I had dumped my blade and I was still waiting for its return from the trustee, but he was still locked in his cell. I had no blade. If the cell doors opened and I was unarmed, I would be at a disadvantage, but then I heard the cells below open and the trustee yelled up, "Abdullah Bey, coming up." He tossed me the knife, which was inside a heavy sweat sock. It still wasn't the best knife, but it would have to do. Everyone, including D, saw the trustee throw me up the knife, so everyone knew that when the cell doors opened, it was on.

I had a few dudes with me on the cellblock and so did D. Everyone was armed, I'm sure, but most likely no one was going to jump in. It likely would be a one-on-one. Before the cell doors opened, I quickly made a protective vest, which was two copies of a newspaper taped together. I then tied it around the front of my body covering vital organs, particularly the heart and lungs. I then slipped on an extra-large prison green shirt to cover it up. It was practically undetectable.

When the cell doors opened, the entire cellblock gathered around as me and D stepped to the middle of the tier. I had my knife in hand, but D was apparently unarmed. Also, he had on no protective gear. In fact he wore a short sleeved, skin tight t-shirt. I am sure he knew my knife would penetrate that with ease. D was a former amateur fighter, and I heard his technique was good. He was fairly tall, of slender build, with lean, well-toned muscle. As we stood face to face, I armed and he apparently unarmed, he started crying. He said, "Abdullah Bey, I'm sorry, I should have never got in the middle of that." Finally he said, "Abdullah Bey, I love you man and don't want to fight you."

I'm looking at this young man, hard core dude, with the tears in his eyes as he is looking back at me with admiration and respect, and the thing was, I knew he was telling the truth. He had genuine love for me. There was definitely some fear on his part, but the overriding emotion was love and respect, and because of that love and respect, he honestly didn't want to fight me. That moment haunted me for years and has impacted many of my future relationships with people because I could not comprehend how a person could genuinely love you, but at the same time want you fucking dead. That was too crazy to comprehend.

I believed that the man spoke his heart, but deep down, I also believed that he knew the prison rules well enough to know that I couldn't let it ride. To not address an attempt on my life, in that environment would only invite other attempts on my life. It had to be addressed. I reached under my shirt, I peeled off my protective vest and I threw it at him, telling him, "Get your knife." He reached into his pocket, pulling out a nasty looking blade. Any good hit from that shit would definitely be trouble.

We started going at it for what seemed a fairly long time. One of his blows hit me on the top of the head, but I didn't feel the blade. I only felt his hand. In a boxing match, a heavy puncher can take five blows from a lighter puncher in an effort to simply land one solid blow to the lighter puncher. However, in knife fighting, that strategy is a death sentence. With knives, the best strategy is to hit without being hit, or hit first and hit hardest. I hit him hard, but he definitely hit back, and his knife was better. Someone yelled, "C.O." and the fight ended. D walked slowly toward the mess hall, being discreetly supported by his man Barsheen. I walked toward the mess hall with a buddy by my side, both of us trying to appear nonchalant. The guards, however, knew that something had happened and they were looking closely at everyone for any indications of distress or injury. I showed neither.

While in the mess hall, almost half the prison was in there and everyone was already talking. An inmate sitting across from me at the table pointed his finger towards my neck. I put my fingers up to my neck and my fingers were covered in blood. I looked down at my shirt and the collar was splattered with blood. I took a napkin and I cleaned the wound the best that I could. I had been stabbed on the left side of the neck, right under the chin. Upon returning to the cellblock, I passed the main cellblock officer and he noticed the blood on my shirt, but he didn't say anything. He was a huge White farmer dude from way up north, but was genuinely cool as heck. He was a very good person. He later passed my cell quietly asking, "You OK?"

I said with absoluteness, "I'm good."

He said, with sincerity, "Take care," and he walked away.

Back at my cell, I looked in the mirror at the hole in my neck and it didn't look that bad, although it was still slightly bleeding. I took a four-inch cotton swab, placing it gently against the wound, and the cotton swab practically disappeared inside the wound. Fuck. I wasn't going for X-rays or stitches, so whatever it was it would simply have to be. I cleaned the wound and tried to keep it clean the best I could. Rumor was that D also had holes in him, but he didn't want to go to protective custody. He sent word through his people asking, "Abdullah Bey, can we talk?"

The thing was that, years ago, I already had a very bad experience with allowing a dude I had beef with to stay in the facility, believing the beef was squashed and it almost cost me my life. I wasn't doing that again. I sent word back to D, that, "There is nothing to talk about." The visits to my cell and messages from all over the prison from D's people were persistent and they were coming from people I had respect for. Their position was that they didn't want to go to war against me, but D was their man and they didn't want to see him injured, particularly when D didn't want to fight.

Finally, I sent word that I would talk to him one-on-one when we hit the yard that evening. Everyone was basically relieved; however, many of my people wanted blood, no talking. My thinking was that, I knew D's people didn't want beef with me; it would be a fight they couldn't win. I also knew that D was genuinely sorry for what he had done and although he honestly was no punk, he did not want to fight, specifically with me; his heart wasn't in it. I felt like if I pushed the issue, most people would understand because prison rules are prison rules and D had seriously violated the rules. However, I always despised bullies and I felt that to push the issue would be to appear as some real bully shit on my part and maybe it would. So, even though I could easily justify taking care of D anyway I chose to, I sent word to D that I would talk in the yard.

D hit the yard before I did. My group was held up because of some incident on the cellblock and all inmate movement was delayed. Immediately upon D entering the big yard, Big Boss approached D, telling him to, "Get your knife and meet me in the back of the yard." Big Boss wanted D's blood because of D's confrontation with me.

Big Boss wasn't really that big, but because his little brother was known as Boss too, everyone simply called him "Big Boss" to make the distinction. Big Boss, however, was a ridiculously well-respected inmate out of Brooklyn, New York, and he and his clique rode at the very top of the prison pecking order everywhere they went. I was tight with his younger brother, Little Boss. We had served time together years ago when I first arrived in state prison. Upon learning that I had arrived at Clinton, Little Boss then wrote a letter to Big Boss, telling him who I was and the friendship we had. Big Boss was already at Clinton.

I had heard many stories about Big Boss, some so outrageous that I thought maybe they weren't true concerning his tremendous courage and unbelievable physical abilities. This was long before I had actually met him. We clicked hard as soon as we met and we built a strong friendship and brotherhood. Big Boss subsequently converted to Islam and I became his mentor. Hearing tales of a man's courage is one thing, but experiencing it firsthand is totally different. Big Boss was a man who would say, "You're my brother Abdullah Bey and I love you," and thereafter was readily willing to put his life on the line to demonstrate that brotherhood and that love. I learned for certain that day what many inmates had long known, and had been saying for years: Big Boss was absolutely the real deal. D was completely shook; he and most inmates did not want any problems with Big Boss, none.

Thankfully, I hit the yard before it went down because D was trying to explain to Big Boss that everything was basically cool with him and me, but Big Boss wasn't trying to hear shit. I called Big Boss and the rest of my clique, explaining the situation. The entire yard was filled with tension. D or his clique wasn't sure what the deal really was, particularly after Big Boss had approached them. They were posted up and prepared, but again, they definitely didn't want it. My folks generally wanted D hit and numerous dudes, Muslim and non-Muslim, volunteered to hit him. I said, "No."

I sent word to D to walk the yard with me. This was so everyone could see that we were walking together and talking, not warring. We made peace. I know all too well that some men will tell you it is peace, but at the first opportunity they would take your head off. Their word means nothing. My rule had always been, up to that point, if you have beef in prison, you crush it, period. So, this was a hard call for me because a truce with D, violated a rule I had adopted after almost losing my life behind bars. I had to now trust that this peace is genuine and not just a ruse to rock me to sleep. So, here we go again. I would risk it. I believed D.

Some of my people were cool with the decision to let it go; others not so much. The next day, a powerfully built inmate who was the enforcer in a Brooklyn drug clique at the prison, Kado, approached me and said with encouragement, "Abdullah Bey, you are the most influential inmate in this prison. Use your power, man," and he quickly walked off. In my mind, though, I believed that I actually had.

The next time I ran into Yaya from the metal shop while in the yard, Yaya was a short, quiet, slightly obese Brooklyn dude, I walked exaggeratedly slow and showed him my injuries, saying to him, "They had better knives, Yaya." I had to play on his emotions; this was for a good cause. Yaya had previously told me upon my numerous requests that he couldn't make and move knives, he just couldn't do it. That day, however, I sensed that something was different. Yaya loved and respected me and I know my injuries seriously bothered him.

A few days passed before I saw Yaya in the yard, but when he saw me, he called me over to an area out of sight of the prison guards. Yaya was walking with a swagger I had never seen before. He handed me a heavy canvas bag he had been carrying; it was very heavy and I heard the clicking of metal inside. I opened it and it was filled with flatheads, metal pressed flat, dangerously sharpened, knives. I smiled broadly and hugged Yaya; he pushed me off with, "Come on, Abdullah Bey." Yaya didn't welcome physical contact like that, Yaya was Yaya. At that prison, we had a tight clique, we had strong unity and now we had the best knives in the prison. No one was better at steel making than Yaya and the knives he made for me were crazy.

The Latino and other gangs soon got the word that Yaya had made and moved numerous knives out the metal shop to the yard. Good. I wanted them to have no doubts that we didn't just have the manpower and unity, we had steel, too, good steel. Peace often is established through strength and we had serious strength at Clinton, and, ultimately, we had peace, too. After that day in the big yard, Yaya walked the prison with a new swagger, like he was the man. I would see him and simply smile.

New Breed of Inmate

IN THE NINETIES, A NEW breed of inmate began to flood the prisons and jails of New York, and these dudes were different. These guys were right from another planet, a different world. These were the relatives of the new crack epidemic plaguing the country. The stories, attitudes, morals, and ethics that these dudes had were completely shocking. I could barely tolerate being near these dudes and they likely knew it.

This new breed of prisoner was either a crack dealer or a crackhead (person very addicted to crack cocaine). In my eyes, each one of these guys was despicable, based upon the stories they told, more so the crack dealer. I heard them gleefully tell stories, the crack dealers, of how they had sold crack cocaine to their own family members, brothers, sisters, sometimes even to their own mothers. They told stories, with laughter, of how young girls, 13 and 14 years old, would get hooked on crack cocaine and how these girls would allow five or six guys in their crew to have sex with them for pieces of crack cocaine. They talked with pride about how some of the neighborhood's "stuck up" women and other ladies, who normally would not give the crack dealer attention, were coerced to have degrading sex in crack houses and stairwells with multiple men or even with animals, often in exchange for small pieces of crack cocaine. These men talked openly about the shootings and the killings of other people over turf wars, that is, who would be allowed to sell drugs on which block. They talked about maiming and shooting drug addicts over the drug addicts failing to pay a small drug debt owed to the drug dealer, debts as low as $20. A dear childhood friend, the son of my mom's best friend, was also killed during that time period over a $20 crack cocaine debt. They killed him over $20 fucking dollars.

In my eyes, these were despicable dudes in their actions. These people, "crack-affiliates," also slowly changed the entire prison culture in some of the worst ways. The idea of there was "honor amongst thieves" eventually went completely out the window.

The prisons and jails were now overrun with a "crackhead" mentality: lie, steal, cheat, double-cross, kill, and snitch, even against your childhood friend, right-hand loyal man, or your own blood brother. This shit was fucking crazy. Prison had changed and a dangerous environment became even more dangerous. Double-crossing and snitching became almost normal while trust and loyalty became rare; treachery was everywhere.

At the time, I didn't understand cocaine or cocaine addiction. I only saw, heard, and understood the effects this drug was having on my present living environment, and on the American neighborhoods and the people who lived there. This was a different world than the one I had ever known and I couldn't wrap my mind around the callousness and heartlessness these dudes displayed. Remorseless and boastful of their deeds as they were, I openly despised these dudes. Although I knew that I was being forced to live around these guys, I also knew that I was going to hurt one of them real fucking soon. My dislike for them was that strong.

The first opportunity came while I was standing on the tier talking to a former Black Panther. He was serving life without possibility of parole for his alleged Black Panther Party activities. There were also strong allegations that he was framed by the government because of his daring to join a group that was committed to the liberation of Black people in America. He was considered a threat to the government and thus was falsely accused and convicted, it was being said. He had already served over 25 years at the time I met him. At the time however, he was simply a mild mannered, humble, fragile, very old man and there was nothing even vaguely menacing about him. He was so well read and deeply knowledgeable on so many different subjects that I enjoyed talking to him, particularly about politics and world affairs. Talking to him was like having a one-on-one with a top-flight college professor. His depth of knowledge on so many issues was definitely professorial.

While talking to him one day on the cellblock as we were waiting to be allowed into the yard, this crack addict comes aggressively barreling by, pushing past him and me to get to the front of the yard line. No respect for the rules of the prison or people around him, "crackhead mentality." Drugs, drugs, drugs, and more drugs was the singular focus of so many of these newly arrived inmates, forget everything and everyone around them, nothing else mattered. He was likely rushing to get to the yard to catch the prison drug dealers to score some crack before they sold out. The former Black Panther simply laughed lightly. I wasn't laughing, and then I got angry. However, I was angrier with the former Black Panther for his not being angry. How is it that after sacrificing 25 years plus of your life for the love of Black people, this walking symbol of Black failure, a committed crack addict, has the audacity to nearly run you over, without even a simple "my bad," a basic apology? This crack addict didn't even know who this old man he nearly ran over was and he likely didn't even care. I looked long and hard at this old man standing in front of me, with all gray hair, gray beard, ailing health, and I was furious. I turned away from him without saying another word, but I'm thinking to myself, *You don't have to be angry, old dude, but when I get to the yard, for that man disrespecting you, I'm fucking him up.*

Everyone knew something was up as soon as I hit the yard. My clique is asking, "What up, Bey, what's good?" I told them nothing, but they knew something was up, they knew me well. Once they determined no major beef was in the air, they gave me the space I often needed to clear my head. So, I walked the yard alone, which I did at times; I often needed alone time. Some would comment on that tendency and thought I should always walk with security. Clinton, at that time, was one of the most dangerous prisons in New York State. I most often just didn't feel that need.

I scanned the yard for this dude; he was going to get it. There were hundreds of inmates in the yard at the time, and the yard was huge. I didn't see him on my first or second trip around the yard.

The old former Black Panther, however, caught up with me before my third trip around. He asked, "What's up, Bey?"

I said, "Nothing." I wasn't in the mood for talking. Finally, upon being pressed, I relented and briskly told him that this was the penitentiary and that you cannot allow disrespect without checking it. Finally, I told him that I was disappointed with him because for all the sacrifices he had made for the love of people like that fool. That fool not only did not know who he was, he was disrespectful, too. I told him that he "should be upset;" in fact, "You should be pissed off, man."

He looked at me like a father looks at a child who's frustrated that he cannot catch a butterfly, although it appears to be flying so low and so slow. He smiled and said, "Abdullah Bey, if my life's sacrifices were about me, I would likely be mad that he didn't know my name, but the struggle has never been about me."

We talked on that occasion about many things including self-sacrifice, all of which helped me better understand the concept of selfless sacrifice. I marveled at him. The old man's absolute refusal to harbor anger or bitterness toward anyone, including those whom he sacrificed his entire life for, yet who mostly didn't know his name, was amazing to me. I later saw the crackhead who had disrespected the old black man, and my heart was in pain thinking, *you fucking crackhead, you don't have the right to disrespect that old man.* Yet, I understood what the old man took pains to get me to see. "Selfless sacrifice." I got it.

From that point on, I looked at him and things around me a little differently. I began to look much more closely at people who consistently sought the limelight and personal recognition while claiming to do this or that only for "the love of the cause". After talking to this old man, I became much more cynical of blatant attention seekers.

After about a year in Clinton, I was instructed to "pack up". I was being transferred to Fishkill Correctional Facility. My clique was still strong and in good shape to survive an extremely wicked place, so I was comfortable saying farewell; it was time to move on.

Fishkill: Losing my Mom

Upon arriving at Fishkill Correctional Facility, a few miles from New York City, my mindset drastically changed. While way up in the mountains, surrounded by men, many of whom would never be released from prison, and living in an environment that was often so violent and vicious, some died brutal deaths in those prisons, I therefore mostly adapted to simply survive. Large portions of my day while in maximum-security prison were focused on ways of surviving and also keeping the people around me whom I cared for safe.

Fishkill, however, was a medium-security facility and the threat level of violent inmates was somewhat diminished. Fishkill didn't have many lifers there. Most people sent to Fishkill were very close to release from prison and so they were basically trying to chill or they were serving very short prison sentences. Therefore, there were basically no killings, stabbings, maiming, or widespread extortion going on there.

While many of the max facilities were so wild they would make the most peaceful monk grab a piece of steel, Fishkill was different. The atmosphere looked and felt less tense. There was almost no tension in the air. Everyone was laid back, smoking, eating, talking and laughing. There was frequently loud, genuine laughter among inmates there, this was different. There were mostly dorm-style housing arrangements at Fishkill, very few cells. Approximately 25 inmates were housed in the dorm where I was assigned and inmates were allowed to walk around the dormitory pretty freely. This dormitory-style set-up wouldn't work at Clinton. Two or more people would likely have been stabbed every night. I couldn't sleep the first few nights, I stayed up all night just watching. People were snoring, there was no creeping, no hits, just the sound of inmates sleeping fairly peacefully.

I later met an inmate at Fishkill whom I had known from serving time in maximum-security prisons. He went on to tell me about the feelings that he had upon arriving from "max" facilities to medium-security facilities and the time it took for him to adjust to this laid-back environment. He went on to explain that max guys upon arrival at Fishkill were easy to identify because they were often standoffish, and always on alert. He was likely talking about me. He told me that it would pretty much pass, and he was basically right.

After a few weeks at Fishkill, I had depressurized a lot. I slept through the night sometimes and the times I couldn't sleep (I still had those nights), I just began to think. Fishkill housed many "short-timers", people who were serving as little as one year behind bars. So, on a daily basis, guys from my dorm and surrounding dorms were being released. They were being sent home. I often listened to these "short-timers" talk about what they were going to do upon release and I watched their faces when the guards yelled into the dorm for them to "pack up", they were going home. It hit me pretty suddenly, the realization that I had only about three years left on my sentence and that the guards would be telling me one day soon to pack up. That shook me. I thought to myself if they were to release me today, what would I do. I had no marketable skills. Besides being able to make a good shank out of almost anything sturdy, what else did I know how to do? Those sleepless nights had my mind racing, trying to figure out a plan for my future. I knew I didn't have many job skills, but I also knew upon release, I would definitely never be coming back to this place.

In my dorm, there was this older inmate who spent most of his days in the prison law library. Through legal battles and many lawsuits, the state correctional facilities relented and allowed law libraries to be set up within the prisons, and they gave inmates liberal access to them.

This inmate was an older White guy, who would frequently speak openly about the law and its operation in various situations. He was a respected "jailhouse lawyer" and he supposedly had assisted a number of inmates win their criminal appeals even while their real lawyers couldn't.

I questioned him frequently about legal questions and debated with him about issues of law pretty frequently. He informed me I had a good grasp of legal concepts and a better understanding of criminal procedure law than many of the inmates who actually worked in the law library. I went on to tell him that, although I didn't work in the law library, I had spent years studying the law. I had spent hours in the law library doing legal research on criminal procedure and substantive criminal law. I regularly read law journals and books on legal methods and the law. Finally, I informed him I had litigated pro-se, acting as my own lawyer, on a number of lawsuits, including one in Federal Court that was presently in cash settlement negotiation. Although it was not my intent, he was impressed.

He went on to tell me about his outside legal training as a paralegal. He told me that he was making over $100 an hour working for some attorneys as a paralegal. He said he would do most of the legal work from start to finish and then pass it to the attorneys. Some attorneys, he said, would then review it, sign off on it and present it to their clients, billing them $300 per hour although he did the many hours' worth of work. He said he definitely felt cheated, but $100 per hour was still more than anyone around him was making. He told me all attorneys, from big Wall Street firms to neighborhood solo practitioners, would pay top dollar for an experienced paralegal. With the large earnings he secured, he said he also picked up an expensive cocaine habit, which eventually landed him in prison on drug charges for a short stay.

He went on to tell me Fishkill had an accredited two-year paralegal program that was run by Marist College. He told me I had a talent and I should definitely consider applying for the program. That night, again I couldn't sleep. This time it was no apprehension of strangers attacking in the night. This apprehension came from not whether I could successfully handle the program. I had no doubts in my academic ability. The doubts came from whether I would be embraced within the legal community as an ex-offender. I thought, I only have three years to release, and so, do I sacrifice two of them chasing some paralegal pipe dream or do I focus more on a trade, like plumbing or carpentry or some other vocational skill?

The White jailhouse lawyer dude told me it was possible, so I thought about it. However, "He is White," I thought. America, I thought, will always give a White man a second, third or even fourth chance. Look what they did for my partner in crime, Jason. At the time, Jason had already been released from prison years earlier and had resumed his life while I was still behind bars fighting daily for my life.

At the time of our arrest, Jason was much older than I was, had a prior violent criminal record and confessed to additional crimes that he had committed alone, apart from the crimes we stood charged with. Yet, they jumped through hoops and bent over backwards to offer him a slap on the wrist while they conspired to crush me and throw me away. My prosecution and eventual sentence was not about rehabilitation, it was about some deep dark stuff that lies in the hearts of some men and some women within the criminal justice system. There were some systemic unjust issues with the criminal justice system and with society at large. My faith in the system was not great. It had been severely damaged many years ago.

As the days passed, I continued to think this thing through. My mind told me that America would never give me a second chance, and that no attorney within America's legal system would allow me, an ex-offender, the opportunity to do legal research, or write a motion or a legal brief, no matter how talented I knew I was. One of my many talents was that I could spot even pinpoint holes in almost any argument, no matter how tight a person believed their point was. Legal argument or otherwise, there is always a hole. Also, I could always see both sides of the argument. I could easily put myself in the other person's shoes, even during very emotional times. I often knew, and appreciated what others were feeling, and how they were thinking. Maybe that's why I get along with people. I often understand where they are coming from and their point of view. I had much to offer anyone who would simply give me a chance. I simply did not have the belief that a second chance would ever happen.

Still, I thought to myself that although America would likely never allow me a second chance at anything academic and the most they may allow me would be a carpentry job or some other work in the construction arena, my heart simply was not there. I did not enjoy working with my hands as much as I enjoyed working with my mind. I remembered reading in some book about ancient Egypt that there was an inscription over one of the monuments saying, "Know thyself." I knew I would not be happy, in the long-term, doing construction work. I also knew that an injury in construction could happen at any time leaving me unable to provide for myself and my family. I wasn't ever returning to prison, that I knew, and so, I needed a career that could hold me down long-term in earnings and be enjoyable. I didn't want to work 25 years at a job I didn't enjoy.

I went to inquire about and eventually signed up for the paralegal program. I figured I would take a chance. I figured that upon my release, having earned the paralegal certificate, if I could convince just a single attorney to give me a chance, I would not let them down. I would do kick-ass work for them, and in return, I could possibly earn enough to survive. I was willing to work for less than $100 an hour. I would do outstanding work for $50 or even $25. I just needed one chance. I decided to go for it.

In the paralegal program, I met professors who were actual lawyers and I had frequent one-on-one talks with them. They told me my view of the criminal justice system was on-point in some places, but definitely off in others. They often conceded that racism and disparity in treatment within the criminal justice system was real, but the total lack of societal opportunity, for ex-offenders was only perceived, some of them thought. They told me there were many people in the legal profession, even Black people, who were given second chances and were doing great. They told me that perception was often reality and if you get a better handle on perception, you can change your reality. I admired many of them although I didn't always agree with their views.

Many of the instructors in the program were White liberals. Today you would call them progressives. They believed in not only giving second chances to people, of all colors, they actually came into the prisons to help assist in that process. These folks, men and women, would sit in the classroom with us inmates for hours, sometimes just talking about life and living, real talk. Conversations beyond just the law, and these folks were lawyers, and PhDs and very educated people. I was at a different place by then, not as closed and guarded and so I opened up more and thus I received more.

These people showed me there were really many people working within the Criminal Justice system who understood that many ex-offenders felt marginalized and often hopeless after getting a criminal conviction, even if the conviction happened while the inmates were still teenagers. These people showed me that not only did many criminal justice professionals and other members of American society fully understand this, but they also were aware of the devastating impact it had on the rehabilitation efforts of some offenders, as well as their behavior upon release. Some of them understood, fairly well, the hopelessness that is felt by many ex-offenders.

In my eyes, a person without hope is destined for minor achievement at best, if any at all. There is no wonder the recidivism rates among released inmates is so outrageously high. The general perception of most men in prison is that upon receiving a felony conviction, your life is basically ruined forever, and your legitimate options are practically zero. Very few believe in a genuine second chance. I am hopeful one day a major societal effort will be put into creating broadened opportunities for ex-offenders and thus dispelling this perception among so many of the criminally convicted that second chances are hard to come by. That perception is absolutely not a recipe for success.

The instructors within the paralegal program successfully convinced me that numerous people were really out there, of all colors and walks of life, speaking up and actively trying to address many real issues, including mass incarceration, disparity in sentencing and increased opportunity for ex-offenders. These mostly White people weren't just talking about it either, they were actually right there, in the flesh, in the trenches, with sleeves rolled up, tackling these issues the best they knew how. I was definitely moved by the actions and sincerity of these people, and not simply by their words. I began to believe that maybe this paralegal thing could work. I desperately needed a viable option to keep me honestly employed upon being released.

I knew that my mother was sick. I also sensed she was actually sicker than my family was letting on. They often kept almost everything from me which they believed would impact my mood. The last time I saw her, she had come to visit me and she looked very frail and thin. Historically, she was always a strong, vibrant and robust woman. My mother had been diagnosed with breast cancer some 10 years earlier. She had fought it into remission, but it was obvious from her frail appearance and unsteady gait, the cancer was back. I was afraid to ask her – I didn't want to hear what I already knew and she never told me. The last time she visited we talked for hours about everything from family to my future upon release. She had definitely become my best friend upon my being incarcerated. She was always there for me, either visiting, sending a letter or on the phone. We came to actually better know and better understand each other during these hard times. We would often talk, heart to heart, and it was great. On her last visit to see me, as usual, we talked for hours while sharing a meal of vending machine food, as there was nothing else to do. We laughed, joked and had a good visit together, as usual. At the visit's end, she held my hands tightly while looking deeply into my eyes, and she said, "Take care of yourself Abdullah, I love you."

I told her, "No question, Mom, I love you too." She definitely held me much tighter and a little longer than usual. As she walked away, she looked back once and waved. She had tears in her eyes and my mom was not the teary type.

Weeks later, my family informed me that mom was terminally ill and that her passing was imminent – likely within days. I immediately reached out to the prison administration and requested from the superintendent for permission to make a "deathbed" visit to my mom. This was a very standard request from inmates who were not high level escape risk and well within the powers of the superintendent to approve. He swiftly denied the request without explanation. His denial was very spiteful because of my reputation for legally challenging genuine abusive administrative policy within that prison and in others as well. He knew me well by name and face. He knew I bothered nobody, was very short, my prison sentence was practically complete, and I was by no means a security risk. Yet, spitefully, he denied my request to visit my mom before she passed away. He would often walk the hallways of the facility and would speak to me upon seeing me. I would politely return his greeting. After that denial, upon me seeing him, he would consciously avoid my eyes and pretend he didn't see me. I never said another word to him as long as I remained in that facility and, thankfully, he never said another word to me.

A few days after the superintendent's denial of my request for a deathbed visit, I was summoned to report to the office of the chaplain, Reverend Houston. He was a short and heavy set Black man. He ran religious services as prison chaplain on Sundays and other days throughout the week for people interested in or committed to the Christian faith. He had his well-practiced somber expression on as he invited me to have a seat. I politely declined the offer to sit and, respectfully, informed him that "I'd rather stand." He went on to explain what I had already known: my mother had passed away that day. I knew it from earlier that day, weird as it may sound, because her spirit visited the prison and she stood over me. He told me if I needed to talk, I could stay or come back later, but I respectfully declined. I didn't need or want to talk to anybody. I just wanted to lie down and clear my head.

Shockingly, there was no prison administration resistance to me attending my mother's funeral. They dressed me in standard prison garb. They shackled me at the hands, waist and feet and walked me to an official prison vehicle. Two correction officers then drove me the two-hour ride down to the funeral home in Bedford Stuyvesant, Brooklyn, New York. During the drive down, Whitney Houston's "I Will Always Love You" played low on the prison car radio. I had never heard it before, and I cried. Being shackled with my hands to my waist, I could not wipe away the tears and they just rolled down my face. I was frustrated because I never wanted anyone related to these prisons to ever see me distressed. They may have noticed because, earlier in the day, they continuously searched my face with their prying eyes for tears. That was their pleasure and I gave them nothing.

The funeral home was packed. As the prison car pulled up, an elderly woman peered into the vehicle exclaiming, "I know who that is, that's Jackie's son, and y'all better take care of him." The punk guards got "shook" by the old lady. They began talking about how many people were there, and should they call base or the local police precinct for backup? I calmed their fears by telling them, "It's a peaceful family" and that they "would be all right." They relaxed a bit and eventually escorted me cautiously into the jam-packed funeral home, sitting in the back where they could make a speedy escape if it hit the fan.

Everybody was cool, and there were no issues. Word spread quickly that I was there and people I hadn't seen in years began coming to the back to say, "What's up?" and give condolences. My dad entered the funeral home, saw me there and bear hugged me with tears in his eyes. That was the first time I believe I ever saw my dad cry. My mother was his first and only love. They were married as teenagers and were partners until the day she passed away. My dad was grieving. After the funeral service, I was hurriedly whisked out of the funeral home, into the prison car, and driven out of the streets of Brooklyn and back up to the Fishkill Correctional Facility.

I was struggling to stay focused within the college paralegal program. My heart and mind were unsettled with the passing of my mother.

However, I knew she would want me to succeed in life and part of that success possibly lay within this program. I had to get my head right. I did complete the program, earning my paralegal certificate. I also earned enough additional credits while attending Marist College's paralegal program to complete the requirements for the awarding of my Bachelors of Arts degree. I previously had earned college credits while taking college courses at Eastern Correctional Facility. I was happy.

The prison held a graduation ceremony for the small number of inmates who graduated the college program and the families of prisoners were allowed to attend. Additionally, prison officials, guest speakers, and college administrators were in attendance. My dad and youngest sister came as my guests. They were happy too. My dad again told me, as he often had, "You are going to do something very special in this life." He said, "God has something special planned for you and I don't know what it is, but I know it." My dad was a very spiritual man, and he often just knew things. The weird thing is, I had generally felt that too. I felt that my life experiences, even during my worst days, were taking me on a journey somewhere. Where, I didn't know, but not to a bad place. These feelings of certainty materialized after I had grown up a bit, matured.

I also knew, I never had an evil, mean or malicious heart. I was misguided as a young man, and thus, I have done some wrong things, but I've never been a mean hearted person. I've always felt that even while some folks in the world were trying to make me feel, and others believe I was some animalistic, worthless criminal and, thus, worthy of any and all the mean-spirited things they or anyone else would do to me. I always knew the Creator knew better. I always believed the Creator knew my heart.

I bothered these people a lot because they knew that I didn't "believe the hype." I manifested my disbelief in their propaganda every day with my bearing, head held high, straight looks in their eyes, and if prodded, I would verbally tell them exactly what I thought about them. The thing is, at seventeen years old, I made big mistakes and was made to pay for those mistakes with 12 and a half years in prison. I served most of that sentence, repentant, sorry for the things I had done and by continuously asking for the Lord's forgiveness for any and all pain I may have ever caused anyone. I often spent hours a day praying to the Creator for forgiveness for all the things I did which injured people including my family, my children, and myself. I did this even while I lived in some of the most vicious environments. Yet, even within these environments, I worked to keep the peace wherever I possibly could, which saved many men from harm. I didn't know what my future held, but I definitely knew my life as a criminal was over. That person was long gone.

The prison guards and administrators however, were not a bunch of seventeen year olds as I was when arrested. The guards were grown men and women beating, robbing, abusing and allegedly killing numerous other men—this, while prison administrators looked the other way. They often set men up to be robbed, raped, beaten, and even killed. They intentionally denied sick inmates medical care and delayed medical attention to inmates on a number of occasions, thus causing men to sometimes lose their lives. This kind of stuff went on every day and in some jails and prisons it was systemic. Then, these same people try to justify their barbaric acts by proclaiming the inmates were "animals." No, you are an animal and I will never bow my head or lower my eyes when face to face with you. I never bought into the hype that any one of these people was better than I – no way, no how. In fact, many of them were worse human beings than I ever was or ever could possibly be. Although they had successfully tricked the general public into believing otherwise, I always believed in my heart that the Creator knew the truth. So, for me, it was okay that the general public didn't have a clue. The Creator and I knew the truth, and they knew that I knew and so they hated my guts.

I am definitely not saying all of the guards or administrators were bad apples. However, a large bunch of them were. Additionally, most of the ones who weren't bad apples knew most of what the bad apples were doing, yet they rarely took a stance against it. There existed one big wall of fucking silence.

College Graduation and
the Parole Board

THE GRADUATION WAS A GOOD day. I felt a real sense of accomplishment. The journey to that point definitely wasn't easy. There were plenty of minefields along the way. One huge minefield along the path to completing college in prison is the inmates and prison staff who often mess with you big time hoping you do or say something to get a disciplinary action, "keep-locked" and thus kicked out of college. You can't attend classes from solitary confinement.

They began calling inmates up to the stage in alphabetical order to be awarded their degrees. They called my name and every emotion hit me at once. I thought of my mother, who was not there, my incarceration, with all of its ups and downs, and all the minefields I had to avoid along the way to this day. With great difficulty, I maintained my composure and rose steadily from my seat. I smiled at my father as I walked to the stage and I was awarded my college degree. I waved broadly to my family from the stage, degree in hand. It definitely was a good day.

After the ceremony and my family had departed, I returned to the prison dorm and immediately began planning my next move. I had served almost twelve years in state prison at that time and my visit to the parole board, and possible release from prison, was less than one year away. I had to have a plan that would keep me out of this shit-hole.

That's exactly what prison was and there was a fierce desire on my part never to return.

The work-release program was a hot commodity at Fishkill. Work-release was a program designed in part to allow inmates who were not security risks the opportunity to be released from state prison early for the purposes of outside employment. From Fishkill prison, they granted work-release requests fairly liberally. Actually, a major reason for the liberal granting of requests for the program and the reason for the program itself was that the prisons had become so overcrowded that they had to do something. The so-called "War on Drugs" and "Get Tough on Crime" prosecutions had left New York State prisons bursting at the seams. Through work-release, inmates would be released from the state prison where they were confined, thus easing prison overcrowding. Particular inmates were transferred to a New York City-based, minimum-security facility. From there, they were allowed to leave that facility a few hours or even days during the week, unsupervised, for work and even home family visits. It was definitely not total freedom from the Department of Corrections, but it was a good start. So, I put my application in for the program. It was quickly denied.

Again, the prison administrators had a dislike for me, mostly because I often challenged their treatment of me and others while under their care, custody and control. Beyond that, I had a good grasp of the law and knew how to litigate – that is, challenge their inappropriate prison actions and decisions to higher authorities, as I often did. I frequently challenged the prison administrators' inappropriate actions and decisions to the Commissioner of the Department of Corrections in Albany, New York, to the New York State Courts, or even to the Federal Court when necessary, which the prison officials hated. Because of my knowledge and my considerable legal abilities, the guards and prison administrators reached a point where they simply stopped blatantly messing with me, often even whispering to their peers who didn't know me to "leave him alone." They knew that I was fairly versed in the law and I would quickly sue or have the New York Attorney General or the Inspector General's office sending investigators to the prison with haste. However, when issues arose where they could deny me this or that request based upon prison "discretion," they excitedly would. They used their power of "discretion" to deny my application for the work-release program. Of course, I challenged that decision, the denial of my work-release application, to the Department of Corrections Commissioner's office, in Albany, New York through the appeal process. My appeal was also denied.

I understood the game very well – you had to "pay to play." I learned early in life that there are repercussions for speaking truth to power. If you are not willing to sacrifice, sometimes much, be wary of playing that game. I learned this while watching the beating my dad took for speaking truth to power concerning the blatant disparity in treatment his son received in the courts. I, being Black, compared to the son of his neighbor, Jason, who was White. The truth hurts and if you injure people more powerful than you, even simply by using words, be prepared for blowback because it probably will come. I was getting blowback from people who had the power of "discretion" of whether to grant my work-release application or deny it. It was denied.

The denials were a disappointment, but not unexpected. Again, I am hip to the game. I also predicted that when I went before the parole board in less than a year, this same "discretion" would be used to deny me release on parole. My sentence was twelve and a half to twenty-five, so I would see the parole board after serving the twelve and a half years. However, upon the discretion of the parole board, they could legally keep me confined for two-thirds of the twenty-five-year sentence, which is over sixteen years. I prepared myself for that very real possibility, and I would soon find out the truth of my apprehension.

Many months before the denial of my work-release application, I had filed a pro-se, no attorney assisted, Federal Court civil rights lawsuit against the State of New York, Department of Corrections, Commissioner of Corrections and the Superintendent/Warden of the Eastern Correctional Facility, where I had been previously confined. In that lawsuit, I challenged their arbitrary and capricious actions within the facility. I had them cornered, in my estimation, and I was looking at a win in Federal Court. I had filed a number of pro-se lawsuits while incarcerated, challenging prison conditions, lack of medical treatment, damage to property, etc. One of them had recently settled and I was awarded $10,000, which would definitely come in handy upon being released.

I am not really a gambling man, but I wanted work-release badly enough that I was going to take a gamble. Many inmates, when they wanted access to information in their prison files or other information related to the running of the prison, used the Freedom of Information Law (FOIL). Those requests were often denied, and you would receive limited information even if the request was granted. Forget that.

When you file a 1983 Federal Civil Rights action in Federal Court, the federal laws of discovery apply. These laws compel parties to release demanded information, liberally and without unreasonable delay. Through mandatory discovery, I always demanded that the defendants, the Department of Corrections, produce everything, including the kitchen sink. Through this process, I demanded a copy of my entire prison file that was in the care, custody and control of the defendant, State of New York, Department of Corrections, and they were compelled by a Federal Court Judge to produce it. It arrived during mail call in a huge manila legal folder.

I reviewed that huge stack of legal documents, meticulously scanning for information that would allow me to win the pending lawsuit against the state of New York for their allowing rampant abuse of power within their correctional facilities thereby injuring inmates. However, I also diligently reviewed my inmate personnel folder looking for their justification for making adverse rulings against me and generally taking hostile postures towards me every day. There was absolutely nothing at all in my file that indicated that I was any kind of security risk or an irrationally disruptive individual. Thus, I knew for certain that the "discretion" used to deny my work-release application was straight bogus.

I was sitting in prison with a fairly clean prison record, having served almost twelve years of a twelve and a half-year sentence. I had earned a bachelor's degree and a two-year paralegal certificate. I had completed numerous internal rehabilitation programs and had earned certificates for them. I was also an instructor in some of these same programs. But I was refused access to a program, work-release, designed for inmates who were a low security risk with demonstrated progress towards rehabilitation. Most inmates around me believed that I would be a "no-brainer" candidate for the work-release program, but I knew better.

Anyway, I had a plan, but it was a big gamble. I contacted the attorneys for the state, and the Court and I informed them that I wanted to arrange a settlement conference to potentially settle the lawsuit I had pending in Federal Court against the Department of Corrections and State of New York, etc. They agreed to talk.

They arranged for me to be escorted on a designated day to a secure area of the prison to take part in a conference call with me and other attorneys who represented the defendants, Department of Corrections, etc.

My proposal was simple: give my application for work-release a fair and impartial review, and if I was found qualified for work-release, grant the application. However, if after a fair and impartial review of all the relevant factors, it was determined that I was a poor candidate for the work-release program, then they would deny my application. I informed them that whether they granted the application or denied it, I would discontinue the Federal Court lawsuit against them.

The state's attorneys went back and forth with me about the particulars – when, how, and why – and eventually they agreed to get back to me because their clients would have to agree. They eventually all agreed and the agreement was drawn up and signed by all relevant parties and I was instructed to refile my application for the work-release program. This particular lawsuit was based upon evident and provable trumped-up charges leveled against me that led to me being sentenced to 90 days solitary confinement with loss of all prison privileges:

phone, visits, packages, etc. I was absolutely confident that I could win the lawsuit and also monetary damages, as I was equally confident that the denial of my work-release application by these folks was based upon straight nonsense.

I also knew that they would, in all probability, deny my re-submitted application for work- release because of the "arrogance of power," they would never submit, even to truth. However, I could still embarrass the heck out of them. Everyone from the Commissioner's office, Warden's office and New York Attorney General's office would be forced to review and discuss my file and with straight faces say, upon review of that file, "You are not a good candidate for the work-release program." They would have to openly conspire to do wrong. This, with the Federal Court watching. I also wanted them to clearly see that I wasn't out to get them by any means. I sincerely and simply wanted them to take a good look at themselves. I wanted them to see what big hypocrites they were. They asked that inmates in their care, custody and control, "Department of Corrections," sincerely work on their rehabilitation efforts, which I demonstrably did. I was diligently working on "reform" and committed to doing nothing but walking the straight path. I wasn't coming back to prison and I took all appropriate steps to avail myself of the programs and educational opportunities presented to achieve that goal. Yet, the State Department of Correctional Services was committed to using its power to deny inmates rights, privileges, and earned opportunities simply because they could.

Finally, I also knew that their arrogance and their blatant refusal to deal fairly and professionally in so many areas of their facilities throughout the state of New York, would make it very easy for me to put them right back on the legal hook. Even if it was simply challenging them in court, because the second denial of my work-release application, was a clear and blatant "abuse of administrative discretion". They were always wide open for legitimate legal challenges. I learned through years of study and experience that life in prison and in the legal profession is always a chess match – you must always have a counter move, and you must always think multiple moves ahead. Anything less is extremely dangerous. I had my next move well planned no matter what they decided to do.

Within a few days of the conference call, I was requested to resubmit my application for work- release. I kept my business quiet and didn't notify any inmates, but a number of the guards knew. The streets were always talking. Although many of the guards despised me because they knew I had good sense and would not tap dance to their savage beat, they mostly had a grudging respect for me.

After a few days of waiting for a reply, the letter came in the mail. My application for work- release had once again been denied. These people are as predictable as can be. I had already begun drafting my legal challenge to the denial because I was far from done with them. However, knowing I had a parole board release hearing approaching soon, I had just given the state a "good will" gesture. I had dropped a solid lawsuit against them in the United States Federal Court in return for absolutely nothing. It was my olive branch offering of the highest order. However, if they used their "discretion" to deny my release from prison at my parole hearing, it was going to be absolutely and ridiculously on. I would become to them a litigation nightmare.

Weeks later, I received notice to appear at my parole board hearing. I was mentally preparing myself for the worst. I arrived at the hearing, which was conducted in a small dingy room of the prison that had a few chairs filled with representatives from the New York State Division of Parole. They offered me a chair.

"Have a seat," one of them said. They immediately began bombarding me with questions, but I felt no hostility from any of them. They wanted to know, "Where would you live?" "Whom would you live with?" and "Do you have a job?" They reviewed my prison file, thumbing through the pages, commenting on all the numerous prison counseling rehabilitation programs I had completed and the certificates for this program or that program I had been awarded.

They commented on the multiple college degrees I had earned, two associate degrees, a bachelor's degree and a two-year paralegal certificate. They also commented on my prison disciplinary record, stints in "keep lock," the fights and solitary confinement.

I arrived before them with no prepared speech. I spoke from the heart, answering their questions truthfully and exhibiting no hostility toward them either. I sat before them knowing and totally confident that I was in no way going to engage in a life of crime as I did as a seventeen year old kid some thirteen years ago. I sat before them knowing that the closest thing to a criminal act I had committed in years was to hurt a few dudes behind the walls who had made hostile moves against me. Every man has the God-given right to defend himself, so that personally didn't count to me. I didn't use drugs or sell drugs at that point in my sentence. I had even stopped smoking weed. I didn't rob, steal, or engage in extortion even when I had the power and influence in the prison to do that and much more. The Creator had given me a second chance. I was genuinely thankful and I was going to seize it.

They couldn't read my mind so I had to tell them much of this and I basically did. It was the truth. I also knew that my prison record would speak for me. I had a few hiccups along the way, but by no stretch of the imagination could my prison record be classified as "bad." The hearing concluded with a, "You will hear from us soon."

I left the hearing feeling that, all things being fair, I would likely be released. An idiot could read my file and see that there was more than enough evidence of "sincere efforts at rehabilitation," which is part of the factors used in determining the granting of parole. However, I also knew that the issue of "discretion" was a beast. Discretion also applies to parole hearings, so they could easily focus on any negatives in my file and disregard any positives, all in the name of "discretion." I understood the game well and I was braced for the nonsense.

The parole board decision arrived in the mail a few days after the hearing. Inmates who had been through the process, some numerous times, told me that if the envelope was thin, you were granted release, because it was simply a one-page letter. However, if the envelope was thick, parole likely was denied and the envelope contained multiple pages of appeal procedure documents. During mail call, the mail delivery corrections officer handed me a letter, from the New York State Division of Parole, and the letter was thin. I stared at it for a few moments without opening it. I finally opened it and the one-page letter informed me that I was being released from prison within a few weeks. I had been granted parole.

All kinds of emotions hit me, but I was generally very happy. Finally, after almost thirteen years in prison, I was coming home. I had to get to the phone and call home. My family was excited. My dad was thrilled and told me that he would get my room in his home ready because he wanted me there. My oldest sister also said that I could stay with her if I wanted to. However, my dad was adamant that I would be living in his home. My dad still had the three-bedroom home in Far Rockaway, with the furnished basement – the home I had lived in before my arrest. I was a little wary about going right back to the exact same place where I had previously lived, and I contemplated whether that would be a good move.

However, I figured that if I was truly committed to doing the right thing, no environment could take me off the right path. I figured that the only one who could take me down the wrong path again was me, and I definitely wasn't going to do that. I informed my family that I would be "staying by Dad."

I had some thinking to do – release was scary. Forget all the happy talk people around me were doing. I hadn't been home in years and I knew the streets had changed. I had to have a solid plan to not just keep me out of prison, but to excel while being out. I was definitely coming for it all. From the time I was a child I was always about being self-sufficient, and thus making money. That mentality hadn't changed.

From childhood I was always a "top-dog" with fly gear, fly jewelry, and fly women. I couldn't see myself coming home and living the life of an average Joe. I just couldn't see it. I had to have a plan to get me where I am most comfortable, the top of the pile. I refused to be an average Joe. However, I thought, "Isn't this the same thinking that got you put in prison in the first place?" That insatiable desire to always be above-average and to be that fly-ass dude.

I had some serious thinking to do and I only had a few more weeks to figure this out. Hours of solitary confinement, "keep lock," and simple time alone in my cell with only my thoughts, did help me to better understand myself. I came to understand that many of the things that I did as a teenager were more for show or to impress other people and it often wasn't really me. I came to understand that my natural disposition was fairly conservative, but my alter ego is flashier than a motherfucker. He needs to be seen. My alter ego needs the spotlight like a fish needs water. However, I also learned and accepted that my natural self really does not. Finally, I realized that most of the times that I had gotten into trouble were during an effort to satisfy my alter ego, impress another person, or rolling with an idiot who couldn't think past go. It was never while I was simply "doing me."

I decided, that going forward, I would follow my own mind and simply "do me" and then let the chips fall where they may. I figured that my natural urge to never be average would take me to good places and that if I simply followed that urge, while walking within the boundaries of the law and commonsense, I was going to be that fly dude anyway. It would just happen naturally. Finally, I had my mind right and your boy was ready to come home.

Some days after receiving the letter granting my parole, I was informed by a corrections officer at Fishkill to "pack up". I was being transferred to a different prison, Mid-Orange Correctional Facility, which was a little closer to New York City. At Fishkill, receiving work-release was a strong possibility, while at Mid-Orange, for most inmates, it was almost a certainty. I only had a few weeks left to serve before release but, still, work-release would put me on the streets almost immediately.

Mid-Orange Correctional Facility

Upon arriving at Mid-Orange Correctional Facility I was extremely hyped, but the good feeling didn't last long. The facility was run very loosely and there were swarms of little motherfuckers, mostly young Queens, Bronx and Brooklyn dudes, running around talking this gangster chronicle bullshit all day long. These guys were all serving small time, between 1 and 3 years, and most had never served time in maximum-security facilities. Many of them also were gang affiliates and they didn't have anything positive on their minds – nothing. This place was a minefield.

My little man Jameer was there, one of the many younger inmates I had taken under my wing schooling and protecting for years while we served time in the harsh maximum-security facilities. He was "short" too – months away from being released. He had already served about 10 years. He told me he simply tried to stay away from the young, want-to-be tough guys that were swarming around the facility. I followed suit. However, it took maximum effort to avoid these dudes. They were everywhere – in the yard, gym, cafeteria, T.V. room, bathroom, dorm area, everywhere. They were difficult to avoid, these dudes, and they were reckless as heck with their mouths, yet, they were mostly little fucking punk-asses.

Jameer and I mostly chilled together, usually talking about finally getting a shot at freedom. I didn't deal with many of the other inmates there. I stayed many hours in the law library, which was my prison job assignment. At Mid-Orange, I was reading 10 or more hours a day mostly in the areas of law, criminal, civil rights and personal injury. I read the New York Law Journal every day to stay abreast of the latest legal news and court decisions. There was also a large classified section in the Law Journal which I reviewed every day. There was often a good amount of postings for "paralegals needed," some paying as much as $100-plus an hour. I was excited.

Most of the little reckless dudes at Mid-Orange would never enter the law library or any other place where there was a book or anything educational. Every now and then, one of them would wander into the law library to ask questions mostly about how to appeal a denial for the work-release program. The thing is, I could talk all day about the relevant law and the best arguments to present when perfecting appeals, etc. However, if you cannot read or write, and many of these young inmates could not, it wasn't information that they could actually apply even if they had legitimate issues for appeal. Still, I did whatever I could to assist anyone who presented themselves for direction.

While serving time in prison, I had always been an educator, the best I knew how to be, for younger inmates and, sometimes, older inmates as well. I benefited greatly from being raised and schooled by older and wiser people, beginning with my father who always gave me "real talk." While serving time behind the walls, particularly my initial years of incarceration, I was always around older and informed inmates. To keep me safe and out of real love, these people often pulled me aside and gave me real talk. Again, not the, "I have to put on a front to protect my prison image" nonsense.

One of the most real things I heard while behind bars was told to me by an old gangster from uptown, T, who was tremendously respected behind the walls. He had gotten fabulously rich selling drugs and was serving a life sentence for drugs and other offenses. He had the "gift of gab," verbal communication that was crazy, and you would often find him surrounded by young and old inmates who were being masterfully entertained by his dramatic story telling abilities. He had the ability and often did make even serving time in a maximum-security prison sound glamorous and fun. He made the life of a gangster, hustler and drug dealer sound so appealing that many of the young dudes in the prison wanted to be just like T.

T's right-hand man at the prison, Abu Barker, grew up with my father, and Abu Barker introduced me to T. T and I were assigned to the same work detail in Eastern Correctional Facility, a cool-out job in the cafeteria stockroom. We would often talk for hours during down time about prison, the drug game, street life, etc. If no food deliveries were scheduled, there was practically no work, so there was a lot of down time. Upon getting to know me, T was impressed with me and he, like many inmates I would meet, and for reasons I still do not fully understand, dropped his mask. They would open up to me and tell me some things that for the sake of their "prison image" they would never publicly utter to anyone.

T told me one time while we were just kicking it, "Bey, you are a smart dude and you can make it." He told me to "Keep suckers out your life, go home and do right man." Then he said the most real shit I had ever heard. He said, "Prison is for losers, Bey," and when I looked at him, he had watery eyes. I will never forget that moment and have never forgotten his words.

As wise as I believed I was before that moment, I still had a slightly glorified image of prison and serving time. Maybe it lingered from all the dudes I watched while growing up, going in and out of prison and then returning to the neighborhood more respected than they were when they went in. I do not know the origins of it, but I do know it was there and T's words poured such cold water on that notion that it died an instant death that day.

At Mid-Orange, when the law library closed, I mostly stayed in my cubicle at the dormitory trying to read and block out all this phony gangster talk these young, broke dudes were kicking all day. They often talked for hours about how they would perfect the drug selling game and other criminal enterprises upon being released from prison. When not in the law library or in my cubicle reading, I walked with Jameer in the small and mostly peaceful yard, often calming him down because these young guys would frequently get on his nerves.

Jameer had grown up a ton since I had first met him many years ago when he would fall out constantly with another one of my little dudes, Waheed, who was a hot-headed real dude from Brownsville, Brooklyn. Jameer would definitely be all right if he could simply avoid hurting somebody at Mid-Orange. I had taught him much over the years we were together about walking through the minefield of prisons, just as older people had taught me. He was good.

However, at Mid-Orange Correctional Facility, many of these young guys had no fathers in their lives to teach them how real men deal with other men. Many of them were not really accustomed to simply shutting the fuck-up and just listening as an informed man talked. Too many had the attitude that *no man can tell me shit* and so they simply tried to learn from their peers, but that is like the blind leading the blind.

These young guys never sat and kicked it "real talk" with men like T, CB, or countless other men behind the walls who were actually real millionaire drug dealers, notorious gangsters, hustlers, pimps and murderers of other men, who in quiet moments, explained to me why they killed.

These young inmates at Mid-Orange never spent hours talking, real talk, to former members of the Black Panther Party and the Black Liberation Army. Men who were serving life sentences for fighting what they believed to be a system that created swarms of misguided and fatherless young Black men, just like them, and then put these same young and misguided men behind bars, often for huge profits or other mischievous reasons.

They had never sat and talked with American "political prisoners" who were so incredibly versed in the issues of political science, geopolitics and the history of African, Caribbean and Black people in the Americas that if they walked into a room full of college Ph.D.'s, many of the Ph.D.'s would voluntarily sit down and listen. These same men also knew so much about navigating the prison environment they had Ph.D.'s in "prison-ology." They could definitely write books on it.

These young inmates at Mid-Orange Correctional Facility generally were lost. As I told a number of them I opened up to because they appeared to have acquired the basic skills of dealing respectfully with another man, "Even if a man is granted work-release or parole, if his mind is not right he will likely return to prison or possibly even be killed." I saw this with my own eyes while serving time. I told them of the numerous dudes, all around the prison system, who had been released onto parole or work-release two or three times, while I had not been released once. These men returned back to prison each time. Others had been killed, sometimes literally within weeks or even days of being released. A good dude, Big Hurt, who was a walking mountain of muscle, and funnier than most top comedians, served years in prison and was killed within days of being released from prison. The common denominator for most of these guys was not that they were necessarily bad guys, but that they mostly didn't have a solid plan to do right. They mostly were going back to the same game that got them arrested in the first place, but the game is mostly rigged against ex-cons. I told them that this so-called war on drugs is being waged in the Black community and that countless law enforcement traps are set-up everywhere to catch dudes slipping and then they are thrown right back into the criminal justice system. About seventy-five percent of released inmates return to prison within three years of being released. I was talking to these young guys at Mid-Orange based on years of experience, and not from some words I had read in a book. These young inmates at Mid-Orange had a lot to learn, but I didn't have enough time left to teach any of them much.

One morning, after only a few weeks at the Mid-Orange Correctional Facility, officers called me to "Pack up". They were transferring me from the Mid-Orange Correctional Facility down to a work-release facility in Queens, New York. Although I had been granted parole, there still was an approximately sixty-day waiting period, prison time owed, before I could actually be released to parole. Finally, they granted me work-release. Although I would only be in the program for maybe sixty days, still I was happy. I was definitely getting closer to being home.

I was also happy to be gone from the Mid-Orange Correctional Facility. That was a truly sad and depressing place. There were hundreds of young guys in that place and the level of straight ignorance, often based upon illiteracy, amongst the young people there was frightening. In fact, most of the young men behind bars are uneducated. Few are high school graduates. Again, they were not all necessarily bad young guys, they were simply lost.

I remember being trained as a literacy coach while at Eastern Correctional under a program sponsored by the Literacy Volunteers of America (LVA). As a literacy coach, I taught dozens of inmates to read and write, assisted many of them in earning their GEDs, and even to enter college. While behind the prison walls, I worked with illiterate inmates in the classroom, in the gym, the yard, or anywhere we could just sit down and kick it. I fed them reading assignments from the news-papers, GED books, and books from my personal collection which I be-lieved they would find interesting after inquiring into what they were interested. Often times, it was some gangster chronicles literature or a book about pimps and street life they were interested in reading, but at least they were reading. The first book I ever read, cover to cover, in my life, I read while in jail. The book was, "Eldorado Red" by Donald Goines, gangster chronicles literature. I thereafter read hundreds of books on a wide variety of subjects.

I found, that after a person learns to read and write, or simply begins reading more regularly, their mind expands. Often, thereafter, their ac-tions changed based on developing a broader perspective of the world.

At Mid-Orange, however, the prevailing culture was so "gangster chronicles" infused, that to pick up a book in the presence of one's "homies" would be perceived as an almost criminal offense. Many of them would just never do it. Voluntarily enrolling in a GED program was therefore unthinkable. Although a good number may have desired to, it was just "not cool."

This kind of confused thinking, education is not cool, was not only prevalent among many of the inmates I've met, but I also noticed it while doing work in the New York City Public School system and even amongst some college kids I later came to meet. I have seen smart kids "play dumb" by the boatload so that other kids won't notice they are smart. Mid-Orange was infested with this confused thinking and it was heartbreaking. There are not really a lot of places for an illiterate person within a modern society besides prison. The majority of the inmates I encountered in prison did not have even a high school education.

I packed up my personal belongings, which was mostly books. I had bags of them along with some legal documents, a few letters and family pictures. I always shared books and gifted books to young and old inmates around me wherever I was. However, the guys at Mid-Orange generally weren't into serious reading, so I dropped some good books, canned food, and other prison valuables on Jameer, said my goodbyes, and I was gone.

The corrections officers at Mid-Orange shackled me once again, at the hands, waist and feet, and placed me in a transport van heading down from these Mountains of New York State to the bright lights of New York City. I was hyped. During the ride to New York City, my mind contemplated all of the wonderful things I was going to get into. Here was my second chance at living, and I had to make the best of it. Entering New York City limits, the lights were bright, the city looked beautiful, and your boy was ready to "get it poppin'."

Work-Release

ARRIVING AT THE WORK-RELEASE FACILITY in Queens, I was unchained. The place was a large warehouse looking facility in Queensbridge, Long Island City, New York. The place, however, was a hot mess. It was dusty, run-down and sloppy-looking on the inside, but I was looking past all of that. As the person doing the new arrival orientation spoke, I listened intently because I didn't want to get snagged on some technicality and be returned upstate. Work-release was considered a privilege, not a right. Finally, they got to the part I wanted to hear. "You could be approved for day passes within a few days," meaning, (visits home).

"Yeah," I thought. I was ready.

While I waited for what felt like long days for a "day pass," I kicked the breeze with guys at the facility who had already been receiving day passes – some guys I knew from the mountains, upstate prisons. Some dudes I actively avoided because they were still talking that gangster chronicles stuff. Unfortunately, many ex-offenders, upon coming home, truly believe that our society systemically marginalize ex-offenders. Therefore, upward mobility for them, they truly believe, is forever blocked. They believe, all they would ever be allowed to do, in this amazing country, while marked as a "felon", is to work at low wage jobs. However, some of these guys were still very young, had served their sentences, and they adamantly believed that to be forever relegated to low wage work because of a mistake they made as a teenager, or very young man, was grossly unfair and absolutely unacceptable. They were not going to willfully accept a future that bleak, they absolutely wanted more out of life. So, they planned to hustle in the illegal trade to achieve that "upward mobility". Although, that was not my plan, I absolutely understood their feelings and their thinking. That belief is so extraordinarily disheartening and so genuinely strong, it can cause havoc in a man's mind.

When my number played, and I was approved for a weekend pass, I immediately called home. My family informed me they would be right outside to pick me up.

"Yes."

Coming Home: First Day Free
After 12 and A Half Years

THE DAY ARRIVED AND I was simply escorted from my housing area through the light security post and to the front door. As one of the guards opened the front door, the daylight rushed in and hit me in the face as I heard someone behind me say, "Have a good visit." All kinds of emotions hit me as I stepped out of the facility and onto the street. I looked up into the sunlight and I praised God. After nearly thirteen years, I was standing in the sunlight with no handcuffs and no chains as a free man. They had released me a bit earlier than the projected time and, thus, my family had not yet arrived at the facility. After pausing in front of the facility for a moment, I quickly walked away from the facility before these people changed their minds. I wasn't taking any chances. However, I didn't know where to go, so I just walked to the corner preparing to cross the street. I froze, and stood a while simply staring at the heavy two-way traffic on this huge Queens boulevard. I had literally forgotten how to cross the freaking street.

After figuring out how to cross the street, I quickly crossed, standing a distance from the facility scanning for my family. I soon heard someone call out to me from a car – it was my big sister. My dad was behind the wheel with my little sister and big sister riding with him. They scooped me up and I rode away from that Queens facility without a single backward glance.

My family and I talked, laughed, and joked as they filled me in on all the latest family business. There was a lot going on. We rode to my great-grandmother's apartment in Bedford Stuyvesant Brooklyn, Brevoort housing projects. She had lived in those projects for maybe 30 years or more and she refused to move – that was her home. She hadn't seen me in over twelve years. She and many others didn't even know I was in prison because my parents simply didn't tell them. We ate together, laughed, joked and it was just great seeing her. I had spent many summer nights staying at her apartment as a child growing up. She babysat my siblings and me as my parents would travel or have a date night.

I arrived by my dad's home in Far Rockaway Queens later that evening. It looked smaller than I remembered, but it was definitely good to be home. Family members came by to check on me and we stayed up late night talking, eating and catching up with each other. It was great seeing the family, many of whom hadn't really visited me while I was away.

When my dad's home finally cleared, he and I kicked it for some more time. My dad was a real dude and he was happy to have his son home. My relationship with my dad had changed tremendously throughout the years going from a dictatorship, filled with my resistance to it, to mutual respect and cooperation. He opened his home to me and gave me the keys to come and go and do what I please without his interference. Now, he would never let me wild out in his home, and he wouldn't allow disrespect from any man. However, he also knew because of the level of respect I had for him as a man, who he was and all he had taught me, I would never disrespect his home anyway.

He gave me the space to grow into myself, make mistakes and bump my head without judgment, and he kept it all in confidence – never talking my wins or losses to anyone in the family. He was my most trusted confidant. I told him many of my plans and never once did he frown upon them. He always simply and sincerely said, "You can do it." I took the upstairs room of my dad's home. I didn't want to return to the basement where I lived as a teen – too many memories of wrong doing. Also, the basement needed lots of repairs and Dad's money wasn't there, and mine wasn't either.

One of my cousins, whom I never got to know while I was a child, hearing I was staying by my dad's place, came around to check on me one day. We hit it off right away. He was my mother's half-sister's son and he definitely was family. He was wild as hell. I clicked with him for numerous reasons, one being he was definitely no joke and well respected in the neighborhood. He was out of Bedford Stuyvesant, in Brooklyn. Also, the clique I had before going to prison was dispersed, married and in different states. I didn't really have the urge to link with them anyway. They hadn't maintained the relationship when I went away and, although I had no hard feelings towards them, I also didn't have the urge to connect with them.

Additionally, I clicked hard with my cousin because my big brother also had failed to hold me down while I was in prison and, therefore, our relationship suffered. We definitely weren't as close as we were years ago. Back as teenagers growing up, my big brother and I were practically inseparable. Additionally, at my time of release from prison, my brother was fighting his own demons. He was going through some serious things in his life and we just didn't connect as we did before I went away. There were no hard feelings on my part towards him or anyone else I knew and loved who had virtually disappeared when I got sent to prison.

I had put myself in prison, my loved ones didn't put me there. I have also learned, what I would do for someone I claimed to love, is just that – "what I would do." I couldn't put my mindset onto anyone else. Finally, I've learned that, until you walk in another person's shoes, you can't accurately predict how you would respond while wearing those shoes. I just don't know. Therefore, I gave everybody a pass and had no hard feelings.

However, the mental and emotional connections I had with these same people were severely dissipated upon my release. Also, I had no honest urge to put strenuous effort into trying to turn back the hands of time trying to "make it like it was." I had too many other things on my priority list, like staying the heck out of prison, connecting with my children, reconnecting with my father and building a legitimate business and career. Besides my man Darnell, who checked on me periodically while I was away, upon my release, I was basically rolling solo.

My cousin, in contrast, was thorough from day one. He told me he didn't know I was in prison. The family told everyone I was away at college. I laughed. Eventually he said he knew better, but he didn't push against the college story for respect for my mom.

My cousin, who was three years older than me, either called or came by my dad's home to check on me nearly every single day. He took me out and about. He had a nice car, and he talked to me about the "new face" of the street game. It had changed tremendously since I had gone away. He showed me the hot hangout spots, restaurants and where the ladies could be found. He loved the ladies and they apparently loved him. I never met a man who apparently knew so much about women. He studied them like I studied the law. He actually ordered and read books on women. If the study of women was taught at college, he would likely have a Ph.D. and be a top instructor in the field.

I watched him do things with women that were amazing to me. Every time he and I went out together, sometimes just to the mall to pick up some new gear, he would meet beautiful women. He would simply stop them, get their number and date them, sometimes that very same night, and often taking extremely provocative pictures of the same woman in the nude or a similar video of them getting it on. I have never, even to this day, met anyone like him. He also was no joke with dudes. The street dudes respected him and wanted no trouble with him, and rightfully so. He had no fear of beef and would quickly put it on a dude and keep it moving with no hesitation.

Watching him, talking to him, and having him rant in detail for hours about women, one of his favorite topics, as well as just doing the dating scene often, helped me quickly get my rhythm back. After 12 and a half years away from the dating game, it was definitely not pretty, initially, watching me socialize with women. In fact, watching me socialize in any social environment was hard to watch, but particularly if women were there. I didn't know what to say, when to say it or definitely how to say it. My tone with everyone was pretty harsh. That's just how I spoke.

Additionally, I couldn't read the various types of women very well, decent or scandalous, honest or deceitful, nor the signs women gave – particularly signs of interest. However, my cousin rarely missed anything. He spotted a scandalous woman quickly and he would often tell me which woman liked me before I even had a clue, often encouraging me to "just talk to her." He was rarely inaccurate.

He also told me I had to step to woman I liked assertively and I couldn't wait for them because, unlike when we were teens, our looks, reputation, gear, etc., got girls often kicking it to us. However, "women generally will not start the conversation, even though you have the looks, the gear, whatever," he would say.

I began to initiate more conversations with woman who I found very attractive. He was definitely correct – women were often extremely receptive. I also began meeting not only very beautiful woman, but also good women. My cousin was impressed with my quick learning curve. I never became as assertive as my cousin, who would literally walk past a jam-packed beauty salon, see a hair stylist he liked, double-back, walk in, and openly tell her with a smile, in front of all of the customers and her co-workers, "You're sexy as hell. We have to hang out sometime." Often he was successful. My ego would likely not allow me to do that – he definitely had me there.

Being home was great although, initially, I was still on work-release. Therefore, I had to return to the correctional facility during the week-days to report in and sleep. Returning back to that place after tasting a bit of freedom was more difficult than anyone could ever imagine. Going back was definitely not easy. Thank goodness, eventually, that ended and I was released from the work-release program to the supervision of the Department of Parole.

Parole Supervision

PAROLE WAS DIFFERENT FROM WORK-RELEASE in that, I was no longer under the supervision of the New York State Department of Correctional Services. I was released from confinement, no more prison bars. So, once released from prison and discharged from the work-release program, the Division of Parole assumed the responsibility of my monitoring and supervision.

Being released from prison, to the supervision of parole, is actually a contract of early release, meaning the parolee must adhere to certain rules, restrictions and regulations or else they could be "violated" and returned back to prison. In my case, I was released after serving 12 and half years of a twenty-five year maximum sentence. One slip up and I could be "violated," returned to prison to serve out the many years I "technically" had not served of my 25-year sentence.

Parole officers, in knowing this, often feel they have tremendous power over parolees. Those parolees know this too and so, when told to jump, most parolees would only ask, "How high?" This reality could be tricky for me, so I could only hope to be assigned to a decent parole officer and not a jerk as I heard some of them actually were.

My initial prayers were answered in that I was assigned to what was rumored to be one of the "coolest" parole officers in the Queens office where I was designated to report. I lived in Queens and so parolees were assigned to the office in the borough or town where they resided.

Parole in those days was crazy. The caseload of each parole office was massive. The prisons were overcrowded, so they began pushing inmates out of prison to work-release, and from work-release to parole. However, that simply swelled the parole officer's caseload, making it almost impossible to effectively monitor everyone in their charge. To ease that problem, the Division of Parole began a program of discharging large numbers of inmates from parole early, usually after three years of supervision free of serious incidents or issues. It became almost automatic in New York at that time that if a person on parole kept their nose clean for three years, they would be discharged from parole supervision. Even if the parolee technically owed many more years on parole, it didn't matter. Early discharge for three years basically incident-free was almost automatic unless the parolee had a life sentence. Lifers didn't get early release.

Trying to keep up with each person assigned to a parole officer's caseload was extremely difficult. The caseloads were huge even with the practice of discharging parolees from the caseload after three years clean. What many of the parole officers did was quickly analyze their caseload to get a sense of who needed that precious time and enhanced scrutiny and who did not. Some dudes really needed extra supervision, no doubt about it. While visiting the massively crowded Queens parole office for my mandated office visits, I was meeting dudes I knew from prison who told me they were still getting it in – committing crimes, mostly drug dealing. Others would come to the parole office and be immediately put in handcuffs because they were fingered out of a photo line-up for some crime.

Still others would frequently visit the office drunk or high on drugs and thus be locked up on the spot or given a warning, depending on numerous factors. The discretion of the parole officer, in cases like that, held tremendous weight.

However, visiting the parole office for bi-weekly check-ins was stressful. Knowing that dudes often went into the parole office somewhat free but often came out handcuffed, chained and shipped back to prison was hard on the brain. Even though I knew going in that I was clean, you just never know. Every time I visited that office for my bi-weekly visits, spoke to my P.O. and then walked out still a free man, I felt the urge to drink, smoke or do something. It was that stressful.

My assigned parole officer, after visiting my home and meeting my family, particularly my dad, and talking to me a few times at his office, didn't sweat me at all. He would pop up at the house every now and then. I was soon switched to only monthly office visits and when I arrived, he would often call me in ahead of other parolees who were there before me. He knew I was serious about my business and I was not out playing games. I really believe that if he had the power to remove me completely from parole supervision, he would have done it. That's how much he respected my mindset and what I was trying to do with my second chance.

Like most of the parole officers in New York City, he also had a huge caseload and had to quickly analyze which parolees he could let breathe a little, could safely give basic "spot checks" on occasion, but it wasn't necessary to pop up at their home and job three or four times a week. He definitely let me breathe, and I respected him as a professional. He was a good parole officer and criminal justice professional, which in my years of experience with the criminal justice system was always hit or miss.

I was home a few months already, yet I still hadn't found a job. One of my terms of parole was that upon release from prison I find and maintain employment. Upon my release from prison, unlike many parolees, I had a few thousand dollars in hand from a lawsuit I had filed and won against the State of New York while I was in prison. However, with no income coming in and life in the big city being very expensive, clothes, food and transportation soon ate up that money.

I sent out at least a hundred resumes, visited temp agencies and followed leads from family, friends and acquaintances. I purchased various newspapers every day, dissecting the classifieds, writing, calling and sometimes putting on my suit and tie and simply walking into establishments with my resume and a smile. Nothing. I came out of prison with three college degrees, two associates, a bachelor's and a two-year paralegal certificate, yet no one would hire me. I tried to fix the 12 and a half year gap in my resume, but I don't know how successful I was in doing that. The big issue, as I would learn, was the lack of work experience – particularly in the paralegal area.

Most of the law firms, before they would even consider interviewing you, wanted your resume to reflect some work experience in a particular legal area (i.e., personal injury, medical malpractice, or insurance fraud). Although the average entry-level paralegal likely didn't know half the things I knew about the law (i.e., substantive law, legal research, legal writing, or legal analysis), they could put the name of a law office where they had previously worked, whereas I could not.

So, although I likely knew more about litigation and the foundations of jurisprudence than most entry level paralegals could ever know, on paper it looked as if I didn't know anything. That is, unless I put on my resume, "I studied law and jurisprudence in the Correctional Facilities of New York State for over 10 years." That, I could not do. I received few callbacks and no interviews.

I was getting frustrated. My dad was patient and simply told me, "It will work out, keep pushing." I was close to thirty years old and living in my father's home. I had to pull my weight. My parole officer was patient as well, but I didn't know how long that would last. I had to make something happen quickly.

I met an older woman while out and about, MB. I am usually a very private person and do not often share my business with others. However, I opened up to her about my entire situation. She had a warmth and sincerity about her that reminded me of my mom and I told her everything. She was an intelligent and empathetic woman, and told me, as for the lack of experience, that I likely wouldn't be hired without it and, therefore, I had to get it. She suggested that I volunteer my legal services to a law office – work for free – and then use that volunteer experience on my resume. She told me that I would be a good fit at a community-based organization where she used to work. She said that they did civil rights work and ran a number of community-based programs for at-risk clients in Brooklyn, New York. She told me that they were affiliated with

Medgar Evers College and that she knew the Director of the Center and would introduce me to her if I were interested.

I was conflicted because it sounded good, besides the working for free part. I was down to practically zero dollars and I could never ask another person for money, not even my dad. I needed income. However, my days were practically free besides job hunting and bonding with my family after years of being away so, I told MB, "Okay." Also, this may buy me some time with my parole situation because the Center was a well-recognized civil rights organization and, although it would be volunteer work, it was still technically work.

The Center

MB MADE THE INTRODUCTION AND I immediately knew this could work. The Director of the Center was an African-American-Caribbean attorney, Dr. Smart. Upon meeting, we talked and I also opened up to her about my entire situation before incarceration and after. She absolutely understood. In fact, she was entirely aware of the issues I faced as well as the numerous other men and women of color who had been released from prison. She told me about the work that the Center was doing concerning prisoner's rights, women's rights, and the rights of immigrants. They were doing a bit of everything. I had massive respect for her.

She introduced me to a number of other people who worked there, including attorneys. She invited me to roll up my sleeves and get busy if I wanted to. Although she had no money in the budget to pay me, it felt good to be connected to some positive people and positive causes. I was in. I began to help with legal research on active cases and memo writing on my findings and conclusions. I conducted the intake of clients when the attorneys were not in the office – getting basic information from them and passing it on to the attorneys. I manned the front desk taking phone calls and messages. I did store runs to pick up coffee and food. I made myself a major asset to the office and not consciously, just by "doing me." I'm a hard worker and I am usually recognized as such. I am also self-motivated, don't need hand holding, punctual, loyal and dependable. I am also competent at most things that I put my mind to and I am a quick study. I fit in pretty well at the Center.

I loved working at the Center, but I still needed cash. My dad, at that time, was swimming in bills and I couldn't have him feeding and clothing me. My cousin was interested in opening a security company that would secure contracts with the New York City nightclubs and bars. I thought it was a good idea and definitely a money-maker. He asked if I would work with him, but we would first have to learn the game, become bouncers and then owners of a security company. He said that he knew some people who likely could get us in and that it paid $125 per night.

The problem for me was that, this could be bad if it went wrong because many parole officers frowned upon parolees doing nightclub work. Although many parolees did it anyway because not many other businesses were open to hiring parolees, I didn't know if my parole officer would violate me if he discovered me doing this kind of work. Although I felt that he likely wouldn't move to violate me, I definitely wasn't sure. I was sure that I was broke and that I wasn't going to rob anyone or sell drugs or do anything illegal. My cousin's hookup offered me the job at $125 a night, two or three nights a week. I took it.

Mom with me at Eastern C.F.

Mom with me at Clinton C.F.

Cool dude with me- Eastern-C.F

Dad with me at attorney
swearing in Ceremony

My summer camp- closing

Dad in Jamaica-much deserved vacation

"Just Chillin"

Black Tie Affair

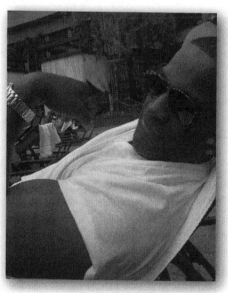

On Vacation-Relaxation

NAAS–and the Tunnel Night Club

THE TEAM I WOULD BE with was "Naas Elite Services". Naas had assignments and contracts with some of the hottest nightclubs in New York City, including the "Tunnel" and "Limelight." The legendary club owner, Peter Gatien, was the owner of both of these establishments. I was assigned to work the "Tunnel," a legendary hip hop, rock and house music nightclub in Manhattan.

My first night on the job was Saturday – hip hop night. The Tunnel was a huge converted warehouse in Manhattan up by the west side highway. It held and attracted close to 2,000 hip hop fans on Saturday nights. It was the hottest hip hop spot in New York City and it attracted all of the hip hop royalty, celebrities, top DJs, and some of the roughest clientele New York City had to offer. The line to enter the club always stretched down the block and around the corner with the ladies' line to the right, the gentlemen's line to the left. Trouble often popped off right on the line with dudes beefing because they were tired of waiting or trying to skip the line.

When I worked the line, I often calmed things down by my approach and conflict resolution skills that I learned from years of dealing with extremely aggressive dudes. However, the challenge with these cats was that they were often high, drunk, or both, and that combination often made situations extremely volatile. Still, I managed that, but I too knew that working this line was like walking a tightrope with no safety net. Things could pop off at any second.

Doing this work would definitely be sticky, particularly on Saturday nights. From all across the tristate area, the drug crews who were often heavily armed, the stick up kids, real gunmen and some just wannabe gangsters all would swing by the Tunnel on Saturday nights. Some of these dudes visiting the Tunnel were really about that life and "real-recognize-real," so I knew them when I met them. However, I learned many years ago that the trick when dealing with real dudes was respect.

If you deal with a man with straight-up respect, any man actually, from a Wall Street attorney to a stone cold killer, usually that respect is recognized and appreciated. However, the quickest way to make lasting enemies or get hurt real bad when dealing with any real dude is dealing with them with open and blatant disrespect. That's a no-go. Respect goes a long way. I don't mean ass-kissing, just a sense that "I recognize you, but I can't accommodate you because of house, club or business establishment rules, but there is no disrespect intended."

Anyway, many of the team still carried firearms, knives, Billy-clubs, brass-knuckles and wore bullet proof vests. It was real like that. Team members were still often shot at, stabbed, cut, or hit over the head with liquor bottles. Although I didn't walk with a firearm, I understood why many of the team did. A manager of the team, Rich, who I believe was law enforcement because all of the police who patrolled the area knew and openly respected him, walked with a .38 caliber snub nose at the small of his back. When he talked to hostile patrons, he often kept his hands behind his back in an apparent non-threatening and non-hostile manner. I knew better. However, he also was very skilled at maintaining order without using force. He knew how to talk to people. He understood conflict resolution and the idea of mutual respect.

Rich quickly noticed how I managed sticky situations without losing my cool and how dudes usually would positively respond to me even while they were often high or drunk. He moved me from the line to the door, which was a trusted and much coveted post. The door definitely was often less tense than working the line. However, at the door you routinely had to turn people away for one reason or another and that took some tact or it could definitely be very volatile. I had that tact and the team supervisors liked that. I rarely had conflict at the door even when having to turn groups of angry dudes away.

Usually, by the time people reached the front door, they were nearly in the club so the frustration of the long line, long wait and often brutally cold weather was replaced with anticipation of a heck of a party. The Tunnel was always a heck of a party, and that was absolutely no hype.

Some of the finest women you want to lay eyes on came through that venue and they were often there by the dozens. Mike Tyson, LL Cool J, Mobb Deep, Big Pun, and many more celebrities visited the Tunnel. Funk Master Flex was the DJ working the turntables many nights that I was there. Flex was a young DJ on the radio at the time, Hot 97 FM, and I liked his style and always thought, "He is going to be very successful." He reminded me of my boy Darnell, super talented.

I now had some money coming in and, although it was risky business, it was better than being absolutely broke or having my dad financially support me when he was already barely getting by. It also allowed me to better focus on the volunteer work I was doing at the Center. As importantly, it permitted me to continue to strengthen family relationships, to take my son and daughter to the mall or simply a movie. My son and daughter were a big part of my life now.

My children were my heart. My daughter and I had always maintained a relationship while I was away and her mother, and particularly her grandmother, made sure to do what they could to make sure our relationship was maintained. They allowed her to visit my family when she came to New York and they would accept my collect calls when I wanted to speak to my daughter from prison. My daughter's mother moved with my daughter to Louisville, Kentucky, a year after I was incarcerated. My daughter was about two years old at the time. Upon my release from prison, my daughter and I connected and built a strong relationship that continues to this day. My daughter is an amazing young lady and we grew our relationship into a strong bound. My daughter is my confidant, loyal advisor and my friend. A daughter's love is so pure and absolute that it is comforting and inspiring beyond belief. My daughter is my heart.

My son's mother and her family were generally a different story. They collectively chose not to allow me to play any part in the parenting of my son after he was born. Even though, initially, my son's mother allowed me to sneak and see my son when her parents were not at home. That changed upon the parents finding me at their home one day visiting my son. They threatened to have me arrested if I ever came around again. Her parents scared her, and her ambivalence toward me drastically changed upon my incarceration. She openly sent word to me that she and her family were going to raise my son and that I would not have any part in his life. Throughout my years of incarceration, from the very first year of confinement, I continued to reach out to her, through letters and messages from family and friends imploring her to "not shut me out." She also shut my family out and they had to resort to sneaking snap pictures of my son (he lived only doors down from my family's home) and sending them to me.

She and her family refused to even bring my son and introduce him to my parents – his grandparents – and his many aunts, uncles, nieces and nephew, all of whom lived only doors away from him. I did instruct my family initially, to respect their opinion because it would only lead to them retaliating against my son's mom. I hoped and prayed they would have a change of heart, or that my son's mother would break free of their influence, move out of their home and do the right thing by my son and me.

Even though my family respected my wishes to not forcefully intrude on the lives of my son and their family, they were also extra kind to my son. For example, my oldest sister was the assistant principal at my son's public school and she used to openly fawn over him. She would write and tell me about it and I would laugh. I'm sure he would go home and tell his mother and grandparents about her extra attention and, although they knew she worked there, they never confronted her about it. My nephew, who was well respected in the neighborhood streets along with his clique, put protection on my son during his school years through word of mouth. My son definitely became suspicious as to why these thorough young men, straight street dudes, were putting protection on him – a square church kid from a square church family. My nephew promised me that he would watch out for my son, and he definitely kept his word.

I continued to send word to my son's mother through family and friends or letters upon finding her address after she had moved out of her family's home. Over the years she continued to adamantly refuse to allow me to see my son although, eventually, she actually did write me a letter explaining her reasons. She explained that in her opinion it was not healthy for his development to know and have visits with a father who was in prison. I was very disappointed, but at least she had communicated and the door of communication was open, or so I thought. She failed to respond to any of my letters after that until many years later.

Years later, when my son was about 12 years old and I was close to being released from prison, my son's mother wrote me a letter explaining that she wanted to talk to me about my son. After all these years lost, I was pissed off at her, but I agreed that we should talk. She forwarded me her home telephone number and I called her. Surprisingly, it was good hearing her voice. I hadn't spoken with her in over ten years. We talked mostly about our son and his life and her present concerns about him. She told me that she was afraid that she was "losing him." She said that he was shutting down to her and that he was doing "poorly in school." She said that his single focus was on knowing and meeting his father.

As I listened intently, it struck me that so many people believe they can be the mother and father, without consideration of what that does to a child. I thought to myself, "I have been reaching out to you for years looking to play a part in his life but now that he's slipping away from you, now you want me to be there." I was happy for the chance, but I was pissed off at her. I felt that it was unjust to my son and unjust to me to have prevented us from knowing each other. She had disappointed me, big-time.

My greatest disappointment was that I had always felt my son's mother was a victim of an oppressive home upbringing and so she rebelled against this extremely strict upbringing in numerous different ways. Getting pregnant was a big embarrassment for her family. The hell she caught before getting pregnant, simply for being a female who could possibly get pregnant, was bad. However, the hell she caught after she actually got pregnant was heartbreaking to hear about. That's why I told my family to not press for a relationship with them and give them space, hoping that her parents would settle down and leave her alone, even if just a little. I cared about her big-time.

I always believed that once things settled down or she got free of them and moved out of their home, she would definitely invite me in to play a part in my son's life. However, she didn't do that. She moved out of the home a few years after my incarceration and she became as resistant to my having a relationship with my son as her parents were. I understood her parents' attitude because they were hardcore religious folks, old, sanctified, holier than thou, and stuck in their ways. However, she didn't have any of those excuses to hide behind, nor was I ever abusive, insane or in any way dangerous to her or my son. So, in my mind, she had no valid rationale or excuse besides, "I just don't want you in his life. Live with it." In my estimation, that is a mean, selfish and vindictive spirit that, yes, will harm me. However, it ultimately will harm our son, and that is what it actually ended up doing. I was very disappointed in her. Still, I just wanted to see my son.

We eventually made plans for her to visit me at Fishkill Correctional Facility, and she promised to bring my son. I was anxious. I wondered what he looked like, how would he talk, how tall he was and what his interests were. All of these thoughts were running through my mind. When I arrived in the visiting room, I spotted her and my son immediately in the crowded visiting room. I walked over to where they were sitting and I hugged her. I hadn't seen her in well over ten years. Although she hadn't changed much in appearance, I could see from the hardening of her face that she had been through some things.

I locked eyes with my son. I just smiled, shaking his hand firmly. My son was extremely handsome, just like his dad. He was very tall at six foot one, and he was still only twelve years old. He was soft-spoken, well-mannered and impeccably groomed. He was very well-spoken and apparently was decently raised. He had the air of a well-raised, somewhat sheltered, middle-class kid. We all talked a long while and my son and I had a good vibe. He was clearly a "momma's boy," but he was obviously yearning to know his father. He reminded me a lot of myself at his age. I loved my mom first and foremost, but I admired my dad and I would have had a void in my soul if I didn't have his masculine energy and masculine example in my life. He was my "dude" for real. I definitely loved my mom, but I moved like my dad. My son watched me from the corners of his eyes, as I talked to his mom or to other visitors or the guards, the same as I did to my father as a young man. At the end of the visit, I promised that we would stay in touch and I kept that promise.

At the Center, people were responding positively to me and I soon became a dearly embraced part of the office staff, although I was just a volunteer. Still, I was one of the first people at work every day and one of the last to leave. I worked as hard as any paid employee would, or maybe even harder. I've always had a solid work ethic. If I agree to do anything, a job or favor, paid or unpaid, I am going to go all out or I am simply not going to do it. That's why, to this day, I hesitate and ponder long and hard before I commit to anything, because once I commit I am all in.

One day, arriving early at the Center as I usually did, I sat at the front desk and greeted visitors, manned the phones and sorted the incoming mail. In the stack of new mail I noticed a job posting looking for a coordinator for a start-up program that would service women, including ex-offenders and other women who were at risk of losing their children to the foster care system. Upon reading it and scanning the qualifications, I believed that I was a good fit for the position. I also noticed that the program was designated to be run out of the Center, and that my supervisor, Dr. Smart, would be the program manager. The phone rang. It was Dr. Smart. She asked if I could retrieve some letter from her desk and deliver a message to a staff member when they arrived. She told me with a laugh that she called the front desk because she knew for certain that "you would be there." Her complimenting my dependability made me feel great. Dr. Smart is an incredible woman. She is beyond kind and caring and I definitely valued her compliment. She also said that she would be in the office soon.

When she arrived, business as usual, I allowed her to settle in, make her phone calls and begin her day's work, which was always a large amount. Thereafter, I interrupted her with a knock on her office door asking, "Do you have a moment?" She invited me to "have a seat." I informed her that I came across a job posting and was wondering would she mind if I submitted a resume in consideration for the coordinator position. She pulled the posting from the stack of papers on her desk and read it. She looked up and said, "I absolutely would not mind." She complimented my work ethic and ability to get along with others. However, she said that I would have to interview for the position against a group of other people and that the office would make the "best choice." All I needed was a fair chance, so I readily said, "Thank you, Dr. Smart. I appreciate the opportunity."

I used my researching skills to take a crash course in foster care, the rules and regulations that apply, the programs already doing this kind of work and the programs they offered within those particular programs. When the office finally called me in for the interview, I was well-prepared. If I didn't get this job, it would not be because I was ill-prepared –no way. In the interview, which took place in Dr. Smart's office, Dr. Smart, the assistant Director to the Center, one of the staff attorneys, and their projects manager were there. I knew them all and they all had come to know me through my months of volunteer work at the Center.

They questioned me hard, but fairly. They asked about my incarceration – why, when and how. I openly told them the entire story. I told them my mindset going in, the struggles I faced while inside, the commitment I exerted to changing my life around and the lessons that

I learned throughout the journey. They were empathetic and openly complimentary to how far I had come. However, they reserved opinion on my hiring and said that I would hear from the office within a few days. I was on pins and needles the entire wait. Although my cousin was sure that I would be offered the position, my attitude was "we'll see." The office called me and offered me the position, starting at $33,000 a year. I was ecstatic. I told my dad and he was happy. He said, "I knew things would open up for you. Congratulations."

With a steady income, I could breathe a little bit and take some financial pressure off of my dad. I could spend time out with my son, although he was perfectly cool eating pizza and watching movies in the house. I could fly my daughter to New York and show her the city – I hadn't seen her in a while because she was still living in Kentucky. I was home from prison for less than a year and things were definitely looking up.

I began in earnest developing the program for the Center from scratch. I had to interview and hire an assistant, develop the training curriculum, identify client sources, print flyers, locate space for workshops, prepare workshop schedules, secure workshop presenters, identify vendors for supplies, draw up vendor contracts and the list went on and on. I was ready for the challenge and I was definitely not going to disappoint the people who had placed their faith in me.

After a few weeks of prep, we launched the program. It was designed to assist parents who were at risk of losing their children to foster care develop basic parenting skills that would prevent them from abusing or neglecting their children. I secured mental health care professionals, parenting coaches, stress management and time management professionals and financial advisors, all designed to give these women tools to better deal with and understand their children.

The women in our program were mandated to be there, mostly by the Court. If they completed the program with a certificate of completion after weeks of steady attendance, and after fulfilling other Court mandated treatment services, they could retain or maintain custody of their children. The results we achieved were good and most of our clients maintained or retained custody of their children and they gained much-needed skills to be better parents.

My monthly visit to my parole officer was approaching and I still hated those visits. Upon being hired as a Coordinator for the Center, I had given up my work at the nightclubs and I had no incidents during my work there, so I was not sweating the visit too much. However, as soon as I arrived at the parole office sometime after being hired by the Center, I knew something was not right. I saw my parole officer as I walked in the main office. However, as soon as he noticed me enter the office, he walked briskly towards the parole supervisor's office and began a whispered discussion with him.

I checked in with the receptionist and immediately thereafter two armed parole officers approached me and escorted me into a back office. My parole officer was there, along with the parole supervisor and the two other armed officers. My parole officer told me to place my hands behind my back as he took out the handcuffs. I asked, "What is going on?" and he said I was being detained for a possible parole violation and I very likely was "going back to prison."

I scanned my brain to figure what angle they were coming from. I was clean as a whistle besides the nightclub job, and that wasn't serious enough for them to be acting like this. Finally, Officer Smith asked me if I was the owner of a business called "A.J. Services," which was a company that was shipping inmates catalog purchased goods, food, clothes, etc., into correctional facilities within New York State. I told him that I was not. He told me he had a confidential informant, within the prison system, that informed the Division of Parole it was my business and I had set it up without notifying or seeking permission from the Division of Parole.

The reality was, I had originated the A.J. Services idea. However, I knew the Division of Parole was so narrow-minded they would never allow me to work an entrepreneurial endeavor that did work with prisoners. They talked rehabilitation, but they were not supportive of ideas outside of the box. They simply supported "get a job and stay out of trouble." When I pitched the idea to people who had some business sense, they saw the potential in the idea and the company was grossing thousands of dollars a month, right out of the gate.

When the company was set up, I informed the partners, the company could not be singularly mine. I would, however, welcome a piece of the pie once the company began turning a profit, and they agreed. So, when Officer Smith asked me if I owned A.J. Services, I truthfully told him no, I did not. The parole officers were adamant it was my company and they had solid evidence against me – "snitches." Finally, I was informed I had to produce the owners of the company within the week or else they were going to move to revoke my parole and return me to prison. They removed the handcuffs and the three-hour or so detention was over and I was free to go – for the moment anyway.

I immediately called my lawyer and told him the situation and told him to contact parole and inform them we will be in the office to talk to them, along with the owner of A.J. Services. My boy Darnell was the major owner and operator of A.J. Services. Darnell had no criminal record and no obligation to meet with these people to explain anything. However, he agreed to do it. My lawyer represented my interest at the meeting, as well as Darnell's interest. However, Darnell's position was, "I don't owe anyone in this office explanation about anything that I do. It is my business and is there anything else that you need to know?" After the meeting, it was obvious and clear that A.J. Services was not my business. Apparently, someone had given them a bum lead.

In reality, even if it was my business, there was no evidence or even a hint of illegality involved in A.J. Services. It was a business designed to address an identified need of thousands of inmates in New York State prisons. It was a store, on the outside, that was willing to deliver all the goodies, cakes, pies, candy, etc., to men and women serving time. I recognized the need while serving time and, having sometimes thousands of dollars in my inmate account, but being limited to shopping in the prison store "commissary," which offered only a tiny list of items and nothing inmates would consider "the good stuff." I knew what that "good stuff" was. I vowed, when I got out, I was going to start a catalog company that catered and delivered food products to inmates, which was a virtually ignored market.

However, I knew the psychology of prison officials and that the Division of Parole would do all they could to block or sabotage an ex-offender from establishing a successful business servicing inmates. That psychology was simply part of their DNA. "It was what it was." A.J. Services grossed thousands of dollars right out of the gate, but because I could not put all my inside knowledge and effort behind the project without risk of getting caught and sent to prison, I was forced to let people run the company who didn't have an "inside track." The business couldn't turn a profit and it went under.

However, looking back, if I had done things a bit differently, I believe it could have worked. Also, if I had simply thought more broadly with "catalog delivery to homes" rather than to prison, I would have struck gold. Years later, "FreshDirect" and other home delivery food services took what I was doing on a small scale, broadened it to homes, and made millions. Life is funny like that sometimes.

Anyway, the parole situation calmed down, but I became like a little parole office celebrity – particularly among the female parole officers. They would see me at the office and go out of their way to compliment me on my entrepreneurial efforts because they thought the catalog company was a great idea. They also balked at the threat to send me to prison for trying to make a legitimate dollar when numerous guys on their caseloads were robbing, stealing and selling drugs. They were mostly women parole officers, and they genuinely respected what I was trying to do and there was no animosity and no hate. Officer Smith also actually understood what I was trying to do and that nothing sinister was going on. However, sometimes within the criminal justice system, employee's attitudes sadly is, it just "is what it is." Everyone with some sense understands that. They may gripe about apparent injustices in whispers among themselves and then they simply "keep it pushing," they move on.

My son and I were bonding quickly, with a few bumps here and there, but overall, we were very cool. I started getting the vibration, however, that his mother was feeling a bit threatened by our fast developing relationship. He and I had gotten very close fairly quickly. My son was a good dude. He was sheltered, but like his mom, they both had that spirit of "do not cage me in or I will rebel." They were both free spirits. His sprouting rebellions are what actually lead his mother to finally allow us to connect because she feared losing him.

My son was smart and charismatic, and the ladies loved him. He was tall, well-built and strikingly handsome. Teenage girls would often openly gawk at him while we were in the streets. He too had a wicked sense of humor and was just fun to be with. The things that challenged our relationship, from my perspective, was that he was spoiled, sheltered, pretty-square, although he didn't think so, and his blinding love of his mother. His extreme protectiveness of her did not allow him the ability to objectively and critically analyze her actions. She had some real nonsense with her and he didn't have the ability to read and dissect it.

For instance, I had discovered through a conversation with him, she had actually never informed him of the true history of how and why he and I didn't meet until he was twelve years old. He was informed it was because I didn't want to be in his life, and never made an effort to be in his life. Unbeknownst to me, that was the lens from which he was viewing me from day one. That was one of the biggest lies ever. Upon learning this fact, sometime into our developing relationship, I told him, "Oh no, that's not true." I gave him times and dates of instances where I reached out to his mother through numerous letters and sent messages through my family and friends. I told him, she even responded to a few letters I had written. Although, at the time, I believed her letters to me had been lost. Anyway, he adamantly refused to believe me and angrily demanded, "Why would my mother lie?" I left it alone. Yet,

I thought to myself, "It is a lie son, and likely one of the biggest lies you have ever been told." I would never refuse to be in the life of one of my children – ever. Yet, he didn't know that. This because he really didn't know me, except what his mother had told him, and I doubt if any of that has been very good.

However, at that point in his young life, I didn't hold it against him. He was too young and emotionally immature to understand how to dig for the truth or even to accept a hard truth. So, although I often had the desire to adamantly tell him "Your mom is a real piece of work," I didn't have the heart to do it. She was his mother and for many years before knowing me, she was all he really had. I got it. I actually didn't want to hurt her, even upon learning of her nonsense, by slowly removing the rose colored glasses he wore when it came to her. Finally, what made my relationship with my son even more challenging, was that he would later make comments, communicating that, I needed to work extra hard to make up for a sin, one that I never actually committed, refusing to be in his life. Dealing with that, was extremely challenging for me.

However, I simply had to trust that one day, if he is a true son of mine, he will see the truth about his mother and the truth about his dad. I've always believed that. So, I just focused on building the relationship between him and me, believing that the other nonsense, in time, would take care of itself. That singular focus was definitely working as we were becoming inseparable. He became my road dog, hanging at my place, shopping with me, hitting up the hot restaurants, movies and just talking. He and I talked a lot about all kinds of things. He's a funny guy.

The coordinator position at the Center exposed me to many people, some of them in positions of power and responsibility at Medgar Evers College. The success of the program also got me recognized as a talented worker and manager by some of these same people. While working as coordinator for the Center, one of the very connected people I met was a young, attractive women named KB. KB was the coordinator for a college-based program that serviced unemployed parents of young children.

While talking to KB, she introduced me to a man who was passing by named AL. AL was the senior job developer for Administrator Kacey, who was one of the most influential administrators at Medgar Evers College. Administrator Kacey was a phenomenal grant writer who pulled millions of dollars into the college as the recipient of grant awards.

Administrator Kacey managed numerous multi-million dollar grant funded programs for the college and she had a huge staff of well over a hundred employees. Administrator Kacey was a big deal at that college and AL was one of her most trusted people. AL was familiar with my program and mentioned there were a number of new projects Administrator Kacey was going after and she would need good people to help her run them. He gave me his business card and asked that I keep in touch. I told him I would.

However, the program I was presently running was my focus at the time and I absolutely wanted to make Dr. Smart and the Center proud. However, some weeks later, I was informed the program was a success, but because of budgets cuts, my program and numerous other programs serving at-risk people were likely not going to be refunded. The much needed services for these women were being defunded and I would likely be out of a job.

The budget predictions were true. The program was defunded and I was out of a job. While at the Center, I had sharpened my legal skills by doing paralegal work, research and writing and learning from some of the most talented attorneys that were employed there. However, I still hadn't acquired enough experience in the minds of most law offices to even give me an interview. I started sending out tons of resumes and nothing.

The Center, too, was a victim of the severe budget cuts and Dr. Smart had to terminate a number of her paid staff. It broke her heart. Dr. Smart considered her workers as family and, although she ran a tight ship, still you knew that even when she called you out it was out of tough love. She was heartbroken over the terminations. It was tough times at the Center. Most other staff members and I were able to apply for unemployment, but that was only good for a few weeks. I needed to find a job.

I had planned to take a trip to Miami, Florida to catch up with some old friends, but with the unemployment situation, I wasn't in the most festive mood. The travel ticket agent wasn't making it any better by demanding I reach the travel office to pick up the tickets before 5:00 p.m. It was already after 4:00 p.m. and their office was over an hour away. Then, by seconds, I missed the train. As I arrived at the train platform, the train doors were closing. I definitely wouldn't make it by 5:00 p.m.

Still, I didn't turn around. Maybe the next train will come soon and get me there miraculously before five or just a little bit after. I waited, but I wasn't optimistic at all. As the subway arrived and the doors opened, I walked into the subway car not feeling great. I was definitely a little down. As the subway doors closed, I heard someone call my name, "Abdul." I turned around to see who it was and it was AL, the senior job developer for Administrator Kacey.

He asked, "How are you?" I simply shook my head. I poured out to him about the job situation, the unemployment, and the job search frustration. He looked at me and said, "Why didn't you call me?" He reached into his pocket and handed me his business card saying, "Call me and we'll meet up next week."

As he exited the subway, I felt good thinking, "Maybe he's not just talking," as some folks often do. I thought to myself, "I'll call him." The train got me into the city in decent time, and the ticket agent was still there. I picked up my travel tickets, thinking "maybe." I had a great time in Miami.

When I returned from Florida, I called AL. He sounded happy to hear from me. He asked what day I was available to meet. I reminded him, I was unemployed, so any day was basically good for me. I asked, "What day works for you?" He laughed, asking did I have time to stop by that day and I said, "Yes." I arrived at his Manhattan office and he was on the phone. He waved to me and gestured for me to have a seat. As soon as he hung up the telephone, it rang again and he started talking. He looked up at me exasperatedly and gestured with his finger. "One minute."

As he talked on the phone, he pulled out a stack of papers and handed them to me. He put the call on hold for a second, simply saying, "Pick the one you want." He resumed his phone conversation. I thumbed through the stack of papers – they were job postings. Most of them were for programs run by his boss, Administrator Kacey, and some of them paid as much as $80,000 per year. I didn't have the education qualifications or experience for some, but still I made a mental note. Others were looking for program assistants and they were ranging in pay from $28,000 to $50,000 and I was a good fit for a number of them.

When AL hung up the phone, he asked, "Did you see anything you like?" I handed him the posting paying $80,000. He read it and laughed saying, "Soon enough." I handed him the other ones paying $28,000-$50,000. He read them and nodded his head in the affirmative. He knew my education background and my work as a coordinator, so he believed I would be a good fit. He called Administrator Kacey. He told her he had someone she "needed to meet." She agreed to meet me and told him to pass me her office number to make the arrangements.

He hung up the phone saying with a smile of satisfaction, "I did my part, it's now up to you." AL was a short and stout African-American man. "Country folk." He had a big heart and I told him, "Thank you, I will do my part." Before I left the office he briefed me on Administrator Kacey's personality, her likes and dislikes. Based upon what he told me about her and what I subsequently learned from others, I knew how I was going to handle the meeting. I definitely had a plan.

I met with KB, who schooled me thoroughly on Administrator Kacey. Then I spoke with Dr. Smart, a great advisor who was well respected on the campus, too. She offered to call Administrator Kacey and she did. They talked for a while as I sat in the office of Dr. Smart. Dr. Smart talked me up, even telling her about my incarceration, my efforts at rehabilitation, the volunteer legal work I did for the Center and the program I had developed from scratch. I was surprised Dr. Smart introduced the incarceration piece. I had planned to do that during the face-to-face. Oh well. Anyway, as expected, it wasn't a disqualifier with Administrator Kacey and I made an appointment to meet her. I always marveled at Dr. Smart's approach to things – it was always straightforward with no chaser. With her, it just "Is what it is." If there is an elephant in the room she is going to ask, "Whose elephant is this?" If the elephant was stinking, she likely will mention that too. "That elephant needs a wash." That's just her personality. There is not a mean bone in her body. She simply calls it as she sees it and she's a beautiful human being.

Administrator Kacey

DAYS LATER, I ARRIVED AT Administrator Kacey's office in Manhattan an hour early. I always arrived early when going to a place for the first time, and particularly for an interview. Some places are hard to find and the search could make you late. I despised being late for anything and being late to an interview was out of the question. I grabbed a cup of coffee at a nearby coffee shop and reviewed my interview notes, anticipating questions and rehearsing my answers. I felt good going in. I was ready.

Arriving at the Administrator's office for our scheduled afternoon meeting, I was informed by a pleasant receptionist that Administrator Kacey was still "in a meeting" and I should have a seat. I later learned the administrator's meetings were often many hours long. Sometimes running deep into the night, particularly when she and her staff were putting the final touches on multi-million dollar grant proposals. That day, the administrator and her staff were working on a grant proposal. After waiting well over an hour, I figured I could either wait or I could reschedule. But the receptionist said the administrator knew I was there and I decided to wait it out.

After a nearly two-hour wait, the administrator stepped out of the conference room area. She was an elderly, fair skinned woman, medium height, very slim and impeccably dressed. I stood up to greet her and before I could utter a word, she firmly grasped my outstretched hand saying, "Hello Mr. Lloyd-Bey, I'm Administrator Kacey. It's nice to meet you." She said, "Walk with me." We walked to an area of the hallway that was private and had a window. She pulled out a cigarette, lit it and said, "I'm not into a lot of small talk and this may be an unorthodox interview." She went on to tell me she had heard "a lot about you" and "you come highly recommended." She sucked hard on her cigarette and tilted her head skyward blowing the smoke in the air. She went on to say she heard I had served hard time and that it was good to see the changes I had made in my life. She went on to say she knew of a young man who was presently serving time and she wanted him to meet me because I potentially could be a "good influence on him."

She invited me into her office to meet with her second in command, Betsy Sipp. Ms. Sipp was a jovial woman from the deep South, and she had a genuine motherly air about her that was very warm and disarming. However, I stayed focused. I would only exhale once I got the job offer. They told me about the position – entry level with lots of room to grow and move up in "responsibility and pay." I listened intently. They then explained the starting salary was $28,000 a year, again with room to grow. She offered me a position. I thanked them for the offer and said, "I am interested." However, I explained, "I am a very good worker" and $28,000 was too low. I would need at least $33,000.

Administrator Kacey paused. She took a long look at me almost as if she was seeing me for the very first time. She took a long pull on her cigarette and after blowing the smoke in the air, she said, "Confidence – I like that." She said, "You may do very well here, Mr. Lloyd-Bey. $33,000 it is. Welcome aboard." I shook her hand firmly, saying, "Thank you for the opportunity, Administrator Kacey."

At that day and time, she had well over a hundred employees working under her supervision. In less than a year of hiring me, I leapfrogged past 80 percent of them, first being named co-division leader of one of her multi-million dollar grant funded programs designed to render academic support services to New York City public schools. Soon thereafter, I was tapped for appointment as Deputy Director of the Office of Youth Development Programs, one of Administrator Kacey's flagship programs. My salary was bumped up to $45,000 per year.

I rose quickly within Administrator Kacey's department for a number of reasons. Besides being an extremely hard worker like her, which she liked, I often stayed at the office well past 9:00 p.m. working on projects, while others had long since gone home. I was also dependable. Often, her workers, as many workers do, would watch the clock and at 5:00 p.m. they were gone. Also, at 9:00 a.m. when they were supposed to be at work, some would often arrive at 9:30 a.m. and, even then, would need time to settle in before actual work would begin. I didn't approach work like that. At eight years old, I used to get up at sunrise and walk numerous blocks to get to the area supermarket before it opened so I could get a post by a cashier and I could pack bags. I hustled hard.

Administrator Kacey knew that at 9:00 a.m., I would be at my desk, and likely I would be there even earlier than that. She soon began to call my desk early in the morning to give me directions to forward to others whenever they arrived at work. I also noticed that after speaking with me early in the morning, the phones at the other cubicles would sometimes ring. I am certain it was Administrator Kacey calling to confirm what she likely already knew – a number of her workers were not in the office when they were supposed to be there.

Since Administrator Kacey had so many projects running, she and her senior people couldn't be at the main office every day – or definitely not at 9:00 a.m. every day. Administrator Kacey had offices in Manhattan and offices all over Brooklyn, as well as numerous offices on Medgar Evers Campus. However, she somehow still knew who was working and who was on cruise-control. That woman seemed to be aware of everything including the fact that I often stayed at the office well after 7:00 p.m., although no one was usually there to tell her and I definitely never did.

Calling people's desk at odd times, I believed, was a tactic she used to see who was around. Additionally, I believe the building security people may have been a source of information as well. They always watched when folks came to work and when they left. Whatever the case, she seemed to know everything about everything, and everything about everybody.

I was working hard upon being hired by Administrator Kacey, but that's just how I always have been. She noticed that about me and she liked it. Additionally, I have always been results-oriented. I honestly never realized there was anything other than results, until much later in life, when I was told that some people actually prefer and value the process, the journey. I later learned that to some people it is not always about winning, it's about the joy of simply being part of the team. For others, it's more about the journey rather than actually reaching the destination.

During those years, my attitude was "forget the journey," I'd gladly ride to paradise with my eyes closed. I definitely didn't see the purpose of stopping to "smell the roses along the way." In fact, if anyone actually stopped my train to paradise to smell some freaking roses, at that point, I would likely have a major attitude.

However, almost everything related to grant funding was "outcome dependent." If you couldn't promise and then demonstrate results, why would anyone hand you a check for millions of dollars? If someone hands you a check for a million dollars, in any arena, you had better get results, and results were all I basically knew. Administrator Kacey loved results. Results to her equated to more grants, and more money, more jobs, and more power – all the things she apparently loved. So, she and I got along extremely well. However, my outlook on things, at times, rubbed the more "enlightened" ones the wrong way, and the lazy ones on the job likely didn't know what to think about me.

When Administrator Kacey appointed me the Deputy Director of Youth Services programs at Medgar Evers College, I was happy. I was so happy I could provide for myself and my family in a better way. I was now comfortably able to secure a nice apartment, a decent car and not worry about bills. I could manage. The job also allowed me the ability to hire some part-time workers. My office usually hired around eighty people to work our summer program, summer camp. We hired teachers, coaches, lifeguards, dance instructors and camp counselors. I pushed to have my son interviewed for one of the "junior counseling" positions at

$10 per hour. Although he was only sixteen years old at the time, he was also very mature for his age, and being the son of the Programs' Deputy Director couldn't hurt. He was hired. He was very happy and so was I.

My son was also living with me at the time, so on payday we would often hit up our favorite restaurant in Manhattan – an upscale Spanish/seafood spot. We would order our usual twin lobsters, fried jumbo shrimp appetizers and get busy. We'd then go catch a movie and then just cruise the city talking.

The new position also brought me back to the Medgar Evers Campus in Brooklyn. My newly assigned office was actually the same office that Dr. Smart had previously occupied. The Center was re-located to offices in another part of the college. As I sat in my new office, the same office I had sat in a number of times while meeting with Dr. Smart, a person I admired dearly, I thought to myself, "Life is funny." I had my first job interview upon release from prison in this office. The office was beautiful. Both Dr. Smart and Administrator Kacey had high standards and great taste.

People from the Center heard I was back on campus and, before I could even settle in, they stopped by the office to see me and congratulate me on my new appointment as the Deputy Director of Youth Services programs. When they entered the office and my receptionist ushered them into my office, formerly their boss, Dr. Smart's office, they just stared, mouth open, and smiled. They applauded my success – they surely always saw the potential in me. However, they, like others around campus and in my life, were pretty amazed at how quickly I had moved up. As I sat in my new office, in my big beautiful leather chair tilted back with my feet on the large mahogany desk, I was happy with my accomplishments as others were as well, but I was absolutely not amazed.

Although thankful and thoughtful about the power of the Most High, I was partly surprised my success arrived so quickly. In less than a year of being hired by Administrator Kacey, I was appointed to help steer one of her top rated programs and was given the much-coveted title of Deputy Director. However, to me, my success was not unexpected because I always expect success. That is, once I started getting my mind in order and I actually matured. As for the journey, I can never predict what will happen along the way, but as for the end result, I expect success and I rarely harbor any other thoughts.

My journey through almost thirteen years of prison was enabled, in large part, to the fact I am rarely moved by incidents that happen along the path to what I define as success. While on the journey to the end result, which is success as I define it in my mind, incidents and occurrences, whether they are good, bad, or otherwise, simply are experiences on the journey to success. The hurt, pain, ups and downs and the temporary wins or losses, I never let blind me to the end result – success.

The end result, of a 12 and a half-year prison sentence, which I always kept vivid in my mind every day, was the vision of me, "Walking out of prison, alive, with my mind, my body and my soul, as unaffected by that wicked experience as humanly possible." I always kept that end result in the forefront of my mind, every day, no matter what else was happening to me or around me at any particular moment in time.

To this day, people tell me I don't get very excited or extremely down about much of anything. Again, that's largely because I truly see most experiences in my life, good, bad or apparently neutral, as simply a small part of a larger picture not worthy of a huge celebration nor worthy of extreme despair. I view each experience as simply part of an emerging picture. So, as I sit in the new office that others may see as a big success, I see it simply as a small part of a larger unfinished picture that's still being drawn. In my mind, I still have a number of mountains to climb. There is, thus, no real celebrating going on at this time – not by me anyway. I was still happy. However, I had plenty more work to do.

The new position was going well. The director I worked under was a cool talented young guy from Harlem, New York, who many referred to as "the wonder boy." He was a favorite of Administrator Kacey, and some also referred to him as Administrator Kacey's "son." He definitely favored her in some mannerisms and skin tone and could actually pass for her son, but he wasn't. A number of people hated him because he was young, smart, talented, hard-working and a favorite of Administrator Kacey. He definitely had her ear and her respect. Although a number of folks hated him because of these things, I liked him, and he and I hit it off big time. I definitely had his back against the hate and he knew it.

Also, we were a good team. He complemented my weaknesses, and vice versa. He was geekish at first blush, although he had his wild side which some would never have guessed. He was extremely intelligent and socially-polished, with a sophisticated persona that sometimes came across to some people as not "keeping it real." That wasn't the truth, but perception is often reality. He held a degree from Columbia University and was light years ahead of most people when it came to the use of technology. He was "geekish," but absolutely not a geek.

In contrast, I was not as socially polished or as sophisticated when dealing with certain issues, especially technology. I was almost techno-logically illiterate. I also couldn't tell you the difference between a black tie event and a white tie event, but he could. Yet very few would claim I didn't "keep it real." I was that roll up your sleeves blue collar worker who was smart, driven and willing to work until I dropped to get the job done.

Additionally, I was competent and thorough in understanding the legal rules and regulations of the various agencies and grant funding sources that we had to deal with. The rules were extremely tedious and complex, but I could dissect them with ease and keep our program in constant compliance. I also was loyal and, although I am comfortable as the leader, if I respect your talents I will play the supporting role without a problem. I definitely respected the talents of the director. That young dude was definitely no joke. Administrator Kacey knew what she was doing when she paired us together and it was "on and poppin'." Our program kicked butt. He and I quickly became standouts.

Administrator Kacey called me to the office in Manhattan from the Brooklyn campus one day saying, "I want to see you in my office." I had been Deputy Director for a few months at that time and I didn't know what she wanted. The director told me before I headed out that,

"Administrator Kacey was awarded a big grant for a start-up program and she wants you to run it." I informed the director I was honored, but I enjoyed what I was doing as Deputy Director. He informed me, "I don't want to lose you and I told Administrator Kacey so." However, he said, "You would be running your own shop and this is an opportunity I am not going to keep you from if you want it."

I met with Administrator Kacey and she explained this was a big grant award and she wanted me to set up and run this new program. I would be given the title of "Program Coordinator" and a significant increase in salary. I would have a personal assistant and a number of workers that would report to me. It was an off-campus program housed in a Homeless Shelter in Brooklyn. I would be charged with setting up the program, which was to identify homeless shelter residents within three New York City shelters who were somewhat employment-ready. I would then give them world-of-work training via workshops, which would include resume writing, job interviewing skills, time management, dress for success, etc. My workers would do the training. After that, my hired job developers would be charged with the responsibility of finding them employment. Our success would be based upon how many of the residents we trained and ultimately found employment.

I was definitely thankful for the vote of confidence and the opportunity she was offering me. She could have picked from the hundreds of other people in her resume file, or from the over one hundred people who presently worked for her. However, she tapped me. That meant a lot to me. However, my heart was not totally into it. My heart was into youth services. To me, there is no better and more rewarding area than helping young people.

For me, youth services was so personal that I saw myself, as well as so many of my friends who went astray, in many of the hundreds of kids our program serviced. They were in need of so many support services, and if they received them they could achieve anything and many of them would be big successes. The deficiencies in the lives of inner-city children are so many it would take another few books to detail. First, there was such a lack of identity which many kids experience, but minority kids felt it much worse. The schools were basically failing to educate many kids. I visited and did classroom work in a good number of public schools, so I saw it first-hand.

Some of the schools were so dangerous, they literally reminded me of some of the prison yards I had walked. The tension was so high, you can literally feel it. The gang bangers and tough guys ran these schools and a conducive environment for learning was absent. No wonder some of the high schools I visited had graduation rates below 50 percent, year after year. For Black males, the numbers were often even lower than that.

The neighborhoods around many of these schools also were extremely dangerous. I heard many stories of students not going to school in fear of the drama they faced. Not from the kids at school, but the hood dudes who hung out near and around the schools. There was heavy gang activity, drugs, violence and intimidation all around many of these schools. The schoolgirls were often harassed by older girls who didn't even go to school. Additionally, they were often harassed by the gang dudes and drug dealers who hung-out around the schools. The school guys also felt most of the same pressures and experienced constant harassment simply while walking to and from school.

Then, the school guards, having been taken over by the New York City police department in a legitimate effort to bring some safety to the area, often did this by having daily confrontations and sometimes straight harassed, even the good kids, who might be simply hanging out with each other before or after school, or simply walking down the block in a group bothering no one. Many of the kids were often stopped, frisked, yelled at, cursed at, and blatantly disrespected by law enforcement.

The teachers and school administrators, in many of the schools, seemed to be mere babysitters and issue control professionals rather than teachers. A few bad students in the classroom often disrupted the entire learning process in the classroom, causing teachers to shift from teacher mode to babysitter and issue control mode. The guidance offices I visited and worked with often were grossly understaffed, with one counselor sometimes having over a hundred students on their caseload. This, when a single student honestly might need literally hours of focused counseling time, particularly when preparing for high school graduation and college entry.

Finally, the parents often are not actively involved in the educational endeavors of their children. Many times they are clueless as to the educational needs or deficiencies of their children. Many didn't know about the graduation requirements, SAT preparation, grants, loans or the college admissions process. When our programs or the schools did parent events, the participation of parents was regularly low. Without the strong support of knowledgeable parents and all of the issues that students, particularly in the inner cities face, many of these kids don't have a great chance at achieving educational success. Someone once said you can predict the number of prison cells a city will need based upon the high school graduation rates of the city's students. If that is true, particularly for Black males, the schools are offering many of them up for prison. They were not graduating in huge numbers.

My youth services program work was personal. I understood the challenges the young people, particularly in the inner-city, faced daily. Through our program's after-school, in school, and summer-time support services, we aggressively confronted these challenges. Now, Administrator Kacey was asking that I take my talents into a new arena. It was one which I was concerned about, homeless services, but definitely not passionate about. However, how could I say "no" to a woman who trusted and believed in me enough to allow me the opportunity to further develop my own potential under her guidance and leadership? I agreed to set up and run her new program.

I met with my program's director, informing him I accepted Administrator Kacey's offer. He gave me outward support. However, I sensed he was pissed Administrator Kacey was pulling me. We were rocking and rolling and had developed big plans to take the office to even higher heights. My leaving was a loss, and he knew it. Others knew it too with some whispering the office would likely crash when I departed. However, that was wishful thinking on the part of some haters. I never believed that. He was going to be fine.

I began receiving many well wishes during my last days at the Office of Youth Development Programs, along with a flood of resumes. I would need to fill positions for the new program. Once the new staff was hired, offices secured, supplies, and machinery set up, we officially moved into the numerous bed homeless shelters. Two were in Brooklyn and a third location on Lexington Avenue in Manhattan which was a women's homeless shelter.

The chief shelter, our program's home base in Greenpoint Brooklyn, already had the Department of Homeless Services staff running the show there. We entered the shelter and set up offices as a guest in their home – and to some long-term shelter workers as an "unwelcome guest." They thought we were looking to take their jobs. The place was run by a shelter Director, Deputy Director, and a number of building and program managers. I entered the building with my office assistant, head counselor, and two job developers. We generally got along with everyone, even though the program was seen as stepping on the toes of some people who were officially or unofficially doing the kind of work we had at that time received hundreds of thousands of dollars to do. There was definitely some envy and hard feelings in the air. I simply instructed my staff of the context under which we were working and to be aware of it. However, we would do our jobs in a professional and respectful manner and then let the "chips fall where they may."

We were there to do a good job, and that we would do. My head counselor was a fairly attractive young woman who was a bit naïve to some things, or she simply put on a good front. She was also going through an emotional divorce at the time, so her head wasn't always in the game. I had no say in hiring her because she was given to my program by Administrator Kacey. The shelter was filled with street-minded dudes, cunning from years of living on the streets, using drugs, and going in and out of jail, and employees hardened by working with this difficult client base. They could smell vulnerability a mile away, and they smelled it all over my counselor.

Again, the counselor was fairly attractive and was the type of woman who could thus get your typical "Simp" (simple-minded man, willing to buy a women's affection) wide open and very infatuated. The Deputy Director at the homeless shelter was that typical Simp, and his nose was wide open for this counselor. If she had any game she could have used his Simp affection to help move the program forward, but, although she may have had the will, she apparently wasn't skilled like that.

She was also having major marital problems. Her marriage had to be less than a year old, and it was collapsing. Emotionally, she was a mess on most days. She was definitely in a vulnerable emotional state and a little naive to the games men play. Her own husband allegedly persuaded her to move from her home state where she lived most of her life and relocate as his wife in New York City, after only knowing him for a short period of time. He allegedly made her many promises that didn't materialize. She was heartbroken, sad, and vulnerable, and the wolves and Simps were circling. Her presence, and daily emotional breakdowns, was a major distraction I would need to work through.

The Deputy Director of the shelter had his own office, but he frequently came to my office, which I shared with the head counselor, and would sit and talk to her. I frequently was at the two other sites I was in charge of, one being a large woman's shelter in Manhattan. However, too often, when I returned to the Brooklyn site, the Deputy Director was camped out in my office talking to her and drinking coffee. She was an older woman, about 30 something years old. However, this was her first real counseling position after graduating with her degree, so I gave her some leverage on things she didn't know. I instructed her it was not appropriate for folks to come to the office to hang out, sometimes for hours at a time (he wasn't the only employee who did this) particularly when we had so much work to get done and were already understaffed.

However, in the following days the Deputy Director began giving me massive attitude, short answers to any question I or my staff had and he went out of his way to not speak to me unless his director was around. However, he did stop visiting the office numerous times a day simply squatting for hour-long visits to talk to my counselor.

One day, upon returning to my Brooklyn office from my Manhattan office, the Deputy Director of the shelter was standing in my office while my counselor was on the telephone going absolutely ballistic on somebody, which I later learned it was her husband. She's yelling and screaming at him about being "tired" and that he was a "liar," etc. I calmly walked to the back of the office where my desk was and before I could hang my jacket up, I heard the Deputy Director say, "Let me talk to him." She then actually handed him the phone, saying, "Maybe he'll listen to you." I was stunned. The Deputy Director then proceeded to scream all kinds of things into the phone about how "great" a woman she was and he should be "lucky" to have a woman like her and that the husband was "no kind of a man." He was so rude and disrespectful to this woman's husband, and to my office, and it was out of line. It was even more uncomfortable because I knew her husband and he was actually a stand-up guy. When the Deputy Director hung up the phone, I respectfully, but sternly requested him to leave my office and I closed the door. She and I had to talk. This situation had gotten too ugly and it had to stop. Before I could begin, she broke down crying and went into detail about her marriage and the stress it was causing her. I listened empathetically, but respectfully informed her it was hurting her work and our project. I allowed her to leave for the day and I made a phone call to Administrator Kacey explaining the situation and that this counselor was not getting it done. Administrator Kacey had her removed from the site and relocated to the Manhattan office.

The Simp, Deputy Director, was furious when he found out the counselor was relocated and went ballistic when he saw me for the first time. He demanded to know "why was she transferred," "is she coming back" and why I couldn't just let that incident with her husband "ride." I respectfully told him, "it just wasn't a good fit" and that I couldn't talk to him beyond that about the situation. He informed me that "you'll need us more than we need you, so good luck." I knew what that meant – he would be shifting into full "program block mode," and that's what he did. I was trying to avoid that, which is why I was trying to not have a full-blown fallout with this guy.

Additionally, the counselor, after being transferred, had a meeting with Administrator Kacey claiming that I only pushed for her transfer because I was "jealous of her relationship" with the Deputy Director. She never claimed harassment or anything. However, they were both trying to make it so messy for me that it would question my ability to get the job done. Administrator Kacey was about her money, and the success of the program meant money while failure meant money lost. Administrator Kacey was not going to lose money and everyone knew it. I definitely did.

For months, Administrator Kacey was mentioning that she was going to name a director for the program. My title was coordinator, which meant I made less money than a director and had less control over day-to-day operations of the program than a director would. Administrator Kacey called me into the office and informed me that she was naming a temporary director to run the program, her right hand girl "Laura." She instructed me to fill her in and bring her up to speed and that I would be reporting to her.

Upon seeing in my face that I was disappointed, Administrator Kacey told me that she had faith in me and that if she didn't, she would have demoted me or fired me as she often does to people. However, she informed me that the "ship needed to be righted" and with this guy blocking our every move, she believed that Laura would come in and right the ship. I didn't even argue with her. I understood Administrator Kacey well. She was about results and I had a hiccup that could prevent the results she wanted, so she introduced a new face.

My staff despised Laura. They were still absolutely loyal to me. We had worked fourteen hour days for months, through the summer's blazing heat and winter's freezing cold, to get that program up, running and flourishing, and now it was simply being handed over on a silver platter to someone they did not particularly like or respect. They felt even more slighted than me because they were not even consulted on the choice and they had sacrificed so much, working with me in the trenches to get that program up and running. However, I understood the Administrator's thinking. She and I, in many ways, were similar in that we were both "results-oriented." That means sometimes feelings would be hurt, and in this instance it just happened to be mine and my staff's. The results to that point were great, but I had definitely hit a bump in the road in the form of a Simp. Yet, that Simp was the Deputy Director in the building where we were guests. Yes, it was possible to work around him or get him refocused in time, but Administrator Kacey wanted the ship to keep moving forward now.

"Laura" was a joke to my staff and me. Administrator Kacey was paying her top dollar and her leadership skills were horrendous. She had poor communication skills, no apparent interest in the program, and she frequently was a "no-show," claiming she was in the field doing work for Administrator Kacey. She didn't demonstrate interest in the staff, and I had to actively work to keep the team's morale up and help keep the program moving steadily. We all knew, however, that she was not going to last. She was not accustomed to this environment. It was grunt work to work in homeless shelters with ex-offenders, active drug users, the mentally ill and difficult clients, but I had a team of hard-core loyal grunts working with me, men and women, and we got things done.

Upon Laura's arrival, my staff and I were actually still running the program. My new counselor, an older, no-nonsense Caribbean woman, was running solid workshops, my job-developers were job placing hard-to-place clients, and my office assistant was wearing many hats helping out wherever she could. I was designing and developing workshops, conducting workshops, meeting with clients and program staff, monitoring the program outcomes and writing progress reports as we moved forward. Laura was a straight figurehead.

When Laura left or got pulled after a few months, people believed I would finally be named director. I was hopeful, but not convinced. My attitude was, "We'll see." The program was now flourishing. The "Simp" Deputy Director must have found a girlfriend or something because he calmed down, and everything was smooth. Laura eventually left the program and I was thereafter called to Administrator Kacey's office to discuss the program's future.

When I arrived at Administrator Kacey's office in Manhattan, I immediately knew some nonsense was coming my way. One of Administrator Kacey's personal assistants, a classy young woman who was always in the loop, upon seeing me smiled broadly as usual, then simply dropped her eyes and shook her head in an effort to tell me without actually telling me, "You are about to hear some real bullshit." Administrator Kacey eventually came out and ushered me into her office, saying, "Have a seat." There was an older, fair-skinned man in the office whom I knew to be Administrator Kacey's husband. I had met him on a number of occasions at office parties or while he waited in the car to pick up Administrator Kacey after late nights working in the office.

I didn't know what his business was, but he was always immaculately dressed and freshly groomed with a fresh haircut and his mustache perfectly trimmed. The running rumor was that he was a stay at home husband. Administrator Kacey went on to explain that she was naming him as the new "director" of the program. The program my staff and I had built from scratch again was being handed over on a silver platter to someone else. She said that he had years of management experience and a master's degree from some university. She said that he would be a good fit to run the program and that I should fill him in on all of the particulars when he arrived on site in a few days.

Administrator Kacey struggled to keep a straight face as she ran this nonsense, and she appeared to be braced for a protest, but I said nothing. I simply nodded my head. He chimed in a few words about how much "I've heard about you," and how he's looking forward to "working with you." Again, I didn't say a word. Upon leaving the office, the husband exited first. Administrator Kacey called me back in and closed the door to say that she appreciated my work, but that I was not "academically qualified" for her to promote me to director. She said she encourages all of her workers to enhance their education and that "your time will come." I respectfully informed Administrator Kacey that I had "essentially been running the program all along" and that she "knew that."

Basically, she was putting her husband on, giving him a high-paying position, and I got that. However, there are cool ways you do things and there are trifling ways to do things. This was trifling. I saw right through it, and she knew it. I lost a ton of respect for her that day, and I'm absolutely sure that she knew that too. As I left her office, I knew for sure that this was simply a small incident on my path to ultimate success. Still, I was pissed off. I also knew I had to get off the fence about going back to school for an advanced degree. I was only working with a Bachelor's degree. I honestly didn't believe there was a man on the planet that could head-to-head outwork me, but there were tons of them who could academically outrank me. They had more advanced degrees and, thus, they had an advantage. I knew, that day, that I would have to put that "you are not academically qualified" nonsense to bed. That I knew for sure.

I returned to the Brooklyn office disappointed, and my staff was, too. They believed that I was the person who could realistically keep that program moving forward, and they believed that I had gotten played. When they heard who the new director would be they were floored. It was a real joke and everyone saw right away what was going on. Administrator Kacey had in me a workhorse and I had a kick-butt staff riding with me. So, she figured she could plop her husband in as a figurehead and he would have to do no work because my staff and I had the program running like a well-oiled machine. He would simply sit back and collect a fat check and be as happy as could be.

When he arrived at the office for his first day at work, that's exactly how it played out. Administrator Kacey had arranged before his arrival on site for a huge office to be set up for him with a 32-inch TV, expensive stereo system, computer, laptop, a miniature golf course and golf clubs.

He called me into his freshly prepared "macked out" office and said in a sincere tone, "You've been running this program, you still are running this program, and if you need anything from me, you simply knock on my door." The man didn't want to know anything about the workings of the program. He didn't want a tour of the facility. Nothing.

He did eventually meet with the other staff members that day. Thereafter he returned to his office, closed the door, and that is where he basically stayed, day in and day out – if he showed up at all. Sometimes he would call me to say he was not coming in that day. It really didn't matter because, even when he was at our site, he did not socialize with us and we did not spend time with him. He simply sat in his office with the door closed. However, on occasion he would call a staff meeting and have everyone report to him so he could report back to Administrator Kacey. The situation was comical. We had to actually sit and take this guy seriously as he conducted a meeting. I knew I had to get out.

I immediately began researching Ph.D. programs, in class and on-line. The problem for me was that I was not interested in any of the programs offered. The only advanced degree I was actually interested in was a law degree. However, because I picked up those felonies as a teen-ager, I knew that the "discretion" of the powers that controlled could legally deny me a law license. In that case, I would have a law degree, but not be licensed to practice law. In most states, you have to have a law degree and then be granted your license to practice law, and to actually practice law without a license is illegal. This was a tough decision. All I kept thinking was "would some stupid decisions I made as a teenager haunt me my entire adult life?" The issue of "discretion" has been often unfavorable to me in the past. "Why should I believe it would change in the future?" This was definitely a tough decision. I would have to think about this one.

After talking to friends and family, particularly my father, about my interest in law school, they were universally in support of it. My dad said, "Your convictions were years ago and you were a kid at the time. If law school is what you want to do, go for it." Others, including a few friends in the legal profession, informed me that it would come down to an issue of "discretion" and, with the particulars of my situation, they believed that it "was possible."

"Discretion" definitely was a word that I knew too well. However, I had no desire to earn an advanced degree besides the law degree. I was definitely going back to school. There was no doubt about it. So I decided to put it in "God's hands." I was going to law school. I had previously toyed with the idea of going to law school, even going as far as having taken the law school admissions test (LSAT). However, I didn't follow through.

I began researching the entire law school admissions process in earnest by pulling articles, calling law schools' admissions offices, ordering booklets and talking to other attorneys. The process was grueling, and that was just getting into a school. I also learned that there was no guarantee I would be accepted upon applying. Admission to any law school was based upon a number of factors including undergraduate grade point average, law school admissions test scores, personal statement, references and the age-old "discretion" of the admissions office. Nothing was guaranteed.

I began studying for the LSAT again. The first time I took it I didn't score well, and I honestly was just going through the motions at that time. This time, I was more focused. Kaplan offered a good prep course for close to a thousand dollars. However, you have to "pay to play," so I signed up. I began working on my personal statement, which I heard could make or break an applicant. I wanted mine to be excellent; I definitely knew that it would be "different." I identified my references, some good people I had worked with as a paralegal and in the business world. I secured my undergraduate transcripts, which were decent. My G.P.A. was solid.

I took the LSAT again, and when the scores came back I was not ecstatic. I always scored well in reading comprehension, legal analysis and writing. However, in math or (as on the LSAT) on the "games" section (which to me was like math and useless to test the ability of an attorney) I never scored well. The low score in the games section of the LSAT again depressed my overall score. I was still going forward and I believed everything else I was submitting was solid, although my personal statement, which detailed everything in my life, was so difficult to write that it took forever. I am a very private person and asking me to write and share personal stories from my life was like pulling out teeth with no Novocain. It was extremely difficult. However, once it was done I believed it would, at minimum, make the admissions office give me a closer look.

I applied to a number of law schools – about ten in total and mostly in New York City, New Jersey and Washington D.C. I avoided the Ivy League schools like Harvard, Yale, and Columbia, because my LSAT scores were not high enough to be a serious candidate. I also wanted to do public interest law. The Ivy League schools would give me a solid education, surely, but also a huge financial debt. Those schools could easily leave a person over one hundred thousand dollars in student loan debt. My focus was going to be in the area of criminal law and some personal injury. I was certain that I could get an equally solid education at a less expensive school, particularly when those two areas of law can often be low earning areas of practice, at least for the first few years in the profession. In any area of law, once attorneys make a name for themselves they can make a great living, though that often takes time.

Also, the experiences I was having working for people and getting short-changed, as other people profited, solidified the notion in my mind that I was not going to work for anyone long-term. My long-term plan was to build my own law practice and to hire folks who were ready to put in great work for the clients I had acquired. My focus was to simply get the law degree, get licensed and eventually build my own law practice, not work for a firm. Finally, I didn't think that many people asked Johnnie Cochran before hiring him, "Well, before I retain you, what law school did you go to?" Most people today don't know what law school Johnnie Cochran went to, but they do know that he was a "great attorney."

Weeks went by and I didn't hear anything from a single law school. I did, however, finally receive a call from Rutgers School of Law-Camden, New Jersey, saying that the dean of the school wanted to meet me. I was ecstatic. I was at least going to be given a hearing by the dean and that was more than all right with me. I arranged for a date and time the following week. Upon researching a bit further, I discovered that the law school was way out in New Jersey, a few hours' drive from where I lived. Attending that school would mean relocating to New Jersey or commuting many hours there and home every day. This was not good.

Days before my scheduled meeting with the dean at Rutgers-Camden, I received a letter from Rutgers School of Law School-Newark and from CUNY School of Law, at Queens College, offering me a seat in the incoming class. I was hyped. Both were great schools, but CUNY was a noted public interest law school. Also, it was in Queens, New York, a 30-minute drive from my Brooklyn apartment, and it was the least expensive. Some law schools were nearly double the cost of CUNY. Rutgers-Newark, however was tempting in that I was also accepted into a special assistance program designed to assist more minorities to succeed in their law school experience. Many minorities wash out of law school for a number a reasons.

The program was offering additional tutoring, mentoring and job placement assistance upon completion of law school. It was all tempting. However, in my final analysis I believed that, although all those services were helpful, the benefit of going to CUNY, including location, cost and the school's public interest focus, outweighed the benefits being offered by attending Rutgers-Newark.

I also honestly believed the services offered by Rutgers-Newark were wonderful because many minorities, particularly Black men, are overwhelmed by the rigors and demands of law school. Law school can be extremely demanding in terms of time management, financial stress, mental stress, emotional stress and stress on relationships with family and friends. Each one of the above, or a combination of them all, too often sinks people before they can reach graduation. The dropout rate for all people attending law school, and Black males in particular, is fairly high. I wasn't concerned about any of that. I managed money decently, I managed time well, academics never intimidated me, and I had a Ph.D. in stress management. The services offered by Rutgers were wonderful, but I believed that I didn't desperately need them.

I called the dean's office at Rutgers-Camden and informed the office that I was thankful for the dean's offering to meet with me, but that I was going to accept an offer at a school a bit closer to home.

At the time that I received my admission letter to law school, things at the job were getting crazy and I was thankful that I had made my move. First, the program I was working with was in limbo over what I heard was "financial issues." I didn't see how that was possible because the grant was for substantial money, and looking around at the program expenditures and calculating salaries, I couldn't see where all of the money had gone. If it was true that our program was in trouble over financial issues, I couldn't understand how that could be.

However, Administrator Kacey kept total control over the finances of all her numerous programs, including mine, totaling millions of dollars, and only a very select few people could glimpse the financial standing of any individual program. There were rumors floating around for a few years that there was frequent mismanagement of funds by Administrator Kacey's office, but because she brought in so many millions of dollars and so many people, high and low, were "eating well" from her efforts, no one ever called her on it. Anyway, I never received all the details, but I was told that she was removed from her post. Many of her programs financially collapsed after her departure, including ours.

Administrator Kacey's exit left a big void, shaking up the status quo. Many of her handpicked people, as well as numerous other folks close to her, lost their jobs. Applying for and getting accepted to law school at that time seemed to be good timing for me, although Administrator Kacey's successor and I were pretty cool. He and I had done work together in the trenches during my days working with Medgar Evers youth services programs. He was a rising star at the time and he and I hit it off pretty well.

Law school was calling and I was ready to get started. It began the summer of 1999 with a non-credit summer program at the law school, which was voluntary and designed to introduce minority students to the very different world of law school. The program was great because law school was very different from undergraduate school in terms of how you write, read and analyze facts. There is a formula to what's called "legal writing" which is very different from regular writing and it is difficult for some to manage, let alone master. The basic formula is "issue, rule, analysis and conclusion," (IRAC). Trying to master this way of writing and thinking, when for years (since grade school) you simply wrote what you thought and felt, was unbelievably difficult to many.

Additionally, the sheer amount of work that is given to law students, particularly in the first year, is unbelievable. I describe law school as, "They give you so much work that it is humanly impossible to do it all and then they give you just a little bit more." I always believed the process was designed to "weed out" people, particularly during the first year. That is where many students, and high numbers of minorities, either flunk out or simply say, "Forget this, I quit." The workload, and thus the stress level, is honestly that crazy.

Minority law students often are less equipped to succeed in law school. They often have more pressures than other students for a number of reasons. A big one is not having a support structure that is familiar with the law school process. You have no life, particularly during that first year. Thus, if people around you do not get that "you really have no life" during law school because they never met a law student before, which many in the minority community have not, it strains relationships – often to the breaking point.

Thus, the love of the people around you and their feelings of "abandonment" because they just do not understand your absence, mentally and emotionally, absolutely drain you. Trying to succeed in law school, while being mentally and emotionally drained by feelings of loss or being torn between law school and the people you love, including your girlfriend or boyfriend, mom or other family members, is a recipe for law school failure. Additionally, if you are a minority heading to law school, that means you likely had a certain amount of stability in your life up to that point. You are educated and likely working. In minority communities, quite often, if you are the stable one, you are unfortunately often surrounded by a number of unstable people who lean or depend on you for support either mentally, emotionally or financially – and sometimes all three.

The entering law students from minority communities don't always prepare these dependents for what's coming, which is your absence. This is often because they have absolutely no solid idea what they are about to encounter. They are often the first in their circle of friends to attend law school, and are definitely more likely to be the first in their family to do so.

People from the larger society don't as often enter law school from an unstable and uninformed inner-city environment like many minorities do. They may be as personally stable as minority students, yet not have as many unstable people in their environment mentally, emotionally and often financially depending on them. Also, they often have access to more pre-law prep as to what to expect upon entering law school. Even if they do have the same pressures as inner-city minority students, they can better prep people in their lives as to what the future holds. The real truth, though, is even if you prep the people around you as to what is to come, it doesn't always work. Many relationships still splinter and romantic relationships in particular break during law school, including many marriages.

Finally, many of the minority students enter law school broke or financially shaky. They often still have large financial responsibilities. Upon arriving, I met a number of minority students who were attending law school and holding down full-time jobs. They were often supporting themselves with rent, food, and clothes, and many times also financially assisting their parents or family members who were in financially critical situations. The law school advised that you do not work during the first year of law school and, if so, to work the bare minimum amount of hours per week. Not to work at all was unrealistic for many of the students I went to school with, but particularly for the Black and Latino students. There was some envy, I'm sure, for students who could simply come to school, study all day and night, and not have to work at all because Mommy or Daddy was picking up the large law school bill. However, I didn't meet many Black or Latino students who fell into that category. We all mostly worked, including some full-time which was a recipe for law school failure.

The summer program for minority students at CUNY Law School was designed to address many of the challenging issues that law school would present, as well as to give minority students an introduction to the foreign world that is legal writing and legal analysis. It was a good program and I met a lot of cool people there with whom I would later spend a lot of time when classes officially began just a few weeks later in August 1999.

The first day of class was amazing to me. I was finally there. Being finally there, however, meant being introduced to the full blast of law school. I had four classes the first day of law school and in each class the professor gave numerous pages of reading and writing assignments, much of which was due the next class. Legal reading is not the same as reading your favorite romantic or espionage novel. The material is often extremely dense, requiring many readings of the same paragraph or even the same sentence to figure out what the heck they are really trying to say and how it applies to the overall class assignment. It was so much work that it was impossible to get it all completed on time, but you had to figure out a way to do it. That was part of the law school experience – managing tons of work, yet producing a quality end product.

I arrived at law school for the first day of class around 8:30 a.m., and my last class ended around 5:00 p.m. I arrived home around 6:00 p.m., still giddy about the first day, though less so than when the day had begun. I was now thinking, "How am I going to get all of this dense reading and writing assignments done before class begins at 9:00 a.m. tomorrow morning?" It was virtually impossible to do. However, I had to find a way to get it done. I ate a light dinner, climbed in the bed, pulling a sheet over my head to block out the summer sun which was still in the sky, and I simply went to sleep.

I woke up at around 10:00 p.m., made a strong cup of coffee, put the jazz playing low on the radio, and began reading. I read for hours, nonstop, re-reading where necessary, taking extensive notes, and thoroughly analyzing all that I read. I then began the writing assignments, paying strict attention to the IRAC method, identifying the legal "issue," identifying and explaining the legal "rule," "analyzing" how the rule applied to the issue and facts of the case, and then presenting my ultimate "conclusion." It was painstaking and mentally draining work, and when I looked at the clock it was 6:00 a.m. – and I still had more work to do to be ready for my morning class.

By 7:30 a.m. I had all of the work completed. I took a 20 minute nap, a 10 minute shower, got dressed and was out of the house by 8:20 a.m., and was at school, well prepared at 9:00 a.m. That was how I basically spent the next full year of my life, following that same or similar routine. To this day, as an attorney, I often still follow that routine. I work all through the night to prepare for the following day. My mind has accepted it as normal.

The first year of law school was challenging for me in that it was an extreme adjustment process to the tremendous academic workload. I had been out of school for years. Although a few of my classmates would make comments like "I never see you sweat," the reality was that many of my classmates, besides in class, didn't see much of me at all. My routine was to go home after class, eat, sleep, get up and work through the night. I rarely used the computer labs, study halls, quiet rooms, study groups or the library at the school. I had access to a vast law library database on my home computer, LexisNexis and Westlaw, and there was no place quieter than my home. I lived alone at that time and always maintained a serene atmosphere there. Many students felt that if they left the law school and went home, they would be distracted by family, friends, television, telephones, internet, etc., and no work would get done. Some also believed that there was "strength in numbers" and so as long as they stayed in school around the other students, they were somehow safe from academically drowning. This was definitely not true for me. But whatever people thought, worked, and it made them comfortable, and so they did it.

My family and friends were well prepped on my routine and they did not disturb me, and there was absolutely nothing on the Internet or television that could break my focus. I was going to get this law degree and flunking out of law school was not an option. No way.

Many students also hung around the law school and formed numerous study groups, some large and others small. Study groups didn't work for me because my learning style and my patience level, I realized, was different from many others. First, I asked a ton of questions simply to obtain clarity on basic concepts, so some folks wouldn't always have patience with me. However, since I was a kid I always wanted to know, even when instructed to do something by my parents, "Why"? That is often the critical question for me, and not because I don't understand the legal principle or because I am being difficult, rebellious, or an "asshole," as some may assume by my numerous "why" questions. The "why" always catches my attention because if I can understand the "why" I can then introduce a potentially strong counterargument as to "why not?" This includes counterarguments to my parents' argument as to "why" I must go to bed at 8:00 p.m., or "why" a prosecutor is pushing for jail time for a juvenile on a non-violent first offense allegation.

For example, with my parents, once I understand the "why" they want me in bed at 8:00 p.m., "to get a good night's sleep," I can introduce the counterargument as to "why not," to allow me to stay up to 9:00 p.m., "I don't usually fall asleep until 11:00 p.m., anyway." In the case of a prosecution, if a man gets arrested for the possession of an illegal weapon and the prosecutor is asking for a prison sentence of 3 ½ years, and the man's defense lawyer simply counters with a request for 2 years or even 1 year, I believe the lawyer potentially just did the client a serious disservice. Instead of countering with a request for a lower sentence, I suggest pulling the assistant district attorney aside and simply ask, "Why are you offering 3 ½ years?" Get into the mind of the prosecutor, off the record preferably, and sometimes you'll be shocked at what they will tell you. Things like "that is the standard offer for a weapons possession first offender," it's simply "office policy." Now find out "why" that office policy exists and you potentially have the ammunition to secure for your client no jail time and a community-based program, a program preferably designed to address the policy concerns that gave birth to the 3 ½ year offer policy. I've done it.

For me, knowing "what the law is" is simply never enough. I want to know "why the law is" what it is. That is the critical question for me, because to the shock of some, the "why" of some laws, absolutely do not make sense in the overall context of being "fair" and "just." "The Rockefeller drug laws" and the sentencing guidelines for "crack cocaine versus powder cocaine" are just two examples where the "why" behind the law is extremely nonsensical. Ask any prosecutor in the country "why" either of the laws makes sense and you will be shocked, and possibly appalled, at some of the replies. In fairness to some prosecutors, some of them will honestly tell you that it's an office "policy issue," one with which they personally do not even agree.

I make no argument that my approach to the law is better or worse than anyone else's. It's simply often more critical. That is likely because my natural inclination is to seek thorough understanding of things around me, a trait which I likely got from my mother, and then to seek fair and just resolutions of issues, a trait which I likely got from my father. Finally, my first-hand personal experience with the criminal justice system as a child gave me an inside look at the workings of the criminal justice system. The good, the bad and, yes, the ugly.

I saw first-hand, how some prosecutors, at times, do not even see the person they are prosecuting. All they see is the file that they have in front of them and all that is in it. However, the file often does not tell the entire story. Sometimes you have to look beyond the criminal act and try to get a glimpse of the person, which takes more work. But that is why the role of the prosecutor is so important to the criminal justice process. It is so much easier as a prosecutor to take the approach that "this man or woman stands before the court accused of a bad act, thus, they are a bad person."

I saw first-hand, how judges who are supposed to be the balance keepers within the courtroom can become the drivers of the prosecution and actual bullies in the courtroom. I saw how they can completely take over the prosecution and drive the prosecution to a place where the judge wants it to go rather than where the prosecution believes it should go.

I saw first-hand, how court-appointed attorneys, being too afraid to challenge the court because they are paid by the court, and thus fearful of the scorn of the judge, will tell a client off the record that the "judge has a gripe with you" but will not ask on the record or off the record, "Why?" or simply, "How is the position of the prosecution and the court a position that is just?"

In law school, I usually studied alone. However, I had a number of people at the law school that I liked and respected. There were some really good people there. After the first year of law school was completed, I was fairly sure that I would complete this process no matter how challenging it was at times.

One day, I came to school to find a number of students huddled together and some of them were crying. I asked one, "What's up?" I was informed that a number of students had been put on academic probation and that some others were being kicked out of law school because of poor grades. I felt horrible for them because I knew how difficult the law school admission process was and the sacrifices at so many levels you have to make to get in. However, what really annoyed me, particularly about my law school, was that they sold you a bill of goods about all of the academic support that was available upon admission to the school, but I didn't find that to be true. Not at all.

Parole

In my second year of law school, I was actually still on parole. Parole at that time was so overcrowded that a joke amongst parolees was that as "long as you don't get charged with a serious felony during your first three years of prison release and parole supervision, you will be discharged from parole supervision early." That was basically the truth though. "Early discharge" from parole meant that you no longer had to report to parole offices two or four times a month, be subjected to random drug testing, surprise visits to your place of employment or surprise visits and searches of your place of residence. You basically were free of any form of state administrative supervision. For instance, if a person was released from prison after serving 10 years of a 10-20 year sentence, they still owe the state 10 years of the 20-year sentence and they would serve that last 10 years owed on parole supervision. Now, after three years clean and no major incidents on parole, that same person would almost automatically receive "early discharge" and be free from all supervision to ease the parole supervision overcrowding.

There were parolees who, under normal circumstances, would have never been released early from parole supervision who were being released early. This included career criminals, robbers, rapists, and even a few murderers. Parole at that time was simply that overcrowded and, regardless of one's criminal history, if a parolee basically remained "serious" arrest free for three years upon release from prison, they would receive early discharge from parole supervision. It was virtually automatic.

I would sometimes arrive at the massively crowded parole office in downtown Brooklyn (I had moved to Brooklyn so my reporting office and parole officer had changed) and I would sit there literally for hours.

During my many hours' wait at the Brooklyn Parole Office to be called by my new parole officer, Officer Lower, I would meet old acquaintances from prison and be told of all the criminal activity in which they were still engaged. I received numerous offers from them for me to "get down" with their cliques. I respectfully declined. I watched as parolees arrived at the parole office hopping out of fancy cars (BMWs and Mercedes Benzes) filled with hood cats drinking liquor and smoking weed while blasting hard core hip hop music from their expensive car stereos. I listened as parolees plotted their next moves (some legal, many illegal) as they and I waited to be called into the office by our parole monitoring officers. It was getting late and I likely would miss another of my law school classes if I waited any longer, but I had to sit it out. I simply had to wait.

This new parole officer, Officer Lower, was a piece of work and the total opposite of the parole officer I was assigned to in Queens, Officer Smith. Officer Smith was a professional and loved to see parolees do right and would actually encourage and assist them as parole officers are actually supposed to do. Officer Lower, on the other hand, didn't encourage parolees at all. In fact, he came across as a hard-core "hater." His attitude towards me from our initial meeting and his reviewing my file was that, "Yeah you are out here making positive moves, but still I will lock you up with pleasure if you slip up." He never gave a word of encouragement. It was always a position of I am your "adversary" not a supporter. It was a hostile and tension-filled introduction which increased in intensity as the months passed.

At one time, I had been on parole for over four years and I didn't smoke, drink or use drugs. I had been gainfully employed for most of the years I had been released from prison and my take home pay, when employed, was close to what the salary of most of the parole officers in that office at the time were earning, or higher. As a convicted man, or a prisoner, I've always looked any man in the eye (inmates, correctional staff, and the warden) because I never felt any less than any of them. I noticed this tendency of mine often garnered admiration from some, but often animosity from others. This tendency, and some of my other personality aspects, extremely disturbed the new parole officer. He saw me as "full of myself" and was determined to take me down a few notches. My thoughts about him were "in your dreams," and that was the nature of our relationship.

Some of the women parole officers in the Brooklyn office wouldn't openly speak up when they noticed that my parole officer was actively giving me a hard time. However, they would make comments when I came to the office, like "keep your head up." One attractive dark-skinned female parole officer, any time she saw me enter the crowded parole office, would excitedly summon her attractive female friend, another parole officer, and they would simultaneously say, "Hi, attorney," in an exaggerated song like fashion, all with sincere and open respect. My parole officer hated that shit, and he tried hard (but unsuccessfully) not to show it in his envious ass face. He was a super-sized hater.

I am sure other parole officers in the office were aware of the nonsense he was putting me through, yet nobody got involved. Many other parolees at the office definitely knew what was going on. Some were shocked that I was even still on parole, after almost five years of being released without incident. Whether incredulous or shocked at the treatment I was receiving or not, I was definitely interesting talk among the parolees at that office – no doubt about it.

The power of the parole officer is tremendous in the life of a parolee under their supervision. The parole officer can positively encourage and support the efforts of the parolee, or they can refuse to do so. Additionally, they can actively introduce stress levels to the parolee's life in a number of blatant or subtle ways. So much so that the parolee can literally crack under the stress of having a parole officer that clearly wants them to fail. Some actually do crack under the pressure. Parole is extremely stressful enough. Just walking down the street and hoping not to be falsely or mistakenly accused of a crime can weigh heavily on a parolee's psyche. Additionally, the constant idea that one slip up, even a minor one (i.e., not being able to find or maintain a job), can lead to a parole violation and a return to prison, and losing all that you love, including family and your freedom, can simply be overwhelmingly stressful.

Combine that with the knowledge that your parole officer hates the sight of you, and you have stress levels that could crack anybody. Any parolee will admit that the monthly visit to his or her parole officer, even if the parole officer is cool as heck, can be the most stress filled day of one's life, even if you walk in that office as squeaky clean as can be. If your parole officer is walking around with a constant "hard-on" for you, it can make a parolee's life a psychological hell.

Initially, I actively worked to win this parole officer over. I was always polite, even as he went out of his way to annoy and be openly disrespectful in tone with me. Also, he would pop up frequently at my apartment early in the morning, or late at night to "see how you are doing." He would pass his "parole officer" card to my landlord, or to the other tenants in my building if I wasn't around, and tell them to tell me, "I dropped by." He had my school class schedule and he would occasionally call me to the office on days I had class and then keep me in his office waiting for hours to be seen by him. Then he would call me into his office after waiting for hours, ask me one or two questions like "How you doing?" and then say, "Have a nice day." Now, I have to hustle across town in an effort to get to class on time, and I'm sure that made his day.

When I hit the three-year mark on parole, I began inquiring to him about my eligibility for early release from parole. Most parole officers at that time were desperately looking for people to release from their caseload, and usually the release was automatic after three years of parole supervision without serious incidents. He would say, "I will start the process. I will get to it." That was the line he gave me again and again, but he truly wanted me to suffer. He did not want to see me released from parole no matter how well I was doing. As long as I was under his supervision, as far as he was concerned, I would remain on parole. When he finally, put the request in it was denied on a technicality that he was aware of and thus he knew it would be denied. So, I had to wait for him to re-submit the paperwork, he took his sweet time.

The tricky part about parole is, "how do you complain about your parole officer?" and "to whom do you complain?" If I complain to his supervisor, it is going to be "game on" if his supervisor is not a moral and ethical individual. My assumption was that he or she probably was not. That was simply coming from my experience of dealing with so-called "criminal justice professionals," a good number of them were morally and ethically challenged – even the supervisors. If my assumption was correct, and the supervisor is a piece of work, then I will likely be on the "hit list." I understood the game. However, after many months of taking this P.O.'s nonsense, and walking around stressed out, I said, "I can't take anymore." My stress level was that high and my tolerance and patience were both gone.

I sent a letter to my P.O. asking about the early release. I began the paper trail, detailing the many times he told me that he would "begin the process," yet nothing had apparently been done. After he responded negatively to the letter, claiming "I've been busy," I forwarded a copy to his supervisor and enclosed a separate letter to the supervisor respectfully asking for an "inquiry." The parole supervisor was a real piece of work. He was a short, dark-skinned, Black dude with dead eyes. Before he said a single word upon his calling me into his office, I knew that I had to watch my words. I knew that, if I got out of that office, that night, without handcuffs on, it would be a miracle. Additionally, if I did get out of that office, without being arrested, I would definitely have to watch my back. My days as a free man would likely be numbered.

I knew this man, the parole supervisor, on sight. I had met him (rather, people like him) many times before. He hated me and everybody like me and, if one probed deeply enough, he likely did not feel good about himself. He was a company man and although he had a fancy title, "Parole Supervisor," he didn't give two cents about me. This man standing before me was going to co-sign my parole officer's un-ethical behavior with not just "a nod and a wink," but he would now actively support any move made against me. That's how I read it. There was nothing moral or ethical about this man that I could see, in his eyes or on his face. Nothing. What I saw standing before me was a weak, little man that someone had unfortunately blessed with power. I knew him well and I knew that he had the potential to be as treacherous as they come, and so, I would walk easy. I knew all this about this man before he said a single word.

He introduced himself and then immediately began trying to spin me with nonsense. He told me what a "great" parole officer I had and that I was "lucky" to have him. The P.O. then enters the room and both he and the supervisor are speaking in hostile tones, apparently trying to get me to respond out of turn so they can throw the cuffs on me. I don't take the bait. I yes sired and no sired them to death in the most measured and respectful tones possible. I knew if I got out of that office that evening I would be on borrowed time. I had to, first, just get out of there. After it became obvious that all of their yelling, taunting and hostility was not moving me, they relented and told me that I was "free to go." They told me that they would submit the paperwork to have me released from parole when they had "got the time."

I walked out of that office feeling many things, and anger was surely one of them. They were bullies, yet they were both punks. Since the time I was a kid, I despised bullies. Particularly bullies who, at their core, were punks. Most bullies are actually really big fucking punks. Both these men were just that – bullies and punks. However, I always stood up to bullies and this would be no different. I was going to hit back at these dudes, and then "what will be, will be."

When I arrived at home that evening, I began to formulate a plan of action. I knew for sure that if they weren't treacherous enough to straight set me up, that every time I entered that office they would like-ly be very confrontational. I knew for sure that I had to wrap this pa-role stuff up before my next scheduled visit to that office, which was in approximately 30 days. I thought it out and then contacted the people who I believed could assist. First, I had to shine light on the abuse of authority that was going on at that parole office. I learned a long time ago that people are less likely to abuse their authority if they believed the "world is watching." So, I began a letter-writing campaign with myself, my dad and other family members sending out numerous letters to the New York State Governor's office and to the New York State Division of Parole Commissioners' Office in Albany, New York. Then, I followed up with numerous orchestrated phone calls.

The communications to these offices detailed the actions of my parole officer in the Brooklyn parole office as well as the supervisor's, including their attempt to provoke me when I simply dared to ask for an "inquiry" into my parole officer's actions. The letters and calls went on to detail the tremendous effort that I was making to "do the right thing" upon being released onto parole supervision, and the tremendous energy my parole officer was exerting trying to "frustrate" my efforts. Finally, the letters explained that we were looking for intervention and simply for a "fair hearing," and that we believed they could accommodate that humble request and that the letters being drafted to the press detailing the actions of the New York State Department of Parole "need not" be forwarded. They didn't want the embarrassment of reporters inquiring as to why an inmate working on his law degree, with a sparkling post-release record, was being kept on parole supervision and denied early release, while repeat violent offenders and others with extensive criminal histories, were being virtually kicked off of parole.

Responses from the Commissioner's Office came within days of the letters and calls to their office. I was informed by the Commissioner's Office that my parole officer had been contacted, my concerns had been discussed with him, and that he would be contacting me within the week concerning the preparation of the paperwork to have me released from parole. The parole officer called me days later to inform me he was submitting the paperwork to have me released from parole supervision. He again called me days after that to inform me that my paperwork for "release from parole had been approved." I said, "Thank you." I had nothing else to say, nor did he. I never stepped foot in that office again. What a feeling.

Upon entering my second year of law school, I began aggressively exploring different areas of law beyond criminal law and personal injury. There were a number of student clubs and legal clinics at the law school where students interested in particular areas gathered to talk about legal issues in that area, from entertainment law clubs to Christian law clubs. I connected with the entertainment law club. I knew so many people from my nightclub connections, particularly looking to enter the entertainment arena, mostly as producers, singers, promoters and rappers. I knew I could be an asset to that community. I soon thereafter landed a summer internship at Loud Records, an affiliate of Sony Records. I worked closely with the head attorney assisting in reviewing contracts and drafting contracts, collaboration agreements and licensing agreements, which was very enlightening. I learned a lot more about contract law and was not surprised how the business aspect of the entertainment industry can be overwhelming to an artist if they are not fairly well versed in the law.

I learned from reading and socializing more often with industry people that the record deals, if a person doesn't know what they are doing, can be akin to servitude. The record labels will own them. The upfront money that many labels give is simply a loan and that money must be "recouped," meaning paid back to the lender, the record label. Additionally, some signing contracts mandate that the artist pick up the bill for most of their expenditures and, thus, the artist's upfront money can be gone very quickly. Yet, they still are indebted to the record label for that money loaned. Additionally, some labels' standard contracts were locking the artist into six or more albums before they could be a "free agent." That's a whole bunch of albums and most artists aren't "hot" long enough to produce six albums that sell, and then break free from the label to make tons of money on their own. Within that time frame of six albums, the labels, based upon the structure of the contracts, generally get paid top dollar off of all record sales while the artist sometimes is barely getting by.

My office at the record label internship was right next to Chris Lighty's office – a major player in the hip hop music industry. I would often sit and kick it with him about law school and music and he seemed to be one of the most real people in the world. I respected him a great deal because this guy was doing it at a young age. He had money, power and influence and yet he was always so down to earth with his dealings with me. He was never a "funny-style" type dude. I was shocked to hear some years later that he had apparently committed suicide. It appeared to me that he had it all. That young man was doing it for real and I admired him a great deal.

Everyone else at the record label was cool too, from the A&R to the attorney I worked with, as well as the cool and gorgeous personal assistants. They always gave a brother much love. I believe they honestly respected how I was working diligently to get my weight up, and they knew that I was serious about getting it done. However, some of the other interns were mostly very young, corny law school dudes from around the country. I didn't mess with those dudes unless absolutely necessary. One intern, however, was really cool. I believe he was out of Rutgers School of Law-Newark, and he actually was the one who introduced me to the head attorney at the label who then gave me the summer internship. In listening to the other interns though, I believed they didn't really respect the artists because they believed many of the artists didn't understand the business aspect of the music industry and the artists were often belittled by them.

The reality, though, is that artists are artists. They are creative and they are not attorneys or accountants. I respected the artists because, just as they don't do law, I don't sing, dance, rap or produce. They have their personal form of genius. I don't look down on any person because they don't know what I know, so that was some real sucker stuff that I couldn't get with. However, it is true that if a person is going to enter into the business of music, it is mandatory that they get a basic understanding of the business angle. Also, I'd suggest getting a good lawyer to consult with as they move forward. Put the attorney on retainer (on call) to be their advisor so that they can focus on the art while the attorney watches their back.

I also learned from that internship that I didn't have the passion for entertainment law. I liked it, but I didn't love it. The contracts piece, in particular, I thought was not challenging for me. It was too much, the same work every day. However, I definitely pondered bringing a quality entertainment lawyer into my office when I got established. They could handle affairs for artists and I would supervise that work, ensuring it was done to the highest standard that I would set for any law work that had my law office name on it. There seemed to be a definite need for good attorneys in that area, particularly with the quickly changing landscape of the entertainment world and, more particularly, in the music industry.

By the beginning of my third year of law school I was ready to get it over with. I was ready for graduation. I met a fellow law student, who was two grades ahead of me during my first semester in law school (she was in her third year and about to graduate). She told me that she had begun studying for the bar exam as her third year of law school had begun. This was different from most law students who mostly concentrated on bar prep at the end of third year of law school, usually after graduation. She said that many people began bar exam preparation at the end of law school. However, she felt that then only gave them two months to get ready for the bar exam. Law school ended that May and the bar exam is administered that July.

She then claimed, "That was why so many people failed the bar exam. They began studying too late." Her position was that "The only exam that mattered in law school was the bar exam." Why, she asked, were so many students busting their butts in third year in the classroom, but then going into the bar exam unprepared and then failing it? "High classroom grades won't help you on the bar exam," she said. I liked her thinking, although it was far from traditional. Still, I too, began studying for the bar exam during the beginning of my third year of law school. I didn't wait until the end of the third year. I maintained my grades for third year, but my mental energy was split between classroom work and the bar exam prep.

The bar exam was a monstrous exam. It was six hours long for two days in succession. Many folks had to take the exam more than once in order to pass it. Some never actually passed it, even after multiple attempts. I was determined not to be one of those folks. My position was, "I am taking the bar exam one time." That was the promise I made to myself.

During third year of law school, I began studying practice bar exams. I did practice questions, doing a minimum of twenty-five multiple choice questions a day, and then moving up to fifty questions a day. I then added practice essays into the equation. I was studying for the bar exam a minimum of two hours a day, every day for most of my third year of law school, while also studying for the required coursework that was mandated for third year law students. I do not know if any other students were taking that approach, but I didn't meet any, and most who knew of my approach were not in agreement. They mostly felt that the workload for third year law students was heavy enough and that any other distraction could be disastrous. I simply disagreed.

My grades during my last year of law school were not super. However, in my mind, from third year forward, "the only exam that mattered" to me was the bar exam. The bar exam was the ultimate test to determine if a person had the requisite legal knowledge and skills for admittance into the legal profession. I definitely passed all of my classes during my third year and completed all required coursework and was absolutely cleared for graduation.

Many have said that "the stress of law school can work havoc on a romantic relationship," and many relationships and marriages fail during law school attendance. That is true from what I saw. However, I also believe that the high stress levels, the long hours, days and weeks of students working closely together, also builds relationships, and people often "hook up" under those stressful circumstances. There was a lot of "hooking up," both long-term and short-term relationships during law school. I did some "hooking up" too. During my second year of law school I met another law student, Denise, and she and I eventually "hooked up."

I was taken by her looks. She was beautiful and she was simply so different from most of the women I was meeting day-to-day that it was extremely refreshing. She was open, honest, warm and kind-hearted, giving, trusting, and at times, to the extremes. She gave so much of herself to others that her law school grades were actually suffering. I tried telling her that "you have to be a little more selfish and handle your personal business rather than trying to fix everyone else's business." She tried to educate me, saying, "You have to be more giving. You have so much to offer to the world." We kept the relationship quiet throughout the school because we both were fairly private in most of our personal affairs.

Graduation day came and I was hyped. I got "fly," "dressed-to-impress" for graduation. It was a big deal, no question. My dad was very happy too. Graduation day was great. Denise was there, along with my family members and a number of friends. Law school was an amazing experience. However, saying "so long" to law school and friends I had made there was not too difficult to do. I was ready to move on. I definitely knew that I would see many of my law school buddies at different times and places during our careers. But right now, it was time to refine my preparation for the bar exam. I was extremely focused.

I had been studying for the bar exam for almost a year before graduating law school in May of 2002. The bar exam was scheduled for July 2002. Yet again, many students hadn't picked up a single bar exam review book until after graduation. That gave them only two months to prepare for the exam. The exam was a monster. It tested proficiency in so many areas of the law including, but not limited to, criminal law, matrimonial law, property law, contracts, torts, wills, trust and estates. It was an extremely intimidating exam and some of my law school buddies were understandably stressed.

I decided to put together a bar review schedule that I believed would definitely have me prepared to crush that exam. I believe that most people did the same. My plan was to study a minimum of ten hours a day, every day, for the next two months. I believed that if I still were to fail the exam after that kind of intense preparation, then maybe I needed to find some other career interest. However, instead of working through the night as I generally preferred, I decided to set up my study as if it were a 9-to-5 job, with some over-time. I began studying at 9:00 a.m. until 1:00 p.m., usually taking lunch at that time. I then resumed studying from 2:00 p.m. until 6:00 p.m. Thereafter, I would sometimes grab a bite to eat, make phone calls, hit the gym, kick it with friends and family, and then resume study from 10:00 p.m. to 12:00 a.m. After 12:00 a.m., I laid out my study plan for the next day, took my shower and hit the bed. That was basically my daily routine for the entire two months following my law school graduation.

The summer of 2002 was hot outside. It was definitely not easy forsaking the entire summer to study for an exam, and some law students refused to consistently do it. A number of my classmates would call me or email me extending invitations to attend some party or event, which I always declined. Others went to seemingly every "hot" summer event around the city, with some even attending events out of state. I understand that it is difficult to forsake an entire summer by spending it indoors studying. The summer is where it is at for many people. I once-upon-a-time had missed twelve summers straight. I was locked down in state prison, so I got it. I definitely understood how difficult it was to be out of the mix for an entire summer. However, for me, sacrificing a single summer for the accomplishment of a lifetime was well worth it. So that summer was sacrificed – you have to "pay to play".

The Bar Exam

THE DAY BEFORE THE BAR exam, I got sick. I never get sick, but when it comes, it sometimes comes hard. It came hard. I caught a fever that was raging and then alternatively the chills. Every single t-shirt I would put on, within minutes, was so soaked with sweat that it appeared that I had just climbed out of the ocean. I would wring the ocean of sweat out of it and put on a dry one. Within minutes, the same exact thing would occur. No food I ate would stay down – it came gushing out within minutes of consuming. This continued throughout the night and into the day of the bar exam. I may have slept for two hours during that night. I probably should have visited the hospital. I had no energy, a raging fever, and could barely walk. Water wasn't even staying down. I was sick.

I appeared at the bar exam location looking and feeling "out of it." Some noticed but I downplayed it, no excuses, I was rocking this exam. There appeared to be a few hundred people at the testing site. Law students from all of the major law schools from around the entire country were there. The testing site was the Jacob Javits Convention Center in Manhattan, New York. I had been there previously on a few occasions, for the New York Car Show and the "Black Expo," but this was different. I had to rock this exam. They gave us seating and, just my luck, I was seated next to a "pencil-tapper." A young lady annoying as heck, and for whom I felt very sorry because when the exam began, she had a panic attack and "freaked out." They had to escort her out of the exam room.

I was touched by her nervous energy for a second, so when the exam began I couldn't fully focus for a few moments. All sorts of things were running through my mind. I was drawing a blank. Also, I wasn't feeling internally strong. I felt completely out of it with no energy, but I quickly recovered and, opening the exam, I quickly scanned it. The exam was part multiple choice questions and essays. The first couple of questions stumped me, I had no idea what they were asking, so I passed them up, left them unanswered. However, by the time I hit the fourth or so question, I knew the answer unequivocally. There was no doubt that I had gotten it correct. The subsequent 10 or so questions were the same thing. I was absolutely certain about them. I then returned to the first three that had stumped me and they were clear to my mind – I actually did understand them and I answered them. I believe my nerves had blocked out the answer during the first read. There were 50 multiple choice questions on that exam testing areas of New York law. By the time I reached the end of the exam, I was confident that I may have gotten a hand full of them incorrect, but that was about it.

I turned to the essays and began writing them out. I recall while in law school there was a professor who taught New York practice, civil law and rules of New York, and he was known as a great instructor. In fact, it was said that he sometimes gave his class for the final exam practically the exact essay that often appeared on the bar exam. I was skeptical about that because the bar exam questions are closely guarded. That was definitely a coincidence, even if it was true. However, I had taken his class my last semester of law school two months earlier and I remembered working on that final exam like it was yesterday. One of the bar exam essays were almost exactly on point with the professor's final exam. I was ecstatic, and I crushed it. The other essays, I understood each of the issues, related the law well and I wrote strong essays. Nothing on the exam stumped me. I was confident that I didn't just pass the first day's portion of the bar exam, but I was sure that I crushed it.

The first day of the exam was 6 hours long with an hour lunch break. Some went to lunch, and some grouped up to discuss the questions on the exam. I walked to a quiet area and found a bench, laid out and fell asleep. When I awoke, I was drenched in sweat, shivering and still out of it. Still, I got through the day, arriving home later that day feeling okay. Tomorrow we all would return to the test site for part two of the exam. I had to get some sleep or I was not going to make it there. I drank some water and some juice, but it came right back up. I went to bed.

The next morning, I was actually feeling a bit better. I drank some juice and it stayed down. That was a good start. I arrived at the testing site and I was ready to go. They handed out the second part of the bar exam which was 200 multiple-choice questions. They were easy to me. I actually finished the exam early with time to spare. I used that time to review some questions that I may have rushed through. In preparation of the bar exam, I had literally done thousands of practice questions. I wasn't just prepared for the bar exam, I was borderline "over-prepared." Therefore, I more feared missing the obvious by overthinking a question than I feared being asked a question that I did not know.

The day was over, the exam was done and I was happy to have it behind me. I chilled a little with some folks from my law school after the final day of exam, just talking and reviewing some of the questions. A number of my classmates assumed they had failed the exam and others weren't sure. I didn't want to come across as cocky, but I knew I had passed that exam and would be shocked if I didn't. "We'll see." The results would not be in for the July exam until mid-November, right before Thanksgiving. Until then, I still had some summer left and I was ready to get to it.

Employment

W ith law school behind me, I had to now prepare for the world of work. I had to make a living. I only had a few places where I genuinely wanted to work. My goal always was to open my own law practice. I didn't plan on working for anyone, not long-term anyway. Before I could kick my job search into full gear, and only days after the bar exam, I bumped into my old buddy from Medgar Evers College, the Director of Youth Services Programs. He informed me that he was stepping down from that post and that Administrator Kacey was gone. Her replacement, Allen, was looking for a new director. He went on to say that he suggested me and that Allen, who had worked with me before, concurred. He said that they had actually been searching for my contact information for the past week or so.

This was totally unexpected. I wanted to practice law full-time and if I hooked up with Allen, running Youth Services for the college, the best I could do would be part-time law work. I would have to think about this one, but I passed him my number and said, "Tell Allen to call me." Allen called me the following day and we met up within days of that call. Allen was a huge Caribbean man, a fairly young guy, and close to 400 pounds. He was funny, friendly and very likeable. I always personally liked him a great deal. Allen was also well respected in the youth services community in Brooklyn, New York, and he ran numerous Youth Services sites from Beacon programs to a number of on- and off-campus youth services programs. He was also rumored to be on the fast track to a vice president position at Medgar Evers, with a potential $160,000 salary and, as importantly to him, almost complete control of the millions of dollars in grant money held by the college.

Allen confirmed all of the above and he told me that the office of Youth Services was the flagship of his programs and a favorite of the College President. He said with that program in good hands and flourishing, and all other things flowing smoothly, the president would definitely tap him for a dean's position and thereafter a Vice President post. He said from there, if I were to assist, I would be properly compensated and that I would have a friend in him for life. I told him, "We are already friends, Allen, so just focus on the compensation part." He laughed.

I asked what he needed from me and how I could assist? He went on to tell me that he needed me to get control of the Youth Services office and take it to another level. He said that he understood that when the bar exam results came and I got sworn in as an attorney that I would want to practice law full-time. I stressed that point as well. He told me that if I could give him a one-year commitment, that he would make it worth my while, including basic autonomy to run the office as I pleased and with minimum intrusion from him and absolutely none from anyone else.

He told me that he didn't micro-manage. I would have my private office and sufficient staff, so as long as the program flourished, he didn't care about the time I came to work, went home, or took lunch. He said that I could set my own weekly schedule. He said he simply wanted results and subsequently that "promotion to Vice President." That was all good to hear and although I am a workaholic and I rarely take time off, I do enjoy sleeping late to recharge my battery at times, and so, the ability to make my own schedule was definitely good to know.

I asked Allen, "What is the salary?" He said that it was posted at $50,000, but he possibly could squeeze out $55,000. I told him that was insufficient and that for a director's position with my experience and education that was absolutely unacceptable. He went on to tell me that was the locked-in salary, but if I stayed past the first year, he could definitely move the salary significantly higher for the second year and even higher if I stayed beyond that.

Finally, he said there was a "travel budget" for the office. Allen knew that I liked to travel. The travel budget allowed for the Director to attend an array of Youth Services events held all around the country, including Hawaii, Puerto Rico, California, Miami, and Disney World – everywhere. He said the events were fully paid for, including top hotels, meals, and land travel once I landed in the city of choice. He said that he would approve any events of my choosing. I was definitely warming up to the idea.

The starting salary of $55,000 was actually more than most newly hired attorneys in the public interest arena were being paid at that time. The Legal Aid Society and the District Attorney's office were only around $48,000. Although $55,000 was less than I would have wanted, the other perks, including setting my own work schedule and no micro-management, were definitely a stress reliever that I could live with for a year or so. I could also do part-time law work to supplement my income and get it done around my flexible work schedule. However, full-time law practice would be out of the question. I also loved Youth Services, so Allen definitely had my attention.

Finally, I was pretty certain that I had passed the bar exam so that wasn't a real consideration. However, if I actually passed the bar, but was refused a license to practice law based on the issue of "discretion" (I had a felony conviction as a teenager), I would then actually need a job outside of the legal profession. So, I thought, if that were to occur and I was denied a license to practice law, even after passing the bar exam, and then I lost on appeal of that denial, I could then lean on Allen, who would eventually be Vice President, to support my bid for one of those non-legal, $100,000-plus management jobs at the college. My credentials would be in order, having recently earned a law degree. Also, getting "director" experience on my resume, as well as a vice president indebted to me, was definitely a feasible "back-up" plan if, by chance, entry into the legal profession was somehow blocked.

This lengthy meeting, between Allen and me, took place in Allen's "Youth Services" van as it sat parked across the street from Medgar Evers College. I told Allen that I would get back to him in the morning. I slept on it after conferring with a few trusted friends, each who supported my accepting of the offer. I contacted Allen the next day to inform him that "I would do it." He thanked me with real sincerity in his voice. This really meant a lot to him. I asked him, "What's next?" Allen said that I would get a call from the interviewing committee to set up an interview date. He told me that others would be interviewing for the position as well and that the committee I would be meeting with would pick the best candidate. Allen informed me, "You are the best candidate."

He explained, and I agreed that, I had been previously the Deputy Director of the office and was very familiar with the full running of the office. I had, in fact, assisted in the design of the office's programs and procedures. Additionally, I was very familiar with all of the legal requirements related to the grants, as well as all the offices and affiliated personnel connected to the program, including on- and off-campus and I still had great relationships with them all. I could definitely "hit the ground running." Academically, I had a J.D. (a doctorate degree in law), which would be comparable or higher than any other applicant. There was no one interviewing who compared. I was offered the position.

After the interview was completed, Allen called me to say "Congratulations."

I said, "Thanks." I asked, "When do I start?"

He said, "ASAP."

I told him, "I'm ready".

I appeared at the office for the first day to be introduced to my office staff and the college community as the new Director of Youth Services programs at Medgar Evers College. I was happy and anxious to get started. My staff for the academic year, September to June, was small with two full-time counselors, an office assistant, and around six part-time tutors. However, the summer program, from June through August, was different. My office hired and supervised over one hundred people.

Upon meeting and talking to the staff, I thought they were too young and inexperienced in life to offer the young people in our program the level of services I envisioned. Another thing was, upon meeting one-on-one with both of the counselors, it appeared that they were both recently out of college and were just passing through. They had no apparent long-term interest in that office. I was thankful that they would eventually be moving on because they were definitely not what I needed to push the office to a higher level.

Soon thereafter, Allen sent over a counselor from one of his other programs to assist me. He was a hardworking, smart, no nonsense thirty-something year old African guy. I was thrilled with him. He was the stereotypical African dude, hard-working to the extreme and no nonsense. I liked him a lot. His work ethic was amazing. He would stay in that office 14 hours a day, sometimes, if that was what it took to get a project completed. That's always how I approached work and I loved it. He did his work with a focused determination. Simply "get the job done," forget about the clock or that the sun was going down, or the sun was coming up. The work has to be done. That's the kind of worker that I was looking for.

Often, particularly when I first came on as director, I would be in my office working past 10:00 p.m., after arriving at 8:00 a.m., when most of the other offices around the college were closed at 5:00 p.m. Sometimes, when I was leaving the office after 10:00 p.m., my African counselor would still be in his office working on something he and I had discussed earlier. We'd just look at each other and laugh.

My counselor and I together had that office jumping in no time flat. Our program was soon the envy in the Youth Services community and we excelled in numerous metrics, including popularity among students, enrollment numbers, parent and community support and completely fulfilling our grant-mandated obligations. Our program was shining. Allen too was happy. He was, as predicted, promoted first to Dean and then to Vice President. Allen was thereafter received into the tight inner-circle of the President of Medgar Evers College, who happened to be undoubtedly one of the most influential Black men in all of New York City – most definitely in Brooklyn, New York. People now spoke Allen's name in whispered tones. Allen was "the man," and he loved it.

The Character and Fitness Committee

I RECEIVED A LETTER FROM the "Character and Fitness Committee" saying that I was to report to the Character and Fitness Committee to be interviewed for possible admittance to the New York State Bar, the state's attorney licensing board. Upon receiving the letter, I had a rush of mixed emotions. I thought about my childhood and being confused about the world around me and where I fit in. I thought about the mistakes I had made in life and the severe punishments I received for those mistakes. I thought about the tortured journey I had traveled to reach a level of self-understanding and understanding of the world around me. I thought about my parents and the hope and faith they had in me to be the best person I could be, even after all I had experienced as a youth, and likely even with the perceived shortcomings they had as parents. They couldn't always supply the things I craved. I thought about my new friends, all of whom were rooting for me to be successful in this second chance at life. Finally, I thought about what happens if, after all this struggle, strife and long journey to this point in life, the issue of discretion doesn't go my way, and I am ultimately denied a license to practice law in the state of New York. Life is funny sometimes, I thought. So, I would simply put this in the Lord's hands. I said a short prayer.

The hearing officer was an elderly attorney who looked as if he had seen and heard it all. I definitely could not sell him some sob story or spin him. That was fine because I had no intention on spinning him, nor anybody else. I was going to speak from my heart and tell him all he wanted to know and if that wasn't good enough, then so be it. The attorney had in his possession my entire file – the ups, the downs, the highs and the lows. He had it all. This interview, therefore, was simply an attempt to look me in the eyes and get a glimpse of my heart. He wanted to see all that which wasn't in the file, and I surely was going to let him see it. There was nothing to hide.

I intended to tell him where I grew up and how I grew up and all of the influences of the mean streets that grabbed a hold of me at a very early age. I intended to tell him about my parents, who worked such long hard hours to simply keep the lights on, that they couldn't completely monitor all that I did – the good, the bad and the silly. I would tell him about the influences of close friends and elders whom I admired dearly, and of my failures to be able to accurately analyze that these people were not appropriate for a youth's admiration. I would tell him how I drifted into a life of crime and the subsequent incarceration that followed. I would tell him how I nearly lost my life on occasion after occasion while incarcerated and how actually facing potential death, as well as intense introspection, during many months of solitary confinement, as well as a return to God (as stereotypical as it may sound), definitely saved my life. I would tell him how I read my first book while behind bars and then went on to earn my GED, a paralegal certificate and three college degrees. I would tell him how I turned away from idolizing the streets and discovered that an entirely new world beyond the streets existed. I would tell him that I understood the character of a good man and that was the character that I grew into after years of struggle against myself. I would tell him that I wanted to give back and, through law, which I had a talent for, I believed I could do that. All that I intended to tell him, I basically did. However, I left the interview feeling that maybe I could have said more.

Still, I knew that he was a man of faith – a different faith than me, but still a man of God. I also knew that there is only "one God" and that

God was in that room watching over both of us. Of that I was certain. I trusted God with all my heart and all of my soul, and I believed that if this was a righteous man sitting before me, and I sensed that he was, then I was sure that he would see the sincerity in me, even if I didn't say all of what could have been said. I put my faith in that God.

He simply ended the interview by firmly shaking my hand and informing me that I would receive a correspondence from the committee. He gave me neither a decision nor any indication of what that decision would be. This will be a nerve-wracking wait.

Back To Work

WHILE WAITING FOR THE DECISION from the committee, I buried myself into my Youth Services_work, developing the best youth services programs I could produce. My office serviced a number of area public schools, both middle and high schools, providing a list of services including academic support, tutoring, college prep, SAT prep, financial aid counseling, grant and scholarship search assistance and essay preparation assistance for both. My goal was to get as many kids to achieve high academic achievement as possible. Additionally, I pushed to have as many kids graduate high school and attend college as possible. Thus, I needed to provide tremendous support services to achieve this goal. Many of our students had not a single-family member to ever attend college. In fact, the word "college" for many inner-city kids is literally a "scary" word. College was a place where only people "not like them," or anyone in their families, have ever or would ever attend.

A major goal of my program was to "demystify" the word "college" and show these young people that it definitely was a place for them, and that I would help get them there. I began putting emphasis on bringing groups of college-wary kids from the local junior high and high schools to my program, at Medgar Evers College. Allowing them to tour the school and visit the classrooms and meet with college students that looked like them. I also put emphasis on, in addition to academic enhancement services, college tours all along the eastern seaboard. We chartered buses through my office and arranged college tours for our students to universities and colleges in New York, New Jersey, Connecticut, Virginia, Maryland, Pennsylvania and Massachusetts. They were allowed to meet young students, many of whom were minorities like most of my kids. Students they were introduced to often came from New York City, like them, and from neighborhoods and backgrounds like theirs. However, they were enjoying the college experience and preparing for a greater future, just as my kids could do. I needed my kids to see this with their own eyes and then believe that they could do it too.

Many of our kids, upon taking these college tours, had brand new views of the world around them and accepted the reality that they too could get a college degree. Often, after out-of-state college tours, students would tell me that it was not only the first time that they actually had seen a real college, but was also the first time that they ever traveled across a bridge. Many of my kids had never been out of Brooklyn.

I knew well that one's vision is severely limited when the world that one lives in is not expansive. I also knew the great possibilities that existed once one expanded their world. That vision too will expand. I wanted my kids to see the limitless possibilities that were before them. That was my mission.

The Letter

I RECEIVED A LETTER FROM the Character and Fitness Committee some weeks after my interview. I just stared at it. I placed the letter on my kitchen table and mulled around my place without opening it. I had a long day at the office and I was tired. Whatever the decision was, it would likely change the trajectory of my life. I finally opened it. The letter informed me that I was to be admitted to the New York State Bar. I was going to be an attorney. I was humbled. I was scheduled to be sworn in with a group of prospective attorneys in the coming weeks. I invited my family and friends and everyone was ecstatic. My dad was so proud he was beaming. I captured it in a photo we took together that day while I was holding my certificate after being sworn in as an attorney – his pride coming through his entire face. I'm sure if my mom had been there, she too would have felt the same way. It was a very good moment. It was a very good day.

The Job

UPON ALLEN BEING ELEVATED TO Vice President, he swiftly began to change. I always had Allen's cell phone number and he was always accessible if I needed him, which was rarely. Still, he would answer my calls. He swiftly became distant to the point of sometimes not answering his phone at all. I later learned that he had gotten a new phone and only a handful of people had the new number. I wasn't one of them. Allen began appearing for meetings and visits at Medgar Evers College dressed in fancy, ill-fitting suits and walking with a swagger that was different from the very dressed down, humble, friendly and funny Allen that I always knew. Allen appeared to be a man who had become extremely full of himself. It was shocking, but "life is funny sometimes," so "I take it as it comes."

I had been at Medgar Evers College for well over two-years and I did all that Allen asked that I do. He received his promotion and now, getting him on the phone to talk about the promises he had made to me in terms of compensation for my work was next to impossible. I had to literally chase him down. Even then, he talked to me as if I were stressing him out – like I was the problem. I simply reminded Allen of the promises he made to me and that "I had done my part." I now simply wanted him to do his part. At that point, I still hadn't gotten the raise Allen had promised me even, though my efforts had helped him get his promotion. I was underpaid upon being hired and I was presently earning less than other directors. Even so, I was producing better product and had more responsibilities than most of the other program directors.

I also significantly grew my program to Allen's and the president's delight. Additionally, the program was getting wide recognition. We were recently honored for excellence in Washington D.C., where I allowed Allen to accept the award and receive the praise. I had done my part.

I cornered Allen one day coming out of the college with his new swagger, and fancy ill-fitting suit, after payroll told me that my raise and back pay had still not gone through, even after Allen had promised that "it's done." I looked him in the eye after some back-and-forth and I asked him, "Allen, did the raise the president gave you upon your promotion go through yet?" We both knew that it had. For a split second, after dropping his head and then looking up at me, the old Allen was back – jovial, funny, and very likable. He said, "I promise you, I'll get it done." We both walked away likely knowing the end for me working under him was near. I was done with Allen. He likely was done with me too, seeing that he had gotten what he wanted and, therefore, my usefulness to him at that point was at a minimum. I immediately began planning my exit.

Resigning as a Director at Medgar Evers College

THE SUMMER PROGRAM WAS ABOUT to begin within weeks, summer camp. This program was a monster in terms of effort demanded from me. It entailed managing over one hundred staff members for three months of the hot summer and over 500 children. Allen intended to boost that number to 800 children that summer. It also involved dealing with logistics, finding and managing numerous camp sites, dealing with multiple site supervisors and over 500 parents – many of whom demanded attention for this or that matter regarding their children. For the summer camp program, my day would begin at 7:00 a.m. and ended usually at 8:00 p.m., five days per week. At the end of any given day I was absolutely drained. My summer camp, which was absolutely free, for 500 Brooklyn, low-income children, ages 7-16, included basketball, swimming, soccer, dance and an array of academic support activities in many subjects. The upcoming summer camp, of 2005, would not see me as the director. Dealing with Allen's unscrupulous ploys had totally taken my energy. I drafted my letter of resignation and forwarded it to the President of Medgar Evers College, and to Allen.

I sat in my Jeep after resigning, days before the summer program was scheduled to begin, just thinking. I didn't intend to stick it to Allen, but he would now have to scramble to find my replacement, ASAP. I just honestly didn't have the mental energy to continue. I was mentally done. I could not work another day under Allen's leadership. He had completely played me.

After resigning, I sat in my Jeep, as it set in front of Medgar Evers College, and stared at the sky. I honestly didn't have a mapped-out plan upon resigning. All I knew was that I had to get out of there. I had no significant money saved, besides a few hundred dollars in savings and my last check that would be due on payday. That was it. However, I had my law license and I had faith that I could "make it happen." There also was some fear. That steady paycheck a job offers is comforting. How would I pay rent or support myself and my kids, although they were older now and both working? I had to pull it together and I had to move forward. I turned on the ignition to my vehicle and I drove away from Medgar Evers College. I didn't look back.

Hanging my Shingle

I BEGAN A MARKETING CAMPAIGN to get my name out there as an attorney –
printing business cards, networking with other attorneys, as well as making legal information presentations to whatever community based groups
would have me. Early in my legal career, I also spent many days in criminal court, socializing with the court clerks, court personnel and, when
possible, individuals who were waiting to be called before the judge and
their families. I listened to many Legal Aid attorneys, and court-appointed attorneys, in particular, making their introductions to clients after being appointed by the court to represent the client because the client could
not afford to hire an attorney.

Listening to some of these conversations broke my heart because
the advice that too many of them were giving, based upon the facts, as I
heard them, was often defeatist and weak. Ethically, I could not interfere
with an attorney and his client, but maybe some of the clients recognized
something in my face that said, "In no way is that good advice." Some
accused would catch me later and run legal questions by me, and I often
told them the truth as I saw it. They were usually extremely thankful.

One morning, while I was milling around the Brooklyn Criminal
Court watching trials, critiquing attorney performances, observing ju-
ries and their reactions to different attorneys, their styles and presentations, as I often did when things were slow, I ran into another one of my
cousins. He was excited to see me and went on to tell me about how he
was facing jail time on trumped-up charges and that his attorney, Legal

Aid, was not putting up a vigorous defense. He begged me to take the case.

I was reluctant to take a family member's case, but after my passing suggestions to his lawyer and not getting follow-up, I agreed to take the case. My cousin was charged with violating an order of protection and, based solely upon the word of the complaining witness, he was arrested.

His attorney didn't see the weak points of the prosecution as I saw them, and upon my taking over the case and conferring with some more seasoned attorneys, including a law school criminal law professor, they also told me that my analysis was off. The law school professor, with almost twenty years of legal experience, actually asked me, "Are you crazy?" and said, "That argument is going to fail."

At that point, I knew something as clearly as I knew anything – "I did not think like many attorneys." I had noticed this from a number of instances in the past, either while talking to experienced attorneys about the law or while listening to the "talking heads," legal commentators on news shows explaining the law and how certain situations would play out. I also noticed it while in law school, while having legal discussions with other law students. However, I kept dismissing what was blatantly obvious – "I viewed things differently than many people, even attorneys." Things that appeared so obvious and clear to me were not always obvious to people around me, again even other attorneys. Their opinions on issues often differed from mine.

When I first noticed it, it was a little unnerving and I would quietly ask myself, "Why do you continuously see things so differently?" Now people are telling me that my analysis is off. But this isn't the classroom, this is real life and a family member's future is on the line. I cannot be wrong.

So here I stand, a young attorney, again analyzing a fact pattern differently than most people around me, to the point that an experienced law professor, whom I admired dearly, is telling me that I'm so wrong and asking "Are you crazy?" I had already advised my client to reject the prosecutor's plea offer, which would have given him "no jail time," but he would have a misdemeanor conviction, a criminal record. I told him to reject the plea offer because I believed, in my analysis, that the prosecutor actually had no case and that I could get the charges completely dismissed. He agreed to follow my advice. He rejected the plea offer.

My motion, a written request to the judge challenging the police's action and requesting that all charges against my client be dismissed, was already written, submitted to the court and was scheduled for oral argument before the judge. I don't like to lose and, more importantly, I don't want my clients to ever feel pain because of my legal failings. I was upset as I tried to get the voices of other attorneys out of my head. I asked myself, "How could you be so off in analysis when the truth appears so clear?"

The judge appeared on the bench and began calling cases. I had to think fast. I quickly opened up the file and scanned it looking for anything to help my case. I will not lose this case, and my client is not going to jail. I noticed that the prosecutor had requested a number of trial delays before I actually came onto the case. I began calculating the time. A client has a constitutional right to a speedy trial and I noticed that, as of that day, the prosecutor had actually run past the statutory limit. I may have an alternative argument. I may have found a way.

I pulled my client outside the courtroom and explained that I was going to go, with his consent, in a different direction. I was going to argue "speedy trial" violation rather than "illegal arrest." He trusted my judgment and as we re-entered the courtroom, the bailiff was calling my case. The courtroom was packed that day and if this strategy failed, many people would witness this crash. When acknowledged by the judge, I respectfully informed her that I wished to "withdraw my written motion," the challenge to the arrest, and replace it with an oral motion requesting all charges be dismissed based on my clients constitutional right to a speedy trial having been violated. The judge simply starred for a second and then said "request to withdraw the motion is granted."

I then argued with the prosecutors, who resisted the speedy trial motion, and then the judge called an end to the argument and prepared to give a ruling. The judge detailed a client's right to a speedy trial and the prosecutor's obligation to ensure that it occurs. With that, the judge ruled that my motion was granted and that all charges against my client were dismissed. The prosecutor had violated my client's constitutionally protected rights. My client bear-hugged me with a "Thanks, cuz." As we turned to exit the courtroom, the judge called out, "Counselor." I turned to face the judge. The judge asked that I approach the bench and while looking at me for a moment said, "For the record, I was going to rule in your favor on your initial motion. I thought you would want to know." I smiled broadly and said, "Thank you, Your Honor." While in the hallway, a number of people from the courtroom came out and approached me asking for my business card and explaining their legal situations to me. It was absolutely a good day. I chatted with my cousin for a while and then headed out.

After that incident with the judge, to whom I was very thankful for her admission, I came to understand that being different in the way I viewed legal issues from many people, even other attorneys, was not actually a handicap. There was nothing wrong with me. That day, I realized that my unease at not being like everyone else when it came to legal analysis, more particularly criminal legal analysis, was foolish because the reality was, I was generally not like everyone else. My intimate past relationships with the criminal justice system, me having lived the "street-life," having lived with criminals, eating with them, talking to them all day, every day, for many years, hearing their stories concerning police interactions, victim interactions, attorney interactions and judge interactions, the good, the bad and the ugly – combined with my intense academic study of the law – all gave me a unique perspective concerning criminal law matters that most people around me would not possess – not even very experienced attorneys. This made me different, but not in a bad way. I was unique. And so, that day, I embraced my uniqueness.

After court that day, I diligently began reflecting on past instances that were still vivid in my mind where my legal view and analysis had differed from the majority. I began to reflect not simply on the fact that I had differed, sometimes grossly, from the majority, which would actually trouble me. I rather begin to reflect on whether I was actually on or off course in my legal analysis during those instances. Upon this reflection, I discovered that my views and analysis were accurate pretty consistently. This ranged from my analysis of whether there was criminality on the part of an individual accused of a potential crime, or to whether a criminal prosecution would be successful against that individual, based upon the relevant facts and evidence, and why it would or would not be.

I began remembering, even instances of listening to high profile, experienced attorneys, analyzing issues on news shows concerning high profile cases and thinking, "their legal analysis is clearly focused on the wrong issue" and why are they not focusing on issue "X, Y or Z?" Then later, after the verdict, the jury would speak and say, "Our main focus was on "X, Y, and Z," totally dismissing the issues the legal commentators were saying the jury would be focusing on.

That day, I decided to trust my own judgment. I would still confer with other attorneys, but I would not defer to their views. I would trust my own analysis.

My caseload soon began to pick up. Often, men and woman I had previously defended would pass my name to others who were in need of legal representation. Quite often too, I would defend a client against one accusation, getting them a fair resolution, charges dismissed or reduced. They would soon thereafter be in need of representation again on new charges. Sometimes being falsely accused and other times just poor judgment. I also soon discovered that if I did a good job for a client, I would be adopted as the "family attorney and counselor of law." I would thereafter be called on to prepare wills, litigate landlord tenant disputes, and even other criminal charges within that family. What I also soon discovered was that many clients who had criminal court issues also had related Family Court issues.

For instance, I had a client whose jealous ex-boyfriend filed a trumped-up child abuse claim against her, having her falsely arrested on that claim. As I defended against this false accusation, I learned that Administration for Children's Services had moved to remove all of her other children from her custody and that case was being litigated in Family Court. Thus, I found myself doing a good amount of Family Court work, defending clients against actions by the State.

When I initially began my legal practice, I was working from a home office. A criminal law practice, in particular, is not well suited for engaging clients at home for obvious reasons. However, I had to get started and I didn't have the income to afford anything decent in terms of office space. The good thing was that, many initial clients and their families were perfectly comfortable meeting up with me at local restaurants or diners, enjoying a cup of coffee or soda while discussing their relevant legal issues.

My cousin, for whom I had earlier gotten his charges dismissed, reached out to me and informed me that I had a distant cousin who was an attorney and that she and her law partner shared office space within the law office of the legendary attorney Johnnie Cochran. He informed me that he had told her about me and that she wanted to meet me. We arranged to meet for lunch at her Manhattan office.

When I arrived at her office, at 233 Broadway, within the Woolworth Building, which is one of the tallest and most beautifully constructed buildings in New York City, I was impressed. She occupied office space on the fifth floor, space she leased from the Johnnie Cochran firm, and the place was absolutely beautiful. Johnnie Cochran had put his magical touch on that place for certain.

Upon exiting the elevator, there was dark, plush wood paneling everywhere and touches of beautiful gold trimming. To the right of the elevators, as I exited, was a plush waiting area, with the same dark plush wood paneling and a large reception desk and expensive looking short couches. The place looked like money. I was a huge fan of Johnnie Cochran and, although he had recently passed away, I could literally feel that man's spirit in that office. He was truly a giant.

When my distant cousin came out, after the pleasant receptionist informed her I was there, she approached me with big smile saying,

"What's up, cuz?" I hugged her and followed her to her spacious, well-kept office. We hit it off immediately. She and her law partner did a lot of work in federal court and some matrimonial work in state court. I assured her that, if any of that passed my way, I would certainly send it to her. I wasn't doing federal court and matrimonial work at that time.

She went on to tell me that there was a pleasant attorney looking for an officemate. Johnnie Cochran's firm was so large, that it occupied the entire fifth floor of the Woolworth Building. That space was huge, containing numerous beautiful large and mid-size offices, conference rooms, bathrooms, and client waiting areas.

The attorney, who my cousin mentioned, was renting an extra office from the Cochran firm, but the rent was too high for her to comfortably handle on her own. She was diligently looking for a compatible officemate. My cousin wanted me to meet her. Upon meeting her, she was a no-nonsense African-American attorney from down South in my family's neck of the woods. I liked her immediately. After talking for a long time, she informed me that I was welcome to come on board in her office. She said the office was usually unoccupied because she and her other officemate rarely used it. They often worked from home or stayed in court most of the day. She said, collectively, the rent would be manageable and that clients, upon seeing that office layout, would be impressed enough to pay those Manhattan attorney legal fees. I would simply have to add a phone line and get started.

I graciously accepted her offer and, days later, I was sitting in my Manhattan law office, located within the law office of my long-time legal hero, Johnnie Cochran. His office was actually right across the hall from mine and it still was intact. They left it basically untouched upon his passing. I leaned back in my huge leather chair, in my beautiful office, clasping my hands behind my head thinking, "Wow...life is funny sometimes."